A Walk Through Time

To--Sam
The Poets say that the
unexamined Life has not
been worth Livin'. So...
Hope you enjoy my attempt
to get off the Hook. Keep
up the good work at MIM6

Steve Scott
2001

A Walk Through Time

MEMOIRS BY STEVE SCOTT SR.

ISBN: 1-58500-918-0

1st Books-rev. 1/13/01

ABOUT THE BOOK

Welcome to these pages. You are very bold, my friend, to choose to traverse the labyrinth of another person's life. For you surely know that as I lift the veiled curtain on my life, we will face the expected and the unexpected. We will meet heroic people and villains. Together we will encounter forgotten demons, brooding thoughts, fears and longings. Perhaps, to some degree, they will mirror your own. For each one of us before we meet our Maker attempts, in some fashion, to look back on our youth, our life. And when we do, the past dims; the present becomes blurred with the potential of the future and remains just that, potential.

One should be wary as one reads any autobiography, but especially when the author excessively casts himself in a favorable light, accentuating moments of brilliance and minimizing times of glorious blunders. I have struggled mightily to avoid the temptation.

The germ of the idea for this work began as an exercise in conjuring up the earliest episodes I could possibly remember of my childhood. It followed a surrealistic experience while I was falling asleep on a park bench in Boston, Massachusetts, in 1989. But for now, just know that a "tiny voice" persuaded me that there might be some value to my family to record for posterity some of the events that shaped my life and those of the Scott family generations ago. We know that the demanding experiences of our childhood are the same ones that make us resilient in coping with the challenges of the future. I have also come to believe that the better we understand our families, the better we understand ourselves, and the more we will want to leave a better world for our progeny.

My original purpose has not changed, but the nature of the work has broadened from just relating stories from my early childhood to include a full range of early experiences through advancing age. To paraphrase one of my favorite authors, Alexander King, "Mine enemy was getting older." Much older! And a couple of really gut-wrenching (literally) operations on this miserable bag of bones signaled a degree of urgency to any activities that I had left undone.

This book is about my journey within and between two different worlds – one black and one white – going from the mind set of a small boy in a very large and poor black family in a small town in the conservative Midwest, to that of a professional man encountering famous and colorful people and events on a much wider scale. It is about a family of fourteen surviving the bone crushing poverty of the Great Depression, mainly through the heroic, unselfish love of parents who possessed an indomitable spirit. It was never the intent of this book to worry about the "the road not taken," but to target the fact that man's purpose is to build upon his past, thereby attempting to enable others to conquer the unknown future. And what a future it will soon be.

"Man fears time . . . Time fears only the Pyramids," says an ancient Egyptian proverb. But I have long wondered why humans can't move back and forth in time as easily as they move around in space? Why is it that unlike our spatial dimensions, we experience time as a one-way street, boxed inside the present moments like passengers on a train hurdling relentlessly down the tracks of time? We glance back to a memory of a fixed past and forward to – well, who knows? As Tennessee Williams said, "Life is all memory, except for the one present moment that goes by you so quick you hardly catch it going." Perhaps he was right, but I wanted to go a step further. I wanted to pretend to be a "time traveler" to the past and to capture a slice of it before the millennium comes to a close and a new one begins. It is stunning to comprehend that, with any luck, we might just live long enough to witness the beginnings of another thousand years. Another hundred years. Another decade. Another year. Another month. Another day. I suspect that on Saturday, January 1, 2000, people will do what they have done in the past: Kill each other, hate each other, deny even the lowest level of subsistence to others, and greedily grasp for every dollar they can lay their hands on, legally or illegally, while at the same time, praying for some kind of deliverance external to themselves.

Future historians will surely record that the twentieth century witnessed the highest and lowest points of our nature. It will have been certainly the bloodiest in the history of human kind. But, there were also times when our spirits soared as men walked on the surface of another world. Between those two eras were episodes of social and technological change that men of the previous century deemed impossible. In some cases, these changes seem magical and God - like. To me, such gropings by mankind in the past, to find its way to an uncertain future, are cause for reflection. In the final chapter I will offer some views on such matters.

So, with those meanderings, I now embark on a voyage of drifting back into time. But, hold on tight, it may be an old-fashioned buggy ride!

TABLE OF CONTENTS

CHAPTER 7

CHAPTER 8

CHAPTER 9

CHAPTER 10

CHAPTER 11

IN MEMORIAM

This Book is Dedicated to the Loving Memory of:

Parents:Lawrence Dowane Scott Sr.

Violet Elizabeth Scott

Brothers:Marlon Lee Scott

Charles Carlyle Scott

Gary Devon Scott

Sister:Vera Lynn Scott

ACKNOWLEDGMENTS

As I attempted to reduce the gaps between loss of memory and forgetting on purpose, I tapped the rich memories and generosity of my brothers and sisters to make sure I stayed within the boundaries of truth and propriety. Their assistance is gratefully acknowledged and genuinely appreciated. I also apologize to all of them for saying too much about their own personal lives and, in some cases, saying more about some family members and not enough about others.

The reader will also notice that I do not speak of lost loves, although I recall having read a book of the life of Charles Darwin in which he said something to the effect that "A book, according to my taste, does not come into the first class unless it contains some person whom one can thoroughly love, and if a pretty woman all the better." So my lovely wife, Marilyn, will remain that love, and that pretty woman.

It should be acknowledged that all persons and characters mentioned are real; however, I have taken an author's license and changed some names to protect the...Guilty!

I would like to acknowledge several wonderful people, each of whom took a chapter or two and magically transformed my indecipherable writings into typewritten form: Amelia Stewart, Pat Browning, Delisa Springfield, Kim Potochnik, Phyllis Shrader, Amy Oxley, and Mary Ann Tillman. Despite their Promethean efforts, I still needed help from the extremely talented and ever pleasant Mrs. Furniss Holloway to edit and proof the final manuscript. For her arduous and heroic effort and attention to detail, I am eternally grateful.

Finally, I would like to acknowledge the fact that wherever possible I have tried to credit the works and phrases of others. Nevertheless, it is a difficult task to arrive at the ripe old age of three score without having read a great deal, and heard a great deal, which one inculcates into one's personality and being. In many cases, therefore, thoughts of others mirror my own, to the degree that pride of authorship becomes blurred. I'm sure that this book contains some such instances. To those whom I may offend, I sincerely apologize.

PREFACE

Welcome to these pages. You are very bold, my friend, to choose to traverse the labyrinth of another person's life. For you surely know that as I lift the veiled curtain on my life, we will face the expected and the unexpected. We will meet heroic people and villains. Together we will encounter forgotten demons, brooding thoughts, fears and longings. Perhaps, to some degree, they will mirror your own. For each one of us before we meet our Maker attempts, in some fashion, to look back on our youth, our life. And when we do, the past dims; the present becomes blurred with the potential of the future and remains just that, potential.

One should be wary as one reads any autobiography, but especially when the author excessively casts himself in a favorable light, accentuating moments of brilliance and minimizing times of glorious blunders. I have struggled mightily to avoid the temptation.

The germ of the idea for this work began as an exercise in conjuring up the earliest episodes I could possibly remember of my childhood. It followed a surrealistic experience while I was falling asleep on a park bench in Boston, Massachusetts, in 1989. But for now, just know that a "tiny voice" persuaded me that there might be some value to my family to record for posterity some of the events that shaped my life and those of the Scott family generations ago. We know that the demanding experiences of our childhood are the same ones that make us resilient in coping with the challenges of the future. I have also come to believe that the better we understand our families, the better we understand ourselves, and the more we will want to leave a better world for our progeny.

My original purpose has not changed, but the nature of the work has broadened from just relating stories from my early childhood to include a full range of early experiences through advancing age. To paraphrase one of my favorite authors, Alexander King, "Mine enemy was getting older." Much older! And a couple of really gut-wrenching (literally) operations on this miserable bag of bones signaled a degree of urgency to any activities that I had left undone.

This book is about my journey within and between two different worlds − one black and one white − going from the mind set of a small boy in a very large and poor black family in a small town in the conservative Midwest, to that of a professional man encountering famous and colorful people and events on a much wider scale. It is about a family of fourteen surviving the bone crushing poverty of the Great Depression, mainly through the heroic, unselfish love of parents who possessed an indomitable spirit. It was never the intent of this book to worry about the "the road not taken," but to target the fact that man's purpose is to build upon his past, thereby attempting to enable others to conquer the unknown future. And what a future it will soon be.

"Man fears time . . . Time fears only the Pyramids," says an ancient Egyptian proverb. But I have long wondered why humans can't move back and forth in time as easily as they move around in space? Why is it that unlike our spatial dimensions, we experience time as a one-way street, boxed inside the present moments like passengers on a train hurdling relentlessly down the tracks of time? We glance back to a memory of a fixed past and forward to − well, who knows? As Tennessee Williams said, "Life is all memory, except for the one present moment that goes by you so quick you hardly catch it going." Perhaps he was right, but I wanted to go a step further. I wanted to pretend to be a "time traveler" to the past and to capture a slice of it before the millennium comes to a close and a new one begins. It is stunning to comprehend that, with any luck, we might just live long enough to witness the beginnings of another thousand years. Another hundred years. Another decade. Another year. Another month. Another day. I suspect that on Saturday, January 1, 2000, people will do what they have done in the past: Kill each other, hate each other, deny even the lowest level of subsistence to others, and greedily grasp for every dollar they can lay their hands on, legally or illegally, while at the same time, praying for some kind of deliverance external to themselves.

Future historians will surely record that the twentieth century witnessed the highest and lowest points of our nature. It will have been certainly the bloodiest in the history of human kind. But, there were also times when our spirits soared as men walked on the surface of another world. Between those two eras were episodes of social and technological change that men of the previous century deemed impossible. In some cases, these changes seem magical and God - like. To me, such gropings by mankind in the past, to find its way to an uncertain future, are cause for reflection. In the final chapter I will offer some views on such matters.

So, with those meanderings, I now embark on a voyage of drifting back into time. But, hold on tight, it may be an old-fashioned buggy ride!

CHAPTER 1

> How old would you be if you
> didn't know how old you were?"
> Satchel Page

REVERSING THE ARROW OF TIME

It was early fall, 1988. I had just arrived at the Westin Hotel, in Boston, Massachusetts, where I would be staying for a three-day American Gas Association meeting. It also happens to be the place where our journey really begins.

Certain events had led to terribly hectic months back at my office in Indianapolis, where I was Director of Public Affairs for Citizens Gas & Coke Utility. The Utility provided natural gas to some 250,000 residents in the city. Citizens Gas is a unique entity, a public charitable trust whose assets are held in "trust" for all inhabitants of the city. The "trust" provision states, in effect, that the utility's mission is to sell gas to all of its customers at the lowest and most reasonable cost. It gets tricky to follow but, in essence, the City-County Council for years felt it had control of the assets. Periodically the Councilmen would challenge the "trust" concept, hoping to use the assets to fund one major project or another. This time they wanted to use the assets to fund improvements to the infrastructure of the inner city. Both sides of the issue would hurl Herculean efforts into the fight trying to win support of the gas customers. Needless to say, the attempt failed again, and both sides lay prostrate on the battlefield. I was one of the exhausted combatants. Quite frankly, I needed to get away from the stench of the battlefield and I intended to use some portion of the Boston trip for rest and recuperation. I had never

1

been to historic Boston and I wanted to revel in her historic charms.

After checking into the Westin and getting settled in my room, I changed from suit and tie into casual clothes and tennis shoes. Then I headed to the lobby and the concierge's desk. I wanted to know what to see and do in Boston. I had heard previously that the Boston Harbor was not far away, and I wanted to see it.

Walking up to the concierge desk, I noticed that a lovely young lady, wearing a smart navy blue uniform with a white V-neck blouse, was standing behind the desk. She was not smiling. I said in my most confident, experienced travelers' voice, "Young Lady, I am interested in seeing Boston Harbor and visiting a few of the historical sites before dinner. Can you help me?" I must have made a good impression because she perked up immediately. With a warm smile, she answered, "Yes, sir, you're very fortunate to be staying at this hotel, because Faneuil Hall is just about five blocks from here. Just step outside the hotel entrance, turn right, walk four blocks, turn right again, and you'll be right in the middle of hundreds of shops and a walkway that surrounds the Harbor." I was hardly prepared for the good fortune of her next comments.

"You may also be interested to know that many visitors can see many of our historic shrines by taking a walking tour along the Freedom Trail. It's near your destination. It includes some of the following sites: Park Street Church, built in 1809, brimstone for the making of gunpowder was stored in its cellar during the War of 1812. The Granary Burying Ground has the graves of John Hancock, Samuel Adams, Paul Revere, and all the victims of the Boston Massacre. The Old South Meeting House is the place where the colonists held a public protest meeting against the British tax on tea, just before the Boston Tea Party. Paul Revere's house is another place you will see. It was about 100 years old in 1770, when Paul Revere moved in. And, of course, there is the Old North Church, built in 1723. It is the city's oldest church. In 1775, two lanterns in its steeple signaled the British route to Concord. Paul Revere, as you know, rode across the countryside to warn his fellow colonists that the British were coming." I flashed my brightest smile in recognition of her command of historic facts.

She seemed very proud of the fact that I was one of the few hotel guests she was able to help without much effort. I appreciated her attention to providing hotel guests with her services. "Great," I said, "You've been very helpful." I reached in my pocket, retrieved my money-clip and proudly gave her a five-dollar tip, thinking to myself all the while, "Gee, I've come a long way from the early days in Lebanon when I was on the receiving end of grateful tips from generous patrons." And then I had an even more evil thought. "Yes, I'm black, and in a strange land, but I do know how to appreciate helpful service." Shame on me for thinking such devilish thoughts. Nevertheless, she smiled again that warm, inviting smile that on other occasions of my youth I would have taken to be one of promise. I left hurriedly.

I noticed, as I made a right turn at the block, tiny knots of people moving toward a very old, but attractive building about a block away. "Great," I thought, "the building with the interesting facade must be some tourist attraction." Since it was on my way to the harbor, I thought I would just tag along with them. After all, they appeared to know where they were going and walked with an obvious sense of purpose. "I'll just follow them," I thought smiling all the while at my good fortune.

Upon entering the building, I noticed the people going directly toward a window where they were exchanging dollars for what appeared to be some type of coin and heading down a short corridor to stairs leading below ground. "Gee this seems odd," I thought, my countenance turning a bit grim. "This must be some type of picture gallery, or a museum housing ancient relics where I can learn about Old Boston." As I drew closer to the ticket window, I noticed a sign saying "tickets-50 cents." Hmm.

Not a bad price to pay for a glimpse of Boston history. Following the other "tourists," I moved toward the stairs. About halfway down, I saw a cavernous opening. "How can this be?" I stammer aloud. "The old building looked so small from the street." If you haven't already guessed, my museum turned out to be a . . . SUBWAY! Even a primitive in the outback of Australia would have known. But not me. Come on, give me a break. You gotta remember I was tired, and single-minded in my desire to see something "old" in Boston.

I thought it was hilarious. I really did. And indeed I permitted a muffled chuckle to turn into a full-blown laugh at myself, much to the chagrin of other passengers who probably thought I had just escaped the clutches of care givers at an insane asylum. The irony, of it is, I probably did. . . . back in Indianapolis.

Undaunted, I made my way out of the "museum" and continued my intrepid journey toward the harbor area. After turning my last turn, per instructions of the concierge, suddenly I saw the whole world explode into a kaleidoscope of hundreds of people, shops, sail boats, and seagulls. It was all, and more, of what I had been told it would be. Even though I had traveled extensively and had seen many wondrous sights, the view before me was breathtaking. I didn't know what to do first. So, I made my way toward a grassy area where several park benches were unoccupied, and I decided I would just sit for a while and take in the view. I then did what I had never in my life done before. I stretched out on a park bench. "No one knows me in this city. I will just blend in with the tourists and scenery. It will be good for my soul."

Most of us have seen old and young men sleep on park benches everywhere, but to us they were always tramps, bums, men down on their luck. But, believe me, everyone should try it at least once. With my eyes gazing to the azure sky, I slipped into a lower energy state of consciousness. Time began to lengthen. I became only vaguely aware of my surroundings. I could now hear

4

seagulls as they flapped their wings during flight, and chatted with one another. I could barely hear couples coming and going, and lovers whispering quietly to one another.

Suddenly, I had an amazing recollection of a book I had read years before by Richard Bach, titled *Illusions*. In it he talked about everyone's innate ability to conjure up one's own reality, if a person would but tap into life's true nature, "oneness with all things, all peoples, even matter itself." He talked of being able to make a cloud disappear if you concentrated on it long and hard enough and you became one with it. "Hey! You might as well try it, Steve," a tiny voice within me whispered. I did! I picked out a cloud, a tiny one of course, and began to concentrate on it, feeling a part of it, feeling its softness like cotton candy. "It is starting to break up, starting to disappear," I thought with obvious pride. "It really is." For a second it was gone. I dared not blink, but I did, once. It remained invisible. I blinked again, and the void took shape and stayed. Did I really do it? In my mind I knew I did. But, what is more important, who really cares. I discovered in those few moments that it is possible for the mind to do amazing things if one will only be receptive to the possibility of an altered state of reality. It happens when there is a willingness to be a part of all life and to accept nature as a part of our inherent make up.

Realizing that one of my future goals would be to write my memoirs for my children, and that I would have to begin at a very, very early period in my life, I asked myself another question. "Why not try, in my altered state, to recall my earliest memories?" Reverse the Arrow of Time. I continued to relax my mind. I found by association of certain events in my life that I could easily get to five years of age. I knew that to be true because I recalled clinging to my mother's dress as she prepared to attend a PTA meeting one afternoon. I was not yet in kindergarten. I also remember receiving a whipping from Mom for my effrontery. I went further back in time. I was visiting my aunt in Crawfordsville, She was in her bathroom and I was standing in the doorway watching a curious sight. She was going through all manner of bodily contortions as she wriggled and tugged at her undergarment. I realize now she must have been putting on a corset. I recalled her laughing at me and my infant curiosity.

As I went deeper into the past, the next event was truly amazing. Perhaps the best way to describe the event is what many people call an . . . out of body experience. I was now somewhere, sometime that I knew instinctively was at my house at 911 West Pearl Street. I was in a tiny room, dark and sweet smelling. There! Over there, in a shadowy corner of the room I could see a basket about three feet in length, and slightly conical in shape. In the dim light I saw it was painted with wonderful colors and muted shapes of yellows, browns and reddish purples. A tiny baby rested in the basket, and was just beginning to stir. In my mind I knew it was me. Apparently, no one was in the room but me. I had just awakened and someone was coming into the room because it became flooded with light. I was being picked up by someone. Yes, I must have been picked up by a female because the person was soft and warm. I felt safe . . . wanted. It must have been my mother. At that thought, the past was suddenly switched off and I was back on the park bench in Boston.

Did all of this really happen? Yes it did. What did it mean? I do not know. All I know is that it was the earliest point of my life that I remember.

Okay, I apologize for our slight detour. And for the sake of our remaining friends lets return from the mystical, the paranormal. I must now rewind to the rawboned reality of my birth and deal with just the facts so we both can understand them.

It was Thursday, August 25, 1932 – the day I was born. It was not a very auspicious occasion. The nation was caught in the agonizing death throes of the Great Depression. Millions of people lined the streets all across the land, looking for work or food to feed their starving families. But, none of that mattered in the early morning hours to a poor, struggling black couple in a small bungalow at 911 West Pearl Street in Lebanon, Indiana. They didn't know it yet, but they were waiting for the hands of an old General Electric clock to strike nine twenty-six a.m. It is my understanding that is the time I decided that I had enough of the easy, safe, and secure life of my mother's womb. It was time for me to burst forth upon the world's stage, whether it was ready for me or not. It would take several years before I would learn that the world could not care less about this screaming, quivering mass of protoplasm that my mother cradled gently in her arms.

In preparation for writing this chapter, I took the trouble to scan the archives at the Lebanon Library for some sign that events of great import happened on the day of my birth. I was sorely disappointed. According to the front page of the August 25, 1932 issue of, the _Lebanon Reporter_, two calamities occurred. "Irwin Worrell suffered a fractured right foot when he fell from a ladder while doing some carpentry work on his home. He was taken to Witham Hospital for an x-ray and later returned to his home. The other was headlined, "Lebanon Banker and Legislator Expires." "Joseph Coons fell ill and was taken to Witham Hospital. With his physician attending him all night, he passed away. Death was attributed to angina pectoris." The weather forecast for that hot, humid day called for "Increasing cloudiness with showers likely." So, these circumstances heralded into the world one infant Stephen LaRue Scott, born to parents Lawrence Dowane and Violet Elizabeth Scott. My earthly arrival was just a whimper, a non event.

I was disconsolate. I secretly hoped that momentous events were shaping the World, the Nation, my hometown. Some unusual signs were in the Heavens. Give me a violent storm, locusts upon the land, anything. I nearly forget to thank the very helpful librarian and, with head bent low, I left the building.

As I drove back to my home in Indianapolis, I suddenly got a lovely, spiritually uplifting idea. I, Stephen L. Scott, was the important thing that happened that day. And with that victory declared, I could now take my rightful place beside my four brothers and sisters. All too quickly for the health of my mother, seven more brothers and sisters would follow. But, for now I would be number five. Ahead of me would be Arthelma, Lawrence Dowane Jr., Valada, and Marlon, in descending order. What a day after all!

The young Scotts who would eventually follow me, in rapid succession, were Don, Gary, Charles, Vera, Teya, Larry, and Jon. A perfect dozen in all.

Okay, that was the day I was born. That is a historical fact. And it's very comforting to know that I was actually spawned from my parents and not from some "spore" drifting in from outer space, or cloned in a test tube in some mad scientist's laboratory.

LEBANON – THE CITY

My hometown has grown comparatively little since its beginning in 1832. "The Friendly City" as it is called, has grown slowly and sluggishly through the years. Nevertheless, it has risen from a lonely log cabin in the midst of a dense swampland to a thriving city of the fifth class. A review of information completed by the Boone County Historical Society in 1984 reveals some of the following historical data.

Lebanon owes its existence to the Indiana Legislature serving in the General Assembly in 1832. Jamestown, located in the far southwestern corner of Boone County, was originally selected as the county seat when Boone was organized in 1830. The 600 pioneers who made it their home were unhappy because of the difficulty in reaching the out-of-the-way county seat. They protested loudly and long enough that the legislature took note, and on January 16, 1832, they adopted a measure which required the relocation of the county's seat to within two miles of the geographical center of the county.

The legislation also mandated a five-member commission to be in charge of selecting the site and name for the county seat. Named as commissioners were James F. Becket of Hendricks County; Thomas Arnett of Hamilton County; John Belles of Marion County; Adam M. French of Montgomery County and John Harland of Clinton County. They were to meet the second Monday of April 1832 to begin their work.

The commission did not meet until the last day of April or the first day of May, according to records, and then only three of the appointed men appeared. They considered a tract of land two miles northwest of the site which was eventually selected. The land was owned by Martin Henry, who wanted $10 an acre for the property.

The naming of Lebanon was credited to commissioner Adam French. He said he selected the name of Lebanon because tall hickory trees in the area reminded him of the biblical cedars of Lebanon about which his mother had read to him from a history book when he was a child. Perhaps it should also be pointed out however, that French's native home was Lebanon, Ohio.

Lebanon began to grow from these meager beginnings. Woods were cleared to make way for streets and homes. Slowly, more homes and businesses were built in the town as the city worked hard to establish itself as the county's center of government and trade. As the rest of the United States progressed with railroads, telegraph, telephone, gas and coal, paved streets, water works, electric carriages, the automobile, radio, movies, electricity in the home, airplanes, concrete highways and televisions, Lebanon grew with it, but not much.

In the early 1900s there was not a single chain store in Lebanon, and all the industry was locally owned, except for the Boss Glove Factory and the Columbia Canning plant. The principal Lebanon industries, included the Fuller Brothers Mill and Yard, Metzger Lumber Company, the Pinnell-Combs Company. Other small businesses, the condensed milk plant, the poultry house and the saw mill provided work for the town's labor force which in turn bought the farmers' produce, milk, poultry and sawed logs.

All the downtown stores surrounded the court house square: retail businesses, doctors, dentists, lawyers, realtors and insurance companies. Saturday was the big business day in Lebanon. It was the time for country folk to pour into town to do their shopping or just to sit around the town square. The Avon theater was also a main attraction. It is still there! Adler's department store dressed the local women in stylish clothes. Crime was practically nonexistent. Policemen had little to do but occasionally arrest a speeder or investigate minor misdemeanors. Witham Hospital, on the north side of town, provided care for the sick or dying. Oak Hill Cemetery was the final resting place for the latter. My mother and father are buried there on its quiet and peaceful 115 acres. The grave of my brother, Marlon, also rests next to them.

Lebanon High School was located a few blocks from downtown. The grade schools were Harney (where the Scotts attended), Stokes and Central. Lebanon Boys Club on Main Street and the YMCA on North Lebanon Street provided more than adequate recreational facilities. The swimming pool and baseball diamond were located on the north side of town along with Ulen Country Club.

In the early 1900's, Lebanon was amply supplied with public transportation. The Interurban Company operated cars between Lafayette and Indianapolis and through Frankfort and Lebanon, every hour from six o'clock in the morning until late at night. There was also an interurban line to Crawfordsville and one to Thorntown, with cars running every two hours throughout the day over these lines. The Big Four Railroad sent several passenger trains through Lebanon every twenty-four hours and the Old Midland had an eastbound and a westbound passenger train connecting Muncie and Brazil. The trains gave way to the interstate, I-65, during my teen years.

In many ways, the city of Lebanon is typical of the small county seats in other parts of the state of Indiana: small and intimate, with the city square being the hub of major activities. It really is not that strange to realize the sameness of the Indiana cities when one recognizes that most Hoosiers were living on small farms which provided most of their needs, except the social life and group recreation which cities like Lebanon could provide.

But a city is made by people and it may be helpful to know something of the social strata and psyche of Lebanonites. The city was divided, like most cities, by economic status: citizens were referred to as the "Northenders" and the "Southenders." The demarcation point for these two social stratums appeared to be the county courthouse. Any residence or building, including Lebanon High School, that extended north of a horizontal line east of the courthouse was middle or upper-middle class. South of the courthouse, including east and west boundaries, one could find upper lower and lower class residents. This differentiation has never changed, even today. Curiously enough, the young "Northenders" would never outwardly flaunt their social status. My impression was that it was bestowed upon them by their parents and by teachers and local businessmen. Nevertheless, their sons and daughters interacted with us "Southenders" with little regard for our social standing or ethnic condition. My father and mother were well respected and called Mr. and Mrs. Scott when appropriate and/or Dowane and Violet by their close "Northender" friends. My brothers and sisters excelled in school activities, being elected to positions of leadership in almost all organized school programs. My sister, Teya, was "May Queen," and my brother, Marlon, was vice president of his junior class. All of my brothers and sisters held high offices in student affairs and in many other school organizations. Fraternizing between the races was commonplace. The black Scott family was assimilated into the social fabric of the city.

If I have expressed no malice toward my fellow white Lebanonites, and if I have neglected to mention overt acts of racism, such omissions were not accidental. I readily admit that prejudice may have existed in the minds of some whites in the city, but I was not aware of it. I am sure that my brothers and sisters could have written this section with an entirely different slant. But, to paraphrase Lin Yutang, "The wisdom of life consists in the elimination of nonessentials. " In other words, what may have happened seemed not to have affected me in any profound way, as I never let my race become an obstacle in my struggles to achieve any of my personal goals then, or later in life. I will speak more on this subject in a later chapter.

PARENTAL PORTRAIT

The miracle of the black family, as someone once observed, is not that so many black fathers and mothers have fallen, but that so many of them still stand, love, nurture, and give of themselves to their families. That was the essence of my parents.

The family has always been the backbone of the black culture. During the days of sorrow and segregation, millions of heroic fathers and mothers struggled to keep their families together, pay their bills, and educate their children to whatever degree money and circumstance would permit. If they could not do it alone, grandparents, aunts and uncles helped. They held family reunions to insure that family heritage and togetherness prevailed into the future, often in the face of unbelievable odds. Today the black family is under terrible siege; few would debate that fact. But, it was not the case in my day and particularly not in my family. It is with the above backdrop that I now offer a closer insight into one of the two people who never faltered in their steadfast efforts to properly raise their many children.

Dad was born Lawrence Dowane Scott on March 16, 1907, in Decatur, Illinois. He was an only child. Dad was tall, about 6 feet and "lanky," as folks were inclined to say in my day. He was a very handsome man even in his advanced age. This fact did not escape the females who grew up with him, especially in high school, who were all white, of course. On many occasions they told me this, unashamedly. He had large, almost gray, penetrating eyes, shielded by thick bushy eyebrows. Dad was very light-skinned, and most of his other facial features were nearly Caucasian.

I never knew much about his early life; he didn't share much of it with me. He did occasionally talk about his high school days, but they to, remained relatively obscure.

Somehow I always had the feeling that these were dark and painful years for him, but I never knew why. One thing is for certain about Dad, if he chose not to talk about something, no probing or prodding would make him break his silence.

Nevertheless, occasionally a door would open slightly and he would offer a brief glimpse of his inner self. I recall his saying that he and a friend, Charlie Boarders, were the first black athletes at Lebanon High School. Both ran track and field, and according to him, they were standouts as well. Dad's primary track specialty event was the quarter mile run. He would say the challenge of this race was stamina and the willingness to endure pain and to fight through exhaustion. These and other strong characteristics stood him in good stead during his lifetime.

Another youthful episode he related to me was a trip he and three high school friends made to New York City, in a Model-T Ford. A playful smile inched across his face as he told of the car breaking down several times en route as they passed through Ohio and Pennsylvania. But they arrived at their destination safely. The smile broadened as he told of the wondrous sights and encounters they had. That smile led me to believe that a great deal of "coming of age" had taken place there.

I believe most of my brothers and sisters would readily agree with me that Dad commanded respect, never "demanded" it. He earned it by his gentle nature and his devotion to his wife and children. He was a no-nonsense person, the total master of the house. We came when he called and obeyed when asked to do chores or errands. It was never a case of "I'll be there after while," or "Just a minute!" or "Do I have to?" No. You were there, on the spot, and lickety-split.

Dad was not a religious man, but he enjoyed the outdoors and communing with nature. It might be said, paraphrasing lines from Shakespeare's "As You Like it," that he found religion in raising his family, sermons in the running brooks, sermons in wheat and corn fields, sermons in stone, and good in everything.

Old-fashioned virtues ruled our home: no drinking, swearing, lying, cheating, hitting, or fighting, especially with your sisters. A blow above the thigh to any of my sisters brought a swift and defiant response. Dad bought a pair of boxing gloves. He didn't want any of his boys to get hurt. If a squabble broke out between us, he would simply say, "Okay, that's it, let's get the gloves. I didn't like fighting, especially with my brothers. I was slow to anger, but if provoked beyond reason, I would become possessed, and the devil himself would have to take the hindmost. Fortunately, I didn't have to "put the gloves on" very often.

Sometimes Dad had to resort to the rod or belt, particularly if no one confessed to committing a particular offense. "I don't know who started the squabble, or committed the offense so all of you will pay the price with a whipping." Reminiscent of the famous line in the movie "Casablanca," Dad would "round up the usual suspects," brothers' Sonny, Marlon, Don and me, and give us sufficient whacks to make us cry. The secret was to cry early and loud. While we would be "licking our wounds," Dad would go into his room and weep as well. Thankfully, he didn't have too many "notches" on his belt, not from me anyway.

There was excitement in the air when Dad would announce he was preparing a dessert for us. His specialties were lemon meringue pie, candied orange slices, and walnut fudge. The walnuts for the fudge were hand-gathered by my brothers and me during early fall. I enjoyed the wonderful warm, sun-drenched fall days when we would walk along the railroad tracks to a secluded wooded area about four miles from our house. We must have been a curious sight. With gunny sacks over our shoulders, Sonny, Marlon, Don, Gary and I would set out in the sunlit glow of early afternoon in search of our plunder. Half our time was spent "horsing around." We played the game of seeing who could walk on the tracks for the

15

longest period of time. The fall leaves in Indiana are as beautiful and picturesque as one can find anywhere in the United States. Sweet gum, oak, birch and sycamore trees have gorgeous orange, red, purple, and yellow leaves. The woods were a sanctuary where time stood still and cares were forgotten.

Most of the time we were successful in finding walnuts, but that was the easy part. The real work began when we reached home with our bounty. The walnuts for Dad's wonderful fudge had to be prepared by shelling the husks, a messy job. With a hammer in hand, we would use the hard cement surface of the sidewalk of our back porch as our work station. Green stain from the walnut shells would be everywhere, particularly on us, since we had no gloves, stains that never seemed to come off, even with the harsh soaps of the time. They finally just wore off. Nevertheless, it all seemed well worth the effort when Dad filled the kitchen with a heavenly aroma of chocolate cooking in the double boiler pots. Dad was meticulous in his preparation of food but would let us take turns running our fingers along the inside of the pots. We were excellent cleaning agents.

It was about this same time, when I was six years old, that Dad began making trips to Denver and Cheyenne. At the time, he was earning fifteen dollars a week as a valet for the very wealthy Shepard family, who lived at Ulen Country Club. He augmented this income by serving as a waiter at the Country Club and also began earning extra money by driving the Shepards to their summer home in the Rocky Mountains near Denver.

Each summer we would wave goodbye to him as he started the engine to the large Chevrolet van used for the trip. Secretly, I believe Dad loved these trips as a temporary vacation escape from the heavy duties and responsibilities of rearing his large family. There was no question that he enjoyed the grandeur and natural beauty of the old West. His stay in Denver and Cheyenne lasted about three months - June until September. During this time that Dad learned to ride horses and would tell us, upon his return, of the beauty and majesty of the Rocky Mountains. As we sat at his knees, he would tell stories of riding along winding mountain trails, witnessing cattle drives, rodeo shows, and "Frontier Days" in Cheyenne.

One summer he brought back with him a great surprise for the family in a large crate. It was a surprise in more ways than one. The crate was huge. It measured about four feet long, three feet wide and four feet high. When the crate was opened, our mouths dropped. "What is it? We all said as one. It was a cabinet-like structure made of the finest polished mahogany. It was a combination radio and record player, by Stromberg-Carlson, one of the premier names in broadcast music equipment at that time. It must have cost a fortune.

"This is swell," I thought to myself. "Mom could use a new wash tub, a kitchen appliance, living room furniture, new beds for my brothers and sisters, new rugs, linoleum for the kitchen floor. And we get a radio-record player." A bit selfish on my part to think that way, but it was the truth.

Actually, the purchase was neither that inconsiderate nor that impractical. After all, there was no television, and listening to the radio was entertainment for us, moreover, it didn't cost money like the movies did. Like other families across America, we would avidly tune in the radio for our beloved shows. We listened to "The Shadow," "Fibber Mcgee and Molly," "Escape," "The Green Hornet," "The Lone Ranger," "Lights-Out," "Paul Harvey and the News," "Red Skelton," and yes, I will admit it, "Amos and Andy." Still, to my way of thinking, the point was if you couldn't eat it, wear it, keep warm by it, sit on it, or reduce the labor intensity around the house, why buy it.

Dad's radio brought me memories of listening to Joe Louis vs. Max Schmelling when Joe lost the first heavyweight title fight. Joe, carrying the hopes of all black people on his shoulders, made us feel like somebody! Our whole household was depressed for days following that fight. At the next rematch as 70 million Americans listened to their radios, we listened on our new Stromberg-Carlson.

To bring closure to this matter, the Scotts spent many pleasurable hours listening to the Stromberg-Carlson radio. We would buy the newest 78 and 33-1/3 rpm RCA and Decca Records like the Mills Brothers, Billy Eckstine, Sarah Vaughan, Nat King Cole, and Arthur Prysock. We even played "Finian's Rainbow" and other wonderful musicals. Dad, as usual, was right again.

Every house is a sermon
about God's love.
Habitat for Humanity

THE HOUSE ON PEARL STREET

The Scott house was a six-room bungalow. I have no recollection of when it was built, but a good guess would be sometime at the turn of the century. It was certainly not a new house when Dad purchased it. When I was a preteen, the home was painted a pale green. It now has bright yellow siding. Four broad cement steps lead to a front porch that stretches across the front of the house. A small picture window to the left of the front door provides a pleasurable view of Pearl Street. Once inside, one enters a small living room, with three bedrooms on the right. The dining room, just ahead of the living room, is separated by a six-foot wide arch and Immediately beyond the 9x12 dining room is the kitchen, which was quite an ordinary one. Off to the right of the kitchen is the one and only bathroom. That's it! That's all! Those were the physical confines wherein fourteen people had to live and grow, cook dinners and sleep. No room for a library to do studies, no getaway space to be by yourself, and of course, family rooms were nonexistent in those days.

The boys slept in one bedroom with bunk beds stacked around the room. Our father and mother had one bedroom and my sisters occupied the final bedroom. The only blessing was that all twelve were not there as teenagers at the same time. By the time the first six to eight children were teenagers (I was number five in the hierarchy), the second six were toddlers and young children, so they didn't take up as much space as one might imagine.

A couple more items are needed to complete the total picture. The heating appliance for our home was a coal stove. It occupied a great deal of space in the far right

19

corner of the living room. Much later, after remodeling, we had central heating. For most of us, the coal stove provided barely enough warmth, as we huddled around it on the coldest of winter evenings. The trick was to get totally warm, then make a mad dash to the bedrooms. Warm covers were scarce, and late at night, when it was much colder, we could have used several more blankets. We substituted blankets with coats or anything else we could find to snuggle under.

There was a tiny attached back porch just off the main living area where laundry was done. When exiting the rear door one could see a shed that housed coal for the coal stove. It also had a small work area with a grand old workbench. A one-car garage was a part of the same covered area, but it was useless. It had a clay dirt floor. At one point, the garage had several windows; however, as baseballs repeatedly crashed through them, Dad gave up replacing them. As a result, wide, gaping holes replaced the windows.

At one point early on, Dad had an old Oldsmobile housed there. My recollection is that the engine was never started. The car just sat there on cement building blocks, in solitary silence. Where the car came from, I don't know. Since it never moved from the area, it did provide extra-covered space for playing and exploring many of life's wonders with neighborhood kids.

The home itself was flanked by an alleyway on the west side of the house. It was only a half block long and was the access road to a small oil distributing company that was about 150 feet behind our house. The company had four large oil tanks that provided residential fuel oil for many area residents. Directly behind the oil distributing company was the Midland Railroad.

Our backyard was actually quite big, large enough for a small garden which we planted in early spring. It provided much-needed vegetables for the family, usually green beans, lettuce, green peppers, tomatoes and corn. There was very little yard space on either side of the house;

however, there was no fence separating us from our neighbor to the east, giving us increased areas for playing. One large cedar tree to the east and just off the front porch provided a shaded area, but most of the yard area was barren of grass because of our constant trampling. It took a terrible beating despite Dad's heroic efforts as a gardener. The alley I mentioned was covered with cinder ash and gave us, over time, plenty of scrapes and painful abrasions when we fell on it, but it was a very decent surface area for playing basketball next to the old shed where we attached our "basketball goal." We rarely had a net to put on the basketball rim; however, it served its purpose. What did poor kids know? We pretended we were playing at Butler Field House in Indianapolis.

Dad told me many years ago that our house cost $8,000 when he purchased it in the 1920s. The local bank manager didn't want to lend him the money, saying, "You will never earn enough money to pay for it." What a cruel thing to say to a young, black man, or any man who wanted to provide a home for his family. Talk about shattering your manhood as well as your ego! Nevertheless, by the 1950s the house was paid for. Dad was such a proud man when he burned the mortgage in front of us. "That'll teach the b------ds," he said, in so many words. He never swore, you know.

The Scott house is located on the west end of Pearl Street. Pearl Street runs east and west and butts against East Street. Five hundred yards beyond East Street was the elevated Pennsylvania Railroad track. To the east were small, modest homes that extended about a quarter of a mile. Pearl Street ended by the restricted boundary of the "Big Four" railroad track and a large grain processing plant. Pearl Street itself was not paved then. Instead, the street was built with wonderful, red brick with the sidewalks paved with red brick as well. Today, such a street would be priceless. Gorgeous cedar trees lined the street, forming a wonderful canopy of shade. Of course, all of the families living on the street were white, except the Scott family.

One final note about Pearl Street. Seldom did any of us venture beyond it, except to go to school, Memorial Park, Ulen Country Club, and the "ole swimming hole!" Perhaps that sounds amazing to today's more worldly youngsters, but that's the way it was. Why did we need more? We had plenty of friends on Pearl Street.

THE PEOPLE OF PEARL STREET

There is something magical and universally enchanting about the street where you live. I believe this was particularly true of yesteryear. As children living on Pearl Street, it was where our known universe began and ended. It was where you were born and played games with family and neighboring children. It was where you rode tricycles and bicycles. It was where you coveted your neighbor's son or daughter. It was where everyone knew everyone else, and looked out for their well being. It was where "ole Mrs. Jackson," the widow with stringy hair and missing teeth, was a member of some witch's coven. And when you went into the high weeds surrounding her haunted house to retrieve a baseball, these fears made the hair stand up on the back of your neck, as the children who dared you to do it howled with laughter. But when you went away to war, or to make your way in the world, the home and the street seemed so far away it was as if they didn't exist at all. Yet, you knew deep down in your soul that if you could just get back there, everything would be all right; your cares would vanish.

I would like for you to meet some of the neighbors who lived on Pearl Street. But be forewarned. They were all great people, wonderfully diverse as a group. As individuals, they were strange indeed.

All of our neighbors were white, of course, and like the Scotts, poor, but proud. All were good, hard working families, but lacking much in sophistication and education. Life was just much simpler then, and much more brutish as the Great Depression lingered like a choking fog over the Nation and on Pearl Street. The "Roaring Twenties" were gone. All across the land many of the mighty had fallen from their lofty heights. Many of the mighty had lost all they had of their stocks, bonds, and real estate. One in four men was out of work. Herbert Hoover was being blamed for all of Americans woes. FDR would succeed Hoover as President and a "new Deal" would save millions. But, it would be a long time before fear and famine would disappear from the Nations cities and Pearl Street.

When World War 11 began, the men of Pearl Street, who did not go off to war, found decent jobs in Lebanon or Indianapolis. Most worked at Stewart Warner Tool & Dye Company, which was located at the far eastern end of Pearl Street. Dad worked there as well. Other men, living on Pearl Street, found jobs as overland truck drivers, or at the larger manufacturing plants in Indianapolis. Some worked at the Army Finance Center at Fort Benjamin Harrison. Several others worked at Allison Detroit Diesel Engine Company in Indianapolis.

Most of the families on Pearl Street had children. There never seemed to be a moment when the Scotts were not playing at someone's house, or other children were at our home playing games. The usual games prevailed, basketball, baseball and football for the boys. The girls enjoyed "dolls," or "play house," or hop scotch and jumping rope.

In trying to recall the kids of Pearl Street, I am suddenly struck by the inordinate number of families with children who were dysfunctional or otherwise disabled in some way. Something strange had stalked the street.

The Henry Cook family who lived next door to us had four children. In chronological order they were Clint, Betty Jean, Donald, and Geneva. Clint and Geneva were ordinary individuals. Unfortunately, the other two children were not. Betty Jean was nine years older than I and suffered from some unknown malady, unknown to Betty Jean, or to her family. I now believe she was a hypertonic person. Her general appearance reminded one of "Olive Oyl" in the Popeye cartoons. In fact, now that I think about it, she talked like "Olive Oyl" as well. Betty Jean was always screaming in an unintelligible language, either at her parents, or at no one in particular. When she finally got married, she moved out of the city. But when she would

24

return home to visit her parents, she screamed at them and ran out of the house as in days of old.

Donald Cook, was crippled. I would say he was stricken with polio and did wear leg braces and walked with a slow and agitated gait. Donald was a nice looking kid, with coal back hair, finely chiseled facial features, and a strong upper body. In fact when he was very young he joined in all the games played in the neighborhood. He deserves a great deal of credit because his skill and determination never faltered. He was welcomed to join us. He wanted, nor received, special consideration because of his infirmity.

The Butlers, Bill and Marie, were the first in our neighborhood to own a newfangled device called television. Most of the neighbors didn't buy one because they didn't have the money. The Scotts were in that category. The Butlers would open their home to us in the evenings, and a horde of Scotts would descend on their home like locusts. Not only did the Butler's have a television, but they probably had one of the nicest homes on the block. It was a sturdy, two-story brick home that towered over the surrounding bungalows framed with wood or shingle siding. Normally we would sit on the floor of the living room while Mr. Butler lay sprawled on his couch. Watching in amazement as Ed Sullivan introduced the Beetles on his "really big show." We watched old Western movies as the "good guys" out dueled the "bad guys." It was truly remarkable, we thought, that man could send pictures flying through the air.

Mr. Butler was a tall, gangly man in his early fifties, a rough and tumble man and a rather scary sort of individual to us. He had the appearance of a man just ready to board a whaling ship and sail off into the North Atlantic. Actually he was a gentle man. His wife Marie was short and stocky with a round, rosy face. Marie was a born housewife who adored her husband. She also adored my father and mother and obviously enjoyed having the Scott children in her presence. She would bake cookies and pies, and bring fresh vegetables from her garden to my parents.

The Butlers had a daughter named Eunice who was retarded. Although she was more than 35 years old, she had the mind of a child of ten. Nevertheless, she was a delight to be around. Eunice was a "tomboy" and loved to play baseball or just plain "catch" with my brothers and me. She would break out in a wide grin when we invited her to join in our games. She was quite good, too, and had a wonderful curve ball which she threw with pride. Eunice constantly chewed tobacco and would emulate big league pitchers as she spat with abandon. She was tall, with unkempt hair. Her vacant eyes betrayed her lack of general awareness of things of the higher order, except for one thing. She played the sweetest harmonica you have ever heard. What a girl! We loved her!

About two and a half blocks further down the street to the east lived Brett Brentwood. He was a deaf mute. I was always surprised when he would show up at our house using sign language to indicate he wanted to play. Although none of us could use sign language to converse, somehow we understood each other in a limited way. He was darkly handsome and very intelligent. He was six or seven years older than the rest of us and he actually acted his age. The girls along Pearl Street giggled and squirmed when he came near, hoping for more than a fleeting smile or glance. He was tall with wonderfully straight, glistening coal black hair. Brett had an olive complexion that looked like fresh peaches and he was always immaculately dressed. His parents were very protective of him and he could never stay long at play, but when he did, he was welcomed. All of the neighborhood children got along well with him with never any fights or disagreements.

Directly across the street from us lived Wilbur Padgett, his wife Estelle, and their son Paul. He was much older than we were, perhaps mid thirties. Another son Charles was married and lived a normal life, I hope, in another city. Paul was a hopeless alcoholic and never married. He continued to live with his parents; I don't think he worked at all. I believe he hung out at the local pool hall and local bar. Then he would come home to drink his dad's home brew.

Wilbur was not necessarily lazy, but if he had a job I never knew about it. I never saw him working around the house. He appeared to be perpetually lying prone in his porch swing drinking "home brew." Wilbur never made much sense when he talked, mostly because he had nothing to talk about. But he loved the Scott family and we got along well. Estelle liked our mother and was a surrogate mother to us all. She was always on hand to comfort Mom when another little Scott was delivered at our home by Dr. Kern. Good people the Padgetts were, especially to my brothers and sisters. They never complained when we hit baseballs into their yard and windows.

Two houses east on Pearl Street lived Bill Dicky and his family. Bill was in his mid forties when we were kids. Dicky provided the "fireworks" on the block, especially when he was "fired-up" on liquor. He would yell a lot at his wife or walk over to our house and try to make idle conversation with Dad, as his mind wandered in and out of his artificially induced euphoria. Bill was a childlike in his demeanor, but was a rugged, handsome, athletically stocky man with a receding hairline, sort of a poor man's Bert Reynolds type. He actually was a very good baseball player and was a mainstay on a Lebanon baseball team, "The Merchants." The Merchants were a very good baseball team who played host to many surrounding baseball teams, including several from Indianapolis.

Dicky enjoyed coming over to our house, especially when we were playing some kind of sport in the street. We threw footballs and baseballs together. He could throw a football, with perfect spirals, for miles! All of the Scott boys could do the same. Dicky enjoyed playing baseball or "catch" with us. We learned how to catch his "steaming" baseballs bare handed because we didn't have baseball

27

gloves. We learned how to move our hands, at impact, in the direction of the ball's flight without doing much damage to our hands. As we got older and could afford to buy baseball gloves, he taught us how to throw wide, sweeping curve balls, sliders and fast balls. Dicky was good for the neighborhood. Also, he had a gorgeous daughter named Alberta. She was a marvel, with long, slick, onyx black hair, olive skin and perfect teeth. Alberta was very friendly, and about our age. I don't think my sisters played with her very much, but sometimes we boys did! She seemed to be going somewhere constantly but it was outside the normal boundaries of "Pearl Streeters."

Alberta had a much younger brother named "Butch," at least Butch was the only name we ever knew. He was, unfortunately, a mongoloid child, I believe; however, we did treat him with respect and did not make light of his condition. I must also give the Dicky family credit for they loved him dearly and took him everywhere they went and they were unashamed. Butch wouldn't join in any of our games, of course, but he would come to our house to watch us play.

My neighbors and their various conditions do not make for exciting information but there are points to be made about them. Principally, the uncommon number of young kids who suffered abnormal afflictions in such a small, constricted area would lead one to think that something insidious and unknown was invading our block. If that inordinate number of dysfunctional births had taken place in the current times, a health department investigation for a common cause would probably have taken place. If a health hazard existed, it mercifully escaped our home.

I hope the reader gets a favorable sense of the warmth and affection we all felt for each other on Pearl Street, no matter what the individual circumstance. We accepted each other for what we were; racially diverse, poor families that were able to interact at the most common level. I'm not sure that could happen today. I didn't speak about our neighbors to the west. There were six families, and they were more of the same: strange!

THE EARLY YEARS

It would be difficult today for a young person to understand how really different and difficult life was at this time. There was radio but no television. Today more than 99 percent of all households in America have at least one television set. By contrast, only a few telephones were in the homes of the poor then, and these were two and three party line systems. In other words, you could only use the phone when the other parties were not using the line. I always found it interesting that we had to memorize the number of rings that were assigned to our house. One could always pretend the rings were for us, knowing that it was someone else's call. One only had to pick up the phone to listen to another person's idle chatter. Few households had cars during the late thirties and early forties, certainly not the Scott family or most other families on Pearl Street. One walked or rode a bicycle. Automobiles came to Pearl Street and the Scotts shortly after World War 11. Pearl Street was used for dreaming. On warm summer nights, we would lie in the street and search the star-studded skies for meteorites to wish upon. Ours was always the same wish - food, food, food.

But, we did not lead dull lives. We built walking stilts and scooters that were propelled by leg power. Simply built, the scooter was made of a flat foot board with wheels from a pair of old skates, a T-board about three feet high for a handle. Pushed with one foot, balanced with the other, away we would go. The Flintstones would have been proud of this contraption. There were also homemade kites and airplanes to build. My brother Sonny was the premier builder of such devices. No matter what I tried to build, scooter or airplane, it ended up looking like a... swing!

During the summer months, the excitement revolved around special visits to the Guernsey Ice Cream Parlor.

This company manufactured its own ice cream and was famous throughout Boone County for their delicious concoctions. A heaping ice cream cone sold for only five cents.

Other such treats included the visits of the "Iceman" to Pearl Street. He made his deliveries from horse and wagon and later with an old truck. Ice was the only method of keeping food refrigerated during those days. With a cardboard sign in the front window signaling the number of pounds desired, 25, 50, or 75 pounds, the "Iceman" would chip off the prescribed amount in huge blocks, hoist the block to his shoulder and trudge into the house. His was a tough, tough, job. When he disappeared into the house, that was the signal for my brothers, sisters and me to sneak chipped pieces of ice from the back of the truck for snacks. Delicious on a hot summer day. It was a curious thing, but this act of sneaking a piece of ice was not considered stealing by the Iceman nor by anyone else. Sharing simple things made all of us, including neighbors, and the Iceman feel like family.

The alley adjacent to our house was our favorite playground. It was covered with crushed coal cinders which made a great surface area for a basketball court. When I was seven years old, my older brother "Sonny," who was handy with tools, affixed a tomato crate with the bottom cut out against the coal shed wall. This became our first basketball goal. Tennis balls, softballs, tin cans, anything round, we tossed or shot into this makeshift basketball goal. At the Scott house basketball was just invented.

Eventually, the tomato crate was replaced by a round metal hoop and the tennis balls, softballs and tin cans were replaced with a basketball. All of the neighborhood kids would come to our house to shoot baskets. Marlon and I particularly took a liking to the sport and spent hours upon hours shooting baskets. In the rain. In the cold. Even in the dark, with the only light coming from our kitchen window. Little did I know at the time that these back alley days of shooting baskets would lead me to a love affair and career door-opener over the course of the next decade and a half.

Another point of interest in the neighborhood was the local "Mom and Pop" store. However, we called it the "jot em down" store. It meant, if you didn't have any money you could make a small purchase and the owner would "jot down" the amount in his little black book. The store was very close to our house. We could shoot down the alley, cross through Mr. Padgett's back yard, and step right onto the door step of the little store run by the Hudsons. This small store was typical of those found in most small towns during the era. Upon entering the store that was once a two-room house, one's nostrils were flooded with hundreds of nonspecific odors all at the same time. A musky, acrid odor emanated from the old wooden floor, never swept, which held bags of flour, sugar, dry cereals and corn meal. On the left, as we entered the rickety old oaken door were dust-filled wall shelves that contained canned goods such as corn, green beans, hominy, pork and beans, and assorted soups. "Fresh" vegetables and tomatoes, head lettuce and cabbage were located next to the shelves.

Toward the rear sat a large pot-bellied stove with buckets for coal and ashes on either side. An old Dr. Pepper, Coca Cola, Mason Root Beer or Nehi Orange vending machine stood in the far corner. The meat counter, which was directly in front, held bologna, frankfurters, hamburger, pot roast, calves liver, and on Fridays, fish. One would be lucky to find any of the above very fresh. A small freezer cabinet housed the ice cream.

Sitting on top of the meat counter were the candies: candy canes, orange slices, jaw breakers, licorice, Holloway and B-B Bat suckers. And naturally, there also sat the cat, one eye open and the other eye shut, he would oversee the comings and goings by day and bring fear to the hearts of mice by night.

How important a slice of Americana these little stores were at the time. They were a haven for little children with a penny, nickel, dime or quarter. Screaming, giggling children crowding the store probably would not be tolerated today, but it was an everyday occurrence then.

The Hudsons also cultivated a quarter acre plot of land near the canning factory, where they grew vegetables for their home and for the store. One early evening as I was trudging home from playing baseball at the vacant lot adjacent to the canning factory, I saw a sight I hope never see again in life. There, in the middle of his large garden, was Mr. Hudson, harnessed to a plow, straining mightily as his wife guided it. The whole scene was surrealistic in its irony. Man had replaced the horse as a beast of burden.

When I was seven years old, I became aware of several indignities Dad and Mom had to endure because of our poverty. Most of them involved the lack of money, clothing and food for the family. For instance, late ever Christmas eve, Dad was given the Christmas tree used to decorate the dining area at Ulen Country Club. There would be a rush to decorate it before Christmas day. However, Santa Claus had usually distributed his presents elsewhere, and there were pitifully few left to put under it.

There were the times during the winter, when our coal bin was nearly empty, when my brothers and I would go forging for coal along the railroad tracks near our house where, during the process of off loading coal to local distributors, ample quantities could be found lying on the ground.

In addition to the weekly payment/collection visits of the Prudential Insurance agent, there was home delivery by the milkman and the bread man, but all too many times we could not pay those debts. The deliverymen generally would leave a small order and extend credit to the following week. The milkman had a regular route down Pearl Street. He would come early in the morning in a huge delivery truck, laden with quart and pint glass bottles of regular milk, chocolate milk, and orange drink. As he approached each house, he would usually whistle a merry tune as he walked up the steps to set the milk bottles he carried in a strong wire basket next to the front door. When on many occasions he would ask to collect for the week's delivery but there was no money to pay him, we were generally instructed by our parents to inform him that they weren't home. He could collect the following week. He would just smile, knowing full well that my parents were home.

The regular milk had three inches of rich, thick cream on the top. One could either shake the bottle to create a homogenized texture throughout or attack the cream separately. I would opt for the cream. As I savored it, I could easily conjure up cartoon pictures where the cat would look up from his milk bowl, licking his lips with a rapturous grin on his face and the hearty bounty dripping from his chin. But, there was another incident during those lean years that haunts me to this day.

THE CASE OF THE MISSING CHOCOLATE BUNNIES

During these early years, until I was nine years old, there was seldom enough food to satisfactorily feed the large Scott family. I secretly worried that at some point the County might take some of us away to an orphanage. The nation was just emerging from the depression, and if not for the fact that most families were having an equally bad go of it, the County officials might have done so. Fortunately Dad and Mom dutifully and loving kept us together. Most of the time we children shared equally with one another whatever food we had. Except one memorable occasion. I choose this anecdote because it illustrates an aspect of my protean personality. Normally I was easy going and slow to anger, but not this time.

I was in the second grade and it was nearing Easter. Dad had waited table for a large gathering at Ulen Country Club that Thursday night. Late that evening, he brought home a large cache of the most wonderful and inviting sweets one could imagine. I was transfixed by their beauty. There, resting in two large Easter baskets were hundreds of jelly-beans, quarter sized mints and other assorted candies. But what took possession my soul were two large chocolate Easter bunnies about eight inches tall and filled with thick creamy filling. It was Dad's plan to hide the baskets and distribute their contents on Easter Sunday. All of us were given strict instructions to not organize a search party to find them.

The following day at school I dreamed of the chocolate bunnies. I paid little attention to any of the lessons of the day. I couldn't. The math problems the teacher put on the blackboard danced in front of my eyes as chocolate bunnies and green and pink mints. When school was out for the day, I raced home hoping to find Dad's hiding place for the chocolate bunnies and to gaze lovingly at them once more. When I arrived home, I could tell something was wrong the moment I opened the front door. The air seemed heavy with sweet odors. My younger brothers Don, Gary, and Charles had a special glow about them as well, as they licked their lips and rubbed there little bellies. They had found the candies and eaten them all, even the chocolate bunnies filled with delicious cream. Not one crumb was left for me. I felt a crushing sense of loss. I flew into a rage. I hissed between barred teeth, half-formed words of revenge, as I grabbed Don, Gary, and Charles, in turn and began to pummel them with blows. Mom, who was off in the kitchen, hearing the commotion, had to drag me off them. Later that evening, when Dad returned home from work and was told of the theft, off came his belt and additional howls were heard. I never wanted chocolate bunnies, nor have I eaten much candy since.

THE CANNING FACTORY

Another point of major interest in our neighborhood was The Canning Factory. That was our name for the Ladoga Canning Company. During the 1930's and 1940's, the canning factory was a place that cast a spell over me and my brothers and sisters. As a matter of fact, all of Boone County was touched by its presence.

Boone County, as well as northern and central Indiana, is blessed with rich, dark soil that makes for excellent farmland. We were taught in our high school history classes that the end moraine of the glaciers from the Ice Age, scoured the land leaving smooth, rich soil in its wake. This soil provided some of the best crops in the world, particularly, high yields of corn, tomatoes, soy beans, and many other edibles.

Summer and early fall were harvest time for these perennial bumper crops. Fifty to seventy-five trucks would clog the small roads leading to the factory. As the trucks awaited their turn to be unloaded, my brothers and I would admire the crop, then putting on our best "poor little black boys" demeanor, ask the farmers to share some of their bountiful harvest with us. Our faith in their generosity was well placed, for and infinitely we received. We always had a salt shaker with us and would sprinkle it liberally over the rich, juicy and succulent tomatoes. We would spit the seeds and watch them fall to the ground as gentle as summer rain.

It seems very curious to me from the vantage point of today's heavy security, health laws, and misanthropic attitudes, how management at the factory would permit us to wander relatively unrestricted throughout the plant. But they did! Most of the workers knew our family and wouldn't say anything to us. Many of them tossed us cans of recently processed foods for which we graciously thanked them. Their offerings would be a part of the evening meal that very day.

Once the trucks were unloaded, the produce would be placed onto conveyor belts leading inside the factory. The vegetables were cleaned and put into huge vats of boiling water for cooking. The canning factory itself was a farm produce processing plant that operated 24-hours a day, seven days a week. At harvest time it was ablaze with lights and was a beehive of activity. I was fascinated to see the large vats of tomatoes being cooked. The contents were then placed into sanitized empty cans that snaked in a Conga line down a long, curving mechanical belt. The cans moved onto a labeling device and were finally boxed for shipping. From my earliest memories, perhaps four years old, the factory filled the air on warm summer evenings with the sweet pungent odor of vegetables being processed and canned for delivery to homes all across America.

The building was located only four hundred yards southwest of our house, and stretched across 15 acres of land. It was bound on the north by the Midland railroad, on the east by Patterson Street, and on the west by the elevated Pennsylvania Railroad. A well maintained grassy field, about a football field in length, attracted the Scott kids. It was our own private field where we played softball, baseball, football and golf. The owners of the property kindly permitted us to treat it as our own domain.

The factory's management used cheap female labor to do the actual processing. Most were lower class housewives. The work was not particularly onerous, but the women did work long hours, especially during the tomato canning season. Union rules and policies were not in effect then, so wages, hours, and working conditions were substandard.

Mexican migrant workers were imported to do all of the harvesting and hand picking of the tomatoes. Curiously, the Scott family looked forward to their arrival. Only a small band, usually four or five large migrant families, would make up the workforce in our immediate vicinity: fathers, mothers, young women and children; all worked in the fields. They lived on the factory premises in tents under very Spartan conditions.

The Mexican elders must have asked white factory workers if there was a black section or element in the city where they could establish congenial contact. Of course they mentioned the Scotts. The first recollection I had of meeting these Mexican workers is when I was ten years old. Several handsome men, perhaps in their early twenties, knocked on our door to introduce themselves. The leader, who spoke very good English, was named Garcia. He and his contingent sat on the front porch and chatted with my father for a while. The next evening two or three more came to our home. We conducted a wonderful "cultural exchange" program. We would teach them elementary English, and they would teach us elementary Spanish. It was a great experience for me to engage in their repartee at such a young age.

There were side benefits for my older brothers and sisters as well. Although I don't think there was any dating, there certainly was a great deal of covetous longing. Even my beautiful aunts, Harriet and Mary Jo, made excuses to their parents to come to our house on many evenings. They didn't come to see me.

ULEN COUNTRY CLUB

Ulen Country Club Park is located on the northeast side of Lebanon. "Ulen," as we Lebanonites called it at the time, was a place of great opulence and unimagined beauty, especially for those of us unaccustomed and untraveled. Even today, some fifty years later, locals and out-of-towners speak of its beauty.

Many of my early life experiences were centered there. My father and brothers spent much time and toil at Ulen from caddying, waiting tables, performing domestic and garden work to other rich developmental experiences as well. Ulen is worth learning more about; not only about the physical layout and occupants who built homes and lived there, but about Henry Ulen, who conceived it. Much of the following material on Ulen was taken from a June 8, 1977, *Indianapolis News* article written by Mytie Barker, a News staff reporter.

Ulen Country Club Park is really a monument to a man who, as a boy, did not complete the eighth grade and who ran away from home, not once, but several times. He even hitched a ride aboard a freight train heading for Chicago.

One could rightly say Ulen is composed of some 150 people living in some 50 homes, all adjacent to the Ulen Country Club, strictly a residential area with no businesses. There are just two streets (Ulen Boulevard and East Drive), 25 light posts and 15 water hydrants. It was an American success story that few places could begin to match. But there is really much more. The country club is adjacent to the residential area as well as to the 18-hole golf course. The history of the man who was responsible for the entire complex is even more an American success story.

The young Henry Ulen worked at various jobs. For a time, he was a telegraph operator, then became a correspondent for the old *Indianapolis Journal*. He went from there to a Chicago newspaper. After that, he studied law. Sometime after he passed the bar examination and began the practice of law, a firm of engineering contractors engaged young Ulen as its counsel. It seems the contractors were about to default on a contract. Determined to keep his clients out of trouble, Ulen, although possessing no engineering training or experience, set forth to complete the building project. The young man who had grown up around Lebanon found himself involved in a growing number of huge engineering projects in Europe, South America, Iran, Greece, Poland, and other exotic places. No spot was too far away or too big or complicated for Ulen & Company to undertake.

Ulen's outstanding reputation spread from one country to another. Contracts included water works, river and harbor improvements, hydraulic developments, dams, tunnels and aqueducts. As the years passed, and as Henry Ulen grew older, he yearned to return to where he was born and reared. He wanted to come home to Lebanon. Accordingly, he shocked all his business associates by declaring his intention to move his Paris and New York offices to Lebanon, which now became the home office of Ulen & Company. This relocation meant that all of the Ulen executives would have to move to Lebanon as well. Since they were men of great intellect and culture, they wanted handsome homes and surroundings for themselves and their families.

Only superior construction was permitted on the 39-acre tract laid out in large lots. New homes to be built had a minimum allowable cost. All utilities were built underground to alleviate clutter. Eventually Ulen residents clamored for recreational facilities. Henry heard their cry. He built a club house which cost nearly a half million dollars. This was an astounding amount of money prior to 1940. He liked to play golf. He also built an 18-hole golf course designed by a very famous golf course architect. Many prominent golfers played these links. Still growing at Ulen are the famed Grottendorf roses which bloom year round, lining the driveways and the homes, and maintaining their gracious opulence.

The Scott children...Front row left to right...Don, Charles, Gary, Vera. Second row...Marlon, Valda holding Teya, Me, Dowane Jr., Arthelma. I was nine years old. No shown are younger brothers Larry and Jon. Numbers have no relationship to age ranking.

Pearl Street fronting our house – It was our baseball diamond and general playground. It was seldom vacant.

The basketball court adjacent to the garage and the Scott house. Playing basketball with family and friends was a daily affair…rain or shine!

The sidewalk in front of our house gets plenty of traffic. That's youngest brother Jon on the left with Teya, Arthelma, Larry, Vera and Charles. Arthelma is protecting her son, Mike.

44

Card games. Mom is in the center. To her right is sister Arthelma. These games were Friday and Saturday night favorites for the Scotts.

Younger brothers Jon and Larry. They were inseparable in their youth.

My Aunt and Uncle Charles and Inella (Center).

Dad was fond of the West. My Brothers, sisters and I were shocked to learn he became an excellent horseman during his several trips during the summer to Cheyenne and Denver.

The station wagon Dad would drive to Colorado.

Picture taken by Dad. It's one of the first diesel trains to come through the city of Lebanon. Not a bad picture of the Scotts first family automobile, a Delta 88 rocket Oldsmobile.

Ulen Country Club, with the 18th green in the foreground.

Joe Louis came to Lebanon to play at Ulen Country Club. I caddied in his foursome.

Looking north on Lebanon Street from Main Street

Lebanon Swimming Pool in Memorial Park

The banks of Sugar Creek, Much as it looked on the day
we walked and trapped its banks for muskrats.

CHAPTER 2

WHEN HUMILITY AND HELL, LIKE HONOR MEET

Lebanon Memorial Park and Ulen Country Club, two important landmarks in Lebanon, are both located on the northeast side of the city. Ulen, already described as a place of great opulence and unimagined beauty, stood as an island unto itself, surrounded by the plain, the ordinary, the peasant-like existence of the rest of the city inhabitants. Most commoners could only stare through its gates and try to imagine the comings and goings of the rich who dwelled within its boundaries. The gardeners, cooks, and housekeepers who worked there could rightfully return to speak of its beauty. Even today, more than fifty years later, I can easily recall the days when we watched baseball at the diamond, caddied, labored in the gardens at Ulen, performed other domestic work in the huge mansions. I was able to realize then how well the idle rich actually lived. I remember several incidents at Ulen.

Just before approaching Ulen, one passes Lebanon Memorial Park on the west side. For a small city, the park is huge. Lovely old oak, cedar and sycamore trees are everywhere throughout the grounds. Ample picnic areas, barbecue pits, horseshoe pitching stalls, swings, slides, basketball and tennis courts abound. The two high profile areas were the baseball diamond and the huge swimming pool with an island that contained a diving tower. At night, it would be lighted with multicolored lights that would shimmer and dance across the water. Unfortunately blacks in Lebanon could not swim there.

This act of prejudice was hard for my family and the other few blacks living there to understand, because, in most endeavors, we were treated as equals, within the same peer group. I remember my dad telling us just how painful it was. "I went to the mayor one time to discuss this indignity. The mayor was pathetic in his apology. We don't mind you Scotts and other blacks in Lebanon swimming in the pool, but the first thing you know, blacks will be coming from Indianapolis to swim here, you know, and the local people just won't like that. There might be trouble." Obviously Dad was hopping mad, and he told the mayor, "That's a bunch of crap." But, what could Dad do, by himself, in those days? That incident was more than fifty years ago, and the world had not yet been awakened to equality. But I can easily dismiss this sordid subject. I didn't want to swim there anyway. It didn't affect me then and it doesn't bother me now. My poor white friends and I preferred to swim in the "ole swimming hole" which was an abandoned gravel pit on the south side of town.

This much is for sure. The white people in Lebanon knew we grew up with them, explored life's great mysteries with them. This was a fact known to all of the town fathers. My brothers and I held the highest offices in high school and were respected by all of the town's people. One of my early jobs at Ulen involves Mrs. "Mary Winfield." Decency forbids me from using her correct name.

Mrs. Winfield in many ways reminded me of a "frontier woman." She appeared and dressed totally out of character with the other rich women of the day at Ulen. She was short and rather thin and between 45 and 50 years old. Her face was round but seemed to have cracks and wrinkles where they shouldn't have been. Her eyes were gray and sad, almost sullen. Her short hair was perpetually unkempt, with several strands hanging limp outside her "bun" hairdo. I believe a lot of her drained physical appearance had to do with the fact that her young daughter, Sarah, was paralyzed from the waist down, and was confined to a wheelchair with polio. I liked Sarah very much. She was very pretty and about twenty-five years old at the time I worked for Mrs. Winfield. Sarah had soft brown hair and eyes that sparkled showing no pain of her regrettable condition. If it wasn't for her cumbersome leg braces that were almost always covered by a blanket, and a slightly withered hand, one would almost think that, at any minute, she would bolt from the wheelchair, put on shorts, and go play tennis, or race off to the happy haunts of goddess nymphs. I wished that for her. Occasionally, we would sit and talk over lunch in her backyard, after I had worked in the yard all morning. Her mother would fix us milk and sandwiches for lunch. Would anyone believe I was treated that well as "yard help and general gardener"? I had no idea this tranquil relationship would rupture one day soon.

During my second summer of working for Mrs. WInfield, something must have happened to the man who cleaned her house and took Sarah for drives in the park for relaxation and to see her friends. He also took care of Mrs. Winfield's boxer dogs. There were five of them housed in a kennel not far from the main house. Strange that I never saw this man or knew his name. I knew he was a middle-aged white man from the way Sarah would describe him. As it turned out, whoever Mr. "Nameless" was, he was an unknown participant in what was to be a dark day for me.

It all began during the month of late August. All Hoosiers know it does get hot in August. I had finished mowing the yard which normally took a couple of hours. I was busy trimming back some ivy along the front walk. As the time neared noon, Mrs. Winfield appeared and asked if I would like a ham, lettuce, and cheese sandwich with ice cold lemonade. I was dying from heat exhaustion and very hungry. I tried my best not to appear too anxious. I could barely smother a shout of glee. "Yes," I said in a whisper.

I had finished eating my ham sandwich and drinking the lemonade under a shade tree. Mrs. Winfield appeared again after about thirty minutes. "Steve," she said in a hesitant voice. "When you finish trimming the ivy under the front windows, I want you to hose down the dog kennel and pick up the 'dog remains.'" The wonderfully tasting ham sandwich and thirst-quenching lemonade did an instant flop to the bottom of my stomach. I stopped breathing for a second. My countenance darkened as her words echoed in my soul as well. Both Mrs. Winfield and I knew something was about to happen, and it did. I darted a contemptible glance in the direction of the kennel. Somehow words came forth from my mouth unsolicited. "Mrs. Winfield, I don't pick up 'dog remains."

She momentarily turned to stone. Her face blanched as she straightened to her full height, arms akimbo at her sides as she said, "And why not? The other help never refused."

I darted a contemptible glance toward the dog kennel. "Well," I said politely, but somewhat scornfully. "Those are your dogs, and if you want the 'dog remains' picked up you will have to get someone else to do the job."

"Young man, if you don't do as I say, I will tell Dowane (My father). I have always known him to be nothing but a gentleman. I can't believe you would act like this. I've known and respected your family all of these years."

"Well, I'm sorry, Mrs. Winfield, but you are just going to have to tell my father." I walked away from her house, saddened by the whole affair.

She did call Dad that evening, and he did talk to me. He asked me to give him my version of the episode, which I did. I also told him that we all work hard for our money and I am not ashamed of that, but none of us by individual choice have to do things below our dignity. I think I might have been crying. After all, it was the first time I had been fired from a job. I thought I saw Dad secretly wipe a "speck of dirt" from the corner of his eye. I was thrilled, happy and relieved when Dad called her back. I overheard him say, "I respect you very much Mrs. Winfield, but if my son says he isn't going to do that kind of job, then that's the way it must be." And that was that. Dad never said another word to me about it.

I didn't have a personal grudge against Mrs. Winfield, and felt rather sorry that the whole incident had happened. She had been very nice to me personally. Picking up someone else's dogs' remains is probably not a big deal, and in many ways it wasn't; but in retrospect, it was an early signal that I was fighting back in some small way for not being able to swim in the pool at Memorial Park. It could have been my reaction to all of the indignities I had read blacks were forced to endure. The "Little Black Sambo" book the class read in elementary school that left me cloaked in anger while the class snickered. The lynchings I read about in history class. The Jim Crow Law that forced blacks to ride at the back of the bus in the South. The rear doors my dad had to enter at the Country Club. Everything seemed to coalesce into that one brief seismic eruption; refusing to do that job seemed to reflect the only dignity I had at the time. So, in many ways, I must thank Mrs. Winfield for unknowingly making me realize that no matter how poor I was and regardless of my station in life, no one, including Mrs. Winfield, was going to destroy my self-worth. I was slowly cloaking myself with armor that would insulate me from many slings and arrows I would endure later in life. One of the most harmful decisions many of us make in life, to one degree or another, is to think we're not good enough, deserving enough, or worthy enough for respect of our personal beliefs. And this discovery would manifest itself several more times before I would leave Lebanon for good. Alas, it would also happen elsewhere as I "tilted at windmills."

IF AT FIRST YOU DON"T SUCCEED

Ulen Country Club afforded excellent potential for earning money, but there were many other lessons of life learned there. A healthy work ethic was just one of those vital lessons, some of which came the hard way.

My father worked as a waiter at Ulen for most of the club's major dinners and for special occasions. This was his second job. I liked to see him go to work there because it was physically easier on him, but there were also other benefits. The managers knew he had a large family, so they would give him pies, cakes and other leftovers to bring home to the family. We would wait hours for him to come home with these special treats for us. Dad also made a great ceremony out of stacking the considerable coins he would receive as tips from customers - dimes, quarters, fifty-cent pieces and silver dollars. After determining the amount of the evening's take, he would put the tips in a huge jar. Over time, he would wrap them. Surprisingly, it would amount to a considerable amount of money. I learned a great lesson from that and began doing it myself. I still maintain that habit today. Every evening, I put loose coins into a container, and after about three months, I wrap them. Would you believe it sometimes amounts to more than a hundred fifty dollars? Normally, I buy a few shares of a local utility stock with the savings. In a way, it is considered discretionary money, but in the long haul, it is put to good use. I have now noticed my son does the same thing. He has learned, as I did, that big trees grow from little acorns.

This whole process reminds me of a story I remember from my youth. It concerned a Chinese King. It so happened that the King's beautiful daughter had been kidnaped. The little princess was the King's heart and soul. He sent word throughout the land that whoever recovered his daughter could have anything in the kingdom he desired. With great detective work, a kinsman was able to find and return the beautiful little princess to the king. True to his word, the king said to the kinsman, "I promised that whoever could return my little princess to me could have whatever he desired. What is it you would like? I will grant it."

The kinsman said, "Your highness, I would like you to double one bag of grain a day for thirty days. That is my wish."

"What? Is that all you desire my friend? No gold, no silver, no land?" The kinsman said, "Double one bag of grain a day for thirty days, that is my humble wish."

"Your wish is granted," the king said. "So, it is written, so it shall be done."

Well, one can hardly believe how many bags of grain the kinsman accumulated over thirty days. A computer could do the calculations, although it would be fun for anyone to try doing them. Suffice it to say, the number is in the hundreds of millions of bags of grain. And you can easily deduce further that the king had been had. There wasn't enough grain in the whole kingdom, alas, in the world to meet the kinsman's wishes. I'm sure Dad never heard of that story, but in his own way, he was teaching us a very important lesson on how saving money, even in small increments, could reap wonderful benefits.

Dad's basic attire for the waiter's job was a white tuxedo jacket, black bow tie and black trousers. He always looked so handsome, better than any of his coworkers. I never really understood the arrangement of the other three resident black waiters, Bruce, Dusty and "Mingo" Jones. For some reason, we never knew the last names of Bruce and Dusty. Bruce, however looked the part of a waiter, like a real professional. He was tall and dark, and he walked with a light, easy gait. Bruce acted like a sporting kind of person. When I knew him, he was about 60 years old. He seemed to like the Scott family but he never visited our house. Where he actually lived, and what he did when he wasn't working, I don't know. I think he would go to

Indianapolis for a bit of night life. There certainly wasn't any to be found in Lebanon.

Dusty was very short and slightly built. He walked with a slow, deliberate pace and was very dark-complexioned – hence, the name "Dusty," because when he came or went, he looked like a pile of dust. "Mingo" Jones, on the other hand, was much younger. He had the appearance of a Chinese man. He had a light olive complexion and a marvelous goatee draped from a chin that seemed to grow right out of his neck. He was never without his black horn-rimmed glasses and constantly smiled, showing a large gold tooth, right in front, that would blind you with its sparkle. Mingo also played a wonderful trumpet and was in great demand with small jazz groups in Indianapolis. Dusty and Mingo were invited to be a part of our family life and activities. My brothers, Sonny, Marlon, Don and I would play golf with them on Mondays, when caddies were allowed to play golf. They were also invited to play in our Friday and Saturday poker games. They both were a lot of fun, laughing and joking, and both played aggressively; however, they weren't solid poker players and usually lost their money.

At home, Dad taught my older sisters, Thelma and Valada, how to be waitresses. My older brothers, Sonny and Marlon, were given this special instruction as well. I watched them practicing how to set a table and, what is most important, how to carry a loaded tray properly on their shoulders. This extra instruction was a great boost to the family for potential earnings at Ulen Country Club. I watched them carefully, for I knew my opportunity would come soon. One day I finally got my chance to be a waiter, and all would soon regret that I did. I can't recall the exact circumstances that led to my great opportunity. I think one of the Indianapolis pros could not make it, and I got the call.

After donning my tuxedo, I was ready to go. Dad gave me some last minute instructions. "Steve," he said, "whatever you do tonight, watch me. Do what I do, and what I tell you to do. Above all, when you leave or enter the kitchen area, remember you exit the swinging double doors on the right and enter on the right-hand side." Well, that didn't seem too hard!

I said, "Okay, Dad, don't worry, I won't embarrass you." As things developed, that was a big lie!

It started out easily enough, I thought. All the dining guests had arrived and were now seated. Dad said, "Steve, go place the baskets of hot rolls on the tables." Great! That sounds easy enough. I thought, and with a full tray of steaming rolls in baskets, I headed out into the "arena," smiling broadly – it was a mistake. I tried to mask the tight tension that started to creep up the length of my body, causing my eyes to become tiny slits that hinted a sense of urgency. The dinner affair was a local celebration of some sort, with the rich men of the city and their families in attendance. To my great wonder and apprehension, I discovered upon entering the dining area that Susie Lennox was there. Susie was the leading cheerleader for the Lebanon High School basketball team and simply gorgeous! She was about five feet five inches tall, with blue-green eyes and long brunette hair that cascaded well below her shoulders. Her full red lips and perfect teeth made her smile seem like the morning sunlight. She was every boy's dream, black or white. Since I was one of the leading scorers on the basketball team at the time, I was respected and admired, and I must say, we had great hidden affection for one another. Anyway, when I got to her sitting area, our eyes greeted each other warmly. Too warmly! I felt arteries hardening, restricting blood from reaching my brain, causing lightheadedness. I became giddy and dizzy. My serving arm began to fall short of the intended basket placement area. Would you believe, part of the wicker basket caught in Susie Lennox's beautiful hair? For the next few moments I was trapped in hell. The more I tried to get the basket untangled from her hair, the worse things became. Jerry Lewis could not have scripted a skit equal to this horrifying event. The warm biscuits began to fly everywhere, into guests' laps, into water glasses, into salad bowls. Thick bile started to rise in my stomach. Susie's father, visibly strained, looked as if he were about to hurl curses. I groaned involuntarily. We finally untangled her hair from the basket. Then Susie gave me a new lease on life. She smiled at me again. The smile that caused the whole thing in the first place was now in permanent state.

Dad motioned for me to come over to a section of the dining room where he had been collecting empty water glasses. His eyes pierced my soul and his forced smile curled downward and his mouth became a tiny slit. "Take this tray into the kitchen," he commanded, in a low voice that came from a throat that sounded like two irons rubbing together. His obvious annoyance caused me great suffering. So, with pain in my knee joints, eyes out of focus, shortness of breath, sweat gushing out of every pore, and too many other calamities to list properly, I headed for the kitchen with the two swinging doors. With a heavy tray of glasses on my shoulder, I entered the wrong swinging door, the left swinging door, just as Bruce, the waiter, was exiting the right side door with a tray full of entrees on his shoulder. We collided! He did a 360 - degree turn and did not save his tray. I did a 180 - degree turn and didn't save mine either! My pirouette was wonderful, though, for a few seconds. Time stood still, as I watched one glass after another fall in slow motion to the floor. I was in a catatonic state – I never heard a sound, but others did, as they watched my heroic efforts to save the day. Snickers from diners greeted my ears. I was finished as a waiter in that one brief episode. I was never invited back. But through it all, as I glanced over to where Susie was sitting, she gave me one last glorious smile that made the world okay again. Well, I didn't want to be a waiter anyway! And, if I have garnered your sympathy for my plight, you should know that I made one more journey to Ulen Country Club before leaving high school. This time, vengeance would be mine; I would return one day, as the soaring Phoenix, to speak at a Rotary Club luncheon. But, that part of our journey lies ahead.

THE BOTTOMLESS PIT

Most anthropologists who have studied different cultures around the world have found that young boys must perform some task to test their manhood before they enter their teen years. Many of them are very dangerous. For example, diving off very high cliffs, or sitting alone in a dark cave for days, killing a lion. In my day the challenge of coming of age was to swim across the bottomless gravel pit.

The "mother" of all simple pleasures was a visit to the "ole swimming hole," especially since we couldn't swim in the luxurious pool at the north side of Memorial Park. In point of fact, the ole swimming hole was a gravel pit on the southeast side of the city. We didn't need parental permission to bathe or swim in its welcomed waters. We just told someone, usually one of our sisters, that we were going swimming. Sonny, Marlon, Don, Gary, and I would swim for three or four hours at a time during the long, hot summer months. The site was not just the Scott getaway place, but a favorite of our white friends living on the south side as well. It was the poorer section of the city, of course.

Old men told tales around the courthouse square of the hideous creatures that lurked in the domain of the "bottomless pit." Others said that on nights of the full moon these sea creatures could be seen prowling the surface of its murky waters. Such tales just added to the fun and mystery of the place.

I must describe the pit. It was hidden from the main roadside view by waist high vegetation. A small winding dirt road was the only access route, and large cedar trees provided a canopied, misty darkness to its approach. The pit was surrounded on three sides by high cliffs – perhaps twenty-five feet high, and was nearly one hundred yards across. A gentle, crescent shaped beach thirty feet wide gently sloped to the water's edge. At times its waters were a clear azure blue. At other times, when rains failed to cleanse its waters, scum, flotsam and jetsam fouled its waters. Yuck! No matter, it was our Memorial Park pool. The water itself graduated to a depth of. . . . well, it depends on what tall tale one chooses to believe. Was it really fathomless? Quite frankly, to its bare skinned bathers, it was. We began swimming as all beginners do, wading and dog paddling. These brazen activities continued for a couple of years, during the summer months, nearly every day too, rain or shine – no lightening though.

Sooner or later, the big challenge was to swim all the way across the pit. There was no question about swimming the distance. It was a matter of when! And you had to have a witness to this macho achievement. It was a rite of passage, a matter of manhood. Early one hot, lazy day in summer, before school was to begin, I made the commitment to myself that the next day was to be the day for my crossing, the day I would become a man. I was nine years old at the time.

The following day I was filled with excitement at the prospect and challenge of making a successful swim . . . When I arrived at the pit, I tossed my clothes casually upon the water's edge. I alerted the swimmers around me of my intent, and, strapping on my most serious game face, I waded out into the waist high water. Then, with a high, arching leap into the air, sucking in a last gasp of air, I broke the surface of the water, sinking deeper and deeper into its inviting embrace. Leveling off under water, I began to breast stroke mightily. The idea was to cover as much ground under water as I could, shortening the distance to the opposite shore. That plan was soon abandoned as I became aware of how cold and dark it was under the water's surface. Then another surprise. The deep water was not as buoyant as I had reasoned. I was having trouble keeping my body level. Despite furious kicking of my legs, I wasn't going anywhere, fast. I headed for the surface. Gulping for air, I broke clear of the pit's icy clutches. My chest was burning and my sight blurred. I searched for the opposite shore, but I couldn't see it. Then, mercifully, it shimmered into view. I was dumbfounded. Swimming underwater had gained me little, for I had been going sideways. I was still seventy-five yards from my goal. After a few agitated strokes to gain the proper trajectory, I began taking on more water through every bodily orifice. For an instant I tried rolling over and floating on my back. It didn't work. I panicked!

Fear gripped me like a heavy, dark cloak, making my whole body feel like lead. Water flooded again into my eyes. Looking back over my shoulder, I could see that the onlookers had become concerned about my well being, and rightly so. They called for me to return to their side of the shore. Trust me, that was my every intent, but that was also equally impossible for the moment. The long and short of it was . . . . I was drowning! I gurgled a muffled scream. It was not a normal scream. It was high-pitched and afraid. It was the scream of seeing my own death. Luckily, it was only in my head. My companions wouldn't be able to tease me about it later. If there was to be a. . . . later!

Instinctively, I reversed my direction, turned over on my back and began to float toward shore. Thank God, by floating, I gained strength for a few seconds. I turned over again, after a few more minutes and began to make long, desperate strokes to shore. Behind terror stricken eyes I could see two of my friends swimming to my rescue, and, with their assistance, I made it back to shore.

Amid a lot of laughing, jeering and kidding, I waded onto the beach and collapsed in a heap. Not quite a man yet, I had made the effort and felt very good about myself! There is a narrow gap between failure and success. I would have to wait until the following year before I would conquer . . . the bottomless pit!

CHAPTER 3

<u>COMING OF AGE</u>

I have given you shadowy glimpses into some of my family's early years. But, my extended family also helped mold my future character. I can recollect a period beginning when I was four years old. My mom would rotate her children on trips to Crawfordsville, Indiana, some twenty miles west of Lebanon. Crawfordsville boasted a population of about the same as Lebanon. Since our family didn't have a car, a family friend named Welsh would drive over from Crawfordsville in an old, black Ford that clattered and clanked like a threshing machine. He would swoop up a couple of Mom's urchins and chug back along the narrow, pasture lined Highway 32 West to Crawfordsville. Usually these trips were in the summertime when my older brothers and sisters, Sonny, Marlon, Arthelma, and Valada and I were out of school. These mini vacations were great moments for all of us. It was a chance to get away from our cramped quarters at home, where we slept two to a bed.

We would stay with my Aunt Lucille and Uncle Theopolis (Thea). Uncle Thea was a tall, handsome, angular man, dark skinned, with straight hair. He had the deepest voice I had ever heard. It was not menacing, just deep, like it came up from a bottomless pit. Uncle Thea appeared to relish these visits of his sister's children and would take us all around the black neighborhood to see our other relatives. They would greet us with lots of hugs and kisses. And best of all, they would offer tasty candy treats.

My Aunt Lucille was a lovely person. At the time, her graying hair framed a round face with negligible cheek bones. She had an almost oriental look, with almond eyes and small, unpainted lips. She spoke in a high, squeaky voice that blended with her gentle nature. Since she had no children of her own, Mom's children who were lucky enough to get to make these visits were showered with the warmth of Aunt Lucille's loving care. We looked forward immensely to these visits with her.

My aunt and uncle lived in a small, neat home. Their house was located directly across the street from a large wire mill that operated day and night. A low, grating, mechanical sound bathed the area and never ceased. Late at night, sleep came slowly and torturously when it did. Not only did the sound keep me awake, but so did fitful dreams of dogs. They loved dogs. Ugly Bull Dogs. They named them after black big bandleaders. The first one I could remember was "Duke." Uncle Thea told us the dog was named, of course, after the famous black bandleader Duke Ellington. He also had an aquarium which was home to a large, dark gray "mud dog." It was a species of the eel, I guess. At any rate it frightened me terribly. As I peered into the aquarium, it seemed to peer back at me as if it had some apparent knowledge of who I was – a stranger in its midst. And it questioned, perhaps even resented, my being there. So, with the incessant noise of the wire mill, "Duke," and the "mud dog," there were many nights when nightmares ruled my stay.

My aunt and uncle were early risers. I wasn't. But I learned quickly to be one, especially when I would awaken to the most heavenly aromas coming from the kitchen. These were strange odors that were absent from my house. We would scamper out of bed to a breakfast befitting the idle rich. The table nearly buckled under the weight of fresh cold milk, orange juice, biscuits and gravy, mounds of bacon, and all the scrambled eggs one could eat. This was a far cry from the dry cereal or oatmeal that was the staple at home. My aunt and uncle never resented the fact that we were eating them out of house and home. They seemed content to sit back with folded hands and witness the attack on the bounty laid out before us.

The special treatment was not surprising since Crawfordsville was my mom's birthplace. Several other relatives of mine lived there as well. These early trips were when I became conscious of my relatives. My cousin Josephine had four sons, Thomas, Raymond, Chester, and Keith. All but Keith were nearly my age. On reflection I realize that had to warm up to them. The only other blacks I had heretofore been associated with during this period were the Booth and Humble families who were not related to the Scotts.

The Churchills were related to my cousins Charles and Madeline, who lived in Lebanon. Slightly older than Mom and Dad, they had no children. One very curious idiosyncracy they had: Every New Years day they would ask Mom and Dad if one or two of us could "walk through their house" for good luck for the coming year. No outsider was permitted to enter their home until this ritual had been performed. Their request never went begging for volunteers. The favored ones chosen would receive fifty cents and a bag of Christmas candy. I thought the practice was quite weird, but I volunteered every year until I entered junior high school.

Apparently in those days, as opposed to current family practice children called most adults not immediately in the family lineage, "aunt" or "uncle." For instance, there was "Aunt Mae King." She lived on a small farm about seven miles outside of the city limits, on the northeast of Lebanon. She also raised chickens for their eggs, which she sold to select customers in town. There were a few pigs and rabbits for domestic consumption. During the time period in question "Aunt Mae" was more than 70 years old and lived alone. Her farm was of medium size. It had taken a real beating over the years from general neglect; it needed painting badly and weeding. "Uncle George" did the planting and harvesting of the 30 acres or so of wheat and corn.

A visit to Aunt Mae's farm was a true adventure. She would come by the house on a given morning, usually very early on a Sunday, and pick up one or two of us to take back to the farm for a day's outing. We would scramble into the back of her old Model-T Ford and chug along the small, dusty back roads to her farm. It was great for her to do this because it gave Mom and Dad a little bonus time with not so many of us running around the house causing mischief.

When we would go to the farm, Aunt Mae would rightly insist we do a few minor chores. She would send me to the hen house to gather eggs for breakfast. This was a lot of fun. But, when the afternoon came, and I was given the job of chasing down a chicken for dinner, I would try to beg off. No way! However, she would send me to the barn with a silent stare and hands on her hips. Probably the reason I didn't want to go was that once, while gathering eggs, I was faced down by a large black and red rooster. Wings flapping and squawking like mad, he chased me around the barn. Finally, I made my escape by running to the house like the devil himself was behind me. Aunt Mae just laughed. But what did I know about roosters. Nor was I anxious to hand pick a chicken who's impending death would soon provide me with a delicious meal in a few hours. Neither did I like to see Aunt Mae put the chicken on a chopping block with a hatchet in hand. She would hold the hatchet high and, with a strong practiced swing, would flash down with a "thwack" and the head of the chicken was off. The remainder of the body would go flapping around the yard. Poor chicken. Just a few moments before it was running around squawking, proud of the eggs it had left for me earlier that morning. Now it was doomed to go into a boiling hot tub. I reluctantly helped pluck the feathers. But my antipathy toward my fallen friend was soon forgotten when I heard the dinner bell summon me from playing in the nearby pasture. What a sight would greet me when I entered the kitchen. I gazed at a dinner table laden with stacks of golden brown fried chicken, steaming bowls filled with fresh corn, green beans, sliced red ripe tomatoes with onions, and platters of golden brown biscuits. Then my eyes would lock in on a pitcher of ice cold lemonade, which I would tackle first.

Back in Lebanon, many wonderful summer days would find me and my brothers and sisters at my grandfather and grandmother's house, on Lebanon Street. Lebanon Street is the principal thoroughfare that divides the city on a north-south axis. On the north axis lived the upperclass families, with huge well-kept homes constructed of lumber and brick. On the south axis were the lower class homes with paper shingled roofs and low maintenance siding. The front and back yards were small compared to those of the families living on the north side of town. The home of my grandparents, Harry and Eva Scott, was an exception. They had a huge back yard, and we played often in their yard which had a swing set and a basketball goal. We also pitched horseshoes and played badminton on the grassy areas. There was also plenty of room in their back yard for a garden where they raised sweet corn, tomatoes, green peppers and string beans. My Uncle Ray and Aunt Lois lived in an adjacent home that was originally built with the same style as my grandparents. There were no fences separating the lots, so this increased the back yard space. It also permitted room for picnics and barbeques, which usually occurred on Memorial Day and the Fourth of July.

My grandfather was Harry Scott, a man whose memory nearly escapes me, mainly because I was so young when he was alive. I do recall that he was a very dark skinned man, almost inky black. He was small and his hair was curly white. He looked like the typical old black and white photographs of black men taken at the turn of the century. He stood ramrod straight and proud in his well-pressed clothes. His wife, Eva, had a magnificent face with facial features similar to those of American Indians. However, she looked like a white person with her long, white hair that was worn in an upswept bun, but on occasions when I observed her combing it, her hair was much longer than shoulder length. She was a wonderful person who loved her five children, Robert, Dorothy, Lois, Harriet and Mary Jo. My Dad was a step brother to these siblings. They were all extremely handsome children and we loved to be in each other's company. They were also very bright in school. When we all gathered together there was much laughing, joking, storytelling and competition in sports.

But something was wrong. Terribly wrong! Somehow, somewhere in the dim past, there must have been some incident that happened involving Mom and Dad. Throughout my early and teenage years, I don't ever recall my dad going to their house, even though it was only seven or eight blocks away. This estrangement remained throughout my dad's life. I do recall that all of the Harry Scott girls loved and admired Dad and Mom. They would all come to our house on a frequent basis, and were welcomed. But Dad never reciprocated the visits. If there was a family crisis they would all rally around one another to offer support. They would do the same when there was a death in the family. But that was the extent of it. The mystery of the schism remains just that, a mystery. Even to this day.

IN GOOD TIMES AND BAD

Throughout all the family adversities encountered during my early years, my father and mother remained a happy couple. Early pictures of them, tucked away in an old scrapbook, reveal that Dad was handsome and Mom was attractive. The marriage seemed made in heaven by the most trusted of gods. But my father, quite properly for the time, was the dominant personality. My mother, for the first fourteen years of my life, seemed content to be the homemaker, teaching skills and values to all of us that would keep us out of harm's way. They both worked tirelessly to maintain a lifestyle that was both nurturing and sustaining of healthy family values.

Mom's early training, perhaps under the tutelage of her own mother, dealt mainly with domestic chores which were passed along to all of us at an early age. I learned how to sew, iron, and prepare food. My specialties in the cooking department were pancakes, biscuits from scratch, and baking meats. Those dishes were not prepared for the whole family however, they were prepared for me. If I missed a meal for various reasons, I could always hustle up something. In our house, anyone who missed a meal was on his own because normally there was nothing left. Of course, Mom, with twelve children to feed, welcomed any help she could get from us that would lighten her heavy load. She made dresses, sewed pants, and attached buttons using an old Singer sewing machine. For me, it was the old standby – needle and thread. Mom was also adept at knitting, crocheting and embroidering, skills which were passed on to my sisters, Arthelma, Valada, Vera and Teya. I found it amazing to see embroidered figures and designs appear virtually out of nowhere on a blank cloth.

Mom tried to wash clothes once a week, usually on Saturday. Dad had purchased an old gray and green

Maytag washer – no Laundromats in those days. The clothes hung on the clothesline in the backyard. There were two large water tubs affixed to the right side of the washer – one for the first rinse, the other for giving the clothes a final bath. Mom always put a blue rinsing fluid in the final rinse. I think it was called, "La France" bluing. I was told it was for brightening the clothes. The brightening process was a necessity because with Mom's large brood playing hard outdoors all day, anything she could do to aid in getting the clothes clean was critical.

Stationed above the wash tub was a wringer mechanism that squeezed the water out of the clothes. It consisted of two hard rubber rollers about 14 inches wide, one above the other. A clamping device, with taut springs, provided the pressure necessary to squeeze the wash water from the clothes. All garments were hand fed through the wringer very carefully! Of course, this double wringer device was not concerned about who or what was coming through, so inevitably, on any particular wash day, a bloodcurdling howl might ring throughout the house. "Help, help! My hand is caught. My hand is caught!" or "The clothes are caught," or forbid other more delicate body parts. To relieve the agony of the poor soul whose appendage was caught or to unstrap the clothes, one had to lift the clamp bar and the pressure on the rollers, once released, the rollers could be separated wide enough to unstrap the poor soul or garments.

The injuries usually were very slight, causing minor dark bruises and much embarrassment, both lasting for several days. As I recall, this regrettable fate befell all of us at one time or another. My brother, Don, received the most severe mauling. His hand and arm was caught and injured enough to be taken to the hospital, but no permanent damage was inflicted on him by this demonic-like machine.

Dad had absolute control of the Lebanon Reporter newspaper when he arrived home from work. Woe be unto those who grabbed the paper to look at cartoons and let Dad find the paper out of numerical order. All would appear at peace and without care, when he would reach for one of his several pipes and take meticulous pains to prepare it for smoking. First, he would lay claim to his favorite easy chair – patriarchal privilege you know. Sitting next to an end table and to his easy chair was a large canister of Sir Walter Raleigh tobacco. He would then read the paper from cover to cover. What contentment would reign over the entire household at such moments. We watched the pipe smoke spiral upwards, the sweet pungent aroma filling the air. Not only did it have a calming effect on Dad, but this ritual called for a cease of the normal hustle, bustle, and din of noise coming from me, my brothers and my sisters. He didn't have to tell us to be quiet, we just did it. Everyone would do their own individual thing. Mom turned to crocheting, my sisters would iron or repair their clothing, and my brothers and I would play basketball outside or do our chores. These were the quiet hours! There was a scarcity of chairs to sit in comfortably while busying oneself, which created a problem: If anyone who was sitting had to get up to go to another section of the house, there would be a mad dash for the chair he had just vacated. We would either win or lose the battle of the chairs and that was that. Since the boys were constantly admonished to be gentlemen in or outside the home, we always lost that skirmish to the girls. Ladies seated first, you know!

Of course, as every adult my age knows, when Mom said, "Let's make some ice cream!" all the world seemed serene and God's kingdom was good. At our house, when this blissful moment took place it was usually on Sunday, but not just any Sunday. It had to be a bright, cheerful sunny day, all of the Saturday chores over. My brothers, sisters and I had to have been exemplary in our behavior, throughout the week. Finally, we had to be eating fried chicken, green beans, biscuits, and mashed potatoes and gravy for dinner that day. And, of course, homemade ice cream had to be made under the shade of our old apple tree, next to the coal shed. Why Dad permitted that old apple tree to remain standing, I don't know. It produced only small worm-infested apples that fell to the ground and rotted, adding to the weekly clean up chores. Actually, though, the tree was not totally worthless. The large overhanging limbs did provide us with the chance for daring, as we climbed its gnarled limbs and branches. It was a gateway to the roof of the shed where, when our courage was high, we would pretend we were Superman and "fly" out into space and land, not so lightly, on the cinder alley some twelve feet below. It would have saved a lot of skinned knees if we had known about gravity and Newton's Third Law of Motion. But, enough of physics and back to the making of ice cream.

The ice cream maker was, in reality, a metal thermos bottle, sitting in a bucket of ice, with built-in paddles attached to an external handle to churn the device and the ingredients it contained. Crushed ice was placed in the bottom and sides of the container, surrounding the device that held the ingredients. Into the thermos went milk and heavy cream, sugar, vanilla extract and eggs. The metal lid for the thermos was placed on the top of the container and then the work began. Mom would say, "Now who wants to turn the handle first?" NO takers! We would scatter as we made up excuses on the run. "I've got to sweep the floor," "I've got to wash dishes," "I've got to work in the garden." We became the characters in the story of "The Little Red Hen." We all wanted to eat, but no one wanted to do the work. However, after the initial cop-out excuses, we would all take turns churning the ice cream. Usually the person who churned the most would get to lick the paddles clean after the ice cream was ready.

When the process was completed and the ice cream was made, on several occasions fresh fruit-strawberries, peaches or berries- were added to crown the masterpiece. Then it was a simple matter of gorging ourselves until our heads hurt. Compare this to today when a trip to the ice cream parlor for one dip of ice cream in a sugar cone will cost you over $1.50. No chance for a headache there, you don't------------------------get------------------------------ enough.

The God said, "I give you every seed bearing plant on the face of the whole earth and every tree that has fruit with seed in it. They will be yours for food."
Genesis 1:29

HOMO HABALIS LIVES!

Homo Habalis, according to anthropologists, was an earlier form of homo sapien who survived as a species by hunting and gathering food. Archaeologists believe this early form of man first came on the scene some two million years ago. It is believed they hunted small prey, but were also scavengers and gatherers of fruits and berries. Homo Habalis was a stout-hearted brute who traveled across the land living off its bounty. When the food gave out, he moved on to more plentiful grounds.

In many ways Habalis and I lived a similar life in those days, but others in Lebanon could gratefully cry out ABBONDAZA! That's Italian for "Enough! Plenty! Abundance!" The Italians apply it mostly to the discussion of food, but abundance or the lack thereof covers more than food.

About 95 percent of the waking time for most of the world's creatures is spent searching for food, even in today's world. Yes, my friend, those of us who can today cry out, ABBONDAZA, must realize that there are many who cannot relate to the meaning of the word, even if it weren't in Italian.

It is not pleasant to watch the nightly news and see starving children in India, Somalia, the Flavelas in South America, and even the homeless and too many others in America who go in search of food to survive for one more day. Apparently, from the most primitive times, when Homo Habalis crossed to the North American continent, food was the highest priority for survival. The "land of milk and honey" has been, for too many of its inhabitants, an illusion. In the 1930s and early 1940s, it was still an illusion for most Americans. The Scotts, with fourteen mouths to feed, did not escape the awful jaws of poverty and food deprivation of this period.

The Great Depression brought misery and a sense of hopelessness to millions of Americans across the land. Its full fury was captured was recounted, dramatized in John Steinbeck's book, TheGrapes of Wrath. Rewrite that story millions of times, with minor alterations for big cities and small hamlets throughout the land. Americans struggled mightily for ways to feed their families during the Great Depression years. I know it is hard for most of us living in the 1990s to believe that finding food for the table was an ordeal and a major time-consuming effort for most American families. Fast food restaurants like Hardees, Rally's, Kentucky Fried Chicken, Pizza Hut, and grocery store frozen food and the like were not grist for even science fiction writers fifty years ago.

Today, the average American eats and eats some more, and in between he snacks too. Late at night while he watches television, he eats. He eats whenever he's hungry, whenever he thinks he might be hungry. But decades ago, on Pearl Street and other streets around the country, food was frequently found only by handout.

For the first ten years of my life, at the Scott house on Pearl Street, food was indeed scarce. Food, in any ample amount, was something of which dreams were made. But the curious thing about the period was that I never knew I was hungry. All I knew was what other families and individuals today know: I must find something to eat. We foraged for nuts, berries, pears, greens, apples, anything that would fill the stomach. That was the mission, and a mission nearly impossible for a family of fourteen. In many ways it was fun. It took great skill to hit the last apple or pear from the tree with a rock or stick. "I got it," we would say, as a rock or stick hit its mark and the fruit would fall in a lovely arch to the ground. We learned to be excellent marksmen. To hunt for walnuts in the forest, bring them home, remove the green outer skin and preserve the precious nut fruit within was a real adventure. But I hated it when my friends and I would be singled out to receive milk and cookies before school in the mornings, even though the milk served to us in cold glass bottles before school in the mornings was really great. The first two inches were thick, sweet cream. The other kids not targeted for breakfast snacks because their families could afford to feed them would watch the rest of us eating. Only the poor received this gratuity from those blessed souls who knew better than we did what we needed as an endangered species. They knew that what we received was possibly all the true nourishment we would receive for that day. The following episode is indicative of the survival skills we employed.

One winter day, I left school at the end of the day walking the usual quarter of a mile toward my home. Suddenly, I became faint with hunger. I had no energy left to negotiate the last two blocks. I lay down in the grass in front of the home of my friend who walked home with me. His name was Bobby Helms. He was more able to muster his strength than I was, so we just lay in the grass and thought of food. Somehow, I made it home and munched some old popcorn I found lying on the kitchen table, which was all I had to eat that day, besides my bottle of cold milk and cookies. The popcorn tasted great! I survived to search for fruit the next day. I don't remember how my brothers and sisters fared individually during this period. What they ate remains a mystery. Even today I wonder what they ate, but I dare not ask. Another time, during what I perceived was a very bitterly cold winter, I became acutely aware of a mighty hunger! Somehow, my brother Sonny decided that animal fur could be our salvation. We could become fur trappers. Muskrat fur trappers, no less. He got an idea from some of his friends, probably Monroe Cody for one, who lived a few houses to the west of us on Pearl Street. He was much older than any of us and a thug at that. Nevertheless, someone floated the idea that muskrat fur could bring $0.75 per fur on the open market. Well, all of this wealth, from little effort, sounded too good to be true to Scott brothers Sonny, Marlon, Don and me. I should have known if Monroe Cody had anything to do with it, it would be too good to be true. Somehow we got five animal traps and sallied forth to set them along the banks of Sugar Creek. Just think, we said to ourselves, $0.75 times five traps, $3.75 -that was over one-half week's pay for most adults! We'll make that in one day, just by using our brains and outwitting the lowly beast, the muskrat.

I laugh like crazy about this tale today, especially when I conjure up the story of <u>Peter and the Wolf</u> by Sergio Prokofiev. It is, you will recall, the immortal fairy tale about young Peter and his small band of intrepid friends setting out to capture the big, bad wolf. There was Peter and his little pop-gun and his intrepid friends, and Sasha the duck out for the big hunt. Anyway, early one morning, in the freezing cold, we set out for Sugar Creek in search of the elusive but life-saving muskrat. We trudged along the banks of the creek bed, feet wet from fording the shallow creek. We placed the traps in the scrub brush along a wide fork in the creek bed. I had not bargained for the sight I saw just ahead of us. It was a large sewer opening with a steady stream of water gushing forth. I remember seeing excrement, condoms, and God only knows what other manner of filth floating in the muck! We were true young trappers though! Not only did I see things I never expected to see, but the surrounding area smelled to high heaven. I said to myself, do muskrats really dwell near here, and how could their pelts be worth $0.75 a piece, or any price for that matter?

At long last the traps were set, successfully I might add, without trapping ourselves. We quickly began the long walk, about three miles back home. We were proud of ourselves. That night I dreamed a thousand dreams of what we could do with the money that would soon be ours.

New shoes, boots, new sweaters and, of course, sweets of all varieties would be purchased from our bounty. The next morning dawn broke with bright sunshine, just a little cold wind, and with much anticipation. "Just the kind of day trappers' should have when they set out to run their traps," I thought to myself as I dressed warmly for the long walk to Sugar Creek. Did I say warmly? Actually it was any clothing I could find, including shoes with holes in the soles that were stuffed with old newspaper scraps. As we arrived at the area where we had placed the traps, silence was our watch word. The land was desolate as we crossed an area that was near water. Slowly, cautiously, and with great anticipation, we crept closer and closer to the designated spot where our traps were concealed. I, being very resourceful, had secretly hidden behind my back a small wooden club, just in case I had to dispatch the poor beasts trapped helplessly in our traps.

When we inspected the traps, our spirits, nay our souls, were pierced by the sight we saw. Nothing! Nothing! Nothing at all. In this cold, miserable environment all our expectations for instant riches were dashed. Where were the muskrats? People had caught them before. I had seen them stuffed at the furriers. Nothing! We tried two more days – nothing! We couldn't believe it. What had gone wrong? Not even the lowly muskrat would give up his fur, his life to perpetuate ours. We did everything right! We were hunters and trappers, weren't we? Well, Peter didn't get the wolf either.

THE COLORED BOYS OF SUMMER-
THE "BABY LINCOLNS"

The city of Lebanon was well known throughout the State of Indiana as a veritable "hotbed" for basketball talent. It is hard to believe that a small school like Lebanon High School, for more than fifty years, was the only high school in the State that could lay claim to three State basketball championships, 1912, 1917, and 1918.

Lebanon High School was the first school to win back to back championships. It was also in the first championship game in 1911, losing to Crawfordsville. They were in the final game in 1943, losing to Fort Wayne Central.

Yes, basketball was king in Lebanon when I was very young, but the city loved baseball too. Baseball, at Ulen City Park, on a Sunday, in summer fifty years ago, was a major event. The team was called the Lebanon Merchants.

My brothers, Sonny, Marlon, Don and I would go to these games. Most of the time we were a part of a gang of other kids who would "sneak in" the games under a huge canvass sheet which surrounded the main entrance and other easily accessible entry points, to keep kids like us out. The gang of kids were all white of course, and like the Scott boys, we didn't have the 25 cents to buy a ticket. However, it was much more fun to sneak into the ballpark.

But even we had a tough time gaining entry when the "Baby Lincolns" came to town. Oh! That was always quite a day. It seemed all of Lebanon would show-up for the games, as well as farmers from the surrounding areas. After all the "Baby Lincolns" were the "colored boys" of summer, and from the big city of Indianapolis, no less.

Who were these colorful colored boys? Actually, most people never knew nor cared. All the spectators knew was that they played the most exciting baseball they had ever seen. They ran hard, they ran fast, the swung at the ball hard, and they hit it far too. They would slide into bases with such style that dust clouds would totally envelopes with defensive and offensive players. When the dust settled, there would be the "Baby Lincoln" standing on the base grinning as he dusted himself off. On most occasions the umpire would yell at the top of his voice . . . OUT! The umpire could not possibly know for sure whether the runner was safe or out because of the dust cloud, but no one really cared. They were content to witness the running skill of the "Baby Lincoln."

The "Baby Lincolns" were truly babies in the eyes of many. They were too young to go World War Two and hence their name. Pete Olden, or "Uncle Pete" as we call him now, has been a friend of my family for nearly thirty years. As a former "Baby Lincoln," he loves to talk about the team, even today. "Uncle Pete" is more than eighty years old now, and ravaged by time. Nevertheless, I remember him in his youth when he was a pitcher for the "Baby Lincoln." "Uncle Pete" is more than six feet tall and was an imposing figure on the mound. He is still a nice looking gentleman, with a shy, good-natured smile that lights up like morning sunshine when he talks about the team. When I interviewed him for this episode, we both closed our eyes in deep reverie.

"Ya see Steve, the team got its name because all of the players were so young. The oldest guy on the team wasn't twenty- five years old."

"Why do you think that was," I dutifully asked?

"Because the team got started around 1938 and lasted till about 1944. All of the young guys that weren't in the war, played on the team. One of the best pitchers we had was a 15-year-old kid named Bucky Crenshaw. As you know I was a pitcher, but I was kinda wild with my "knuckle ball" and curve ball. But, Bucky, Bucky Crenshaw, he was something else to behold. He could throw a fast ball so hard that his catcher would have to leave it in the catcher's mitt for several seconds while the ball cooled off."

"You used to tell me about Bucky's slow ball, "Uncle Pete." Tell me again."

"Well, as you know Steve, a "slow ball" is also called a "knuckle ball" because it is gripped by the knuckles of the pitcher. Most pitches rotate fast, but a "slow ball" barely rotates. Bucky Crenshaw's "slow ball" never rotated . . . at all! Opposing batters were so mesmerized by watching the ball come toward them that they would just stand there in the batters box and never take their eyes off the ball . . . just watching it as the ball entered the catcher's mitt. They would just stand there, scratching their head in disbelief. The fans loved it!"

Uncle Pete indicated that the "Baby Lincoln" players never made any money playing games. "A blanket would be passed between the fans and at the end of the game there was usually enough nickels, dimes and quarters to keep their uniforms clean, pay their transportation, and maybe enough for a few beers.

"We played all the little towns in central Indiana. You know, Lebanon, Crawfordsville, Jamestown, Elwood and Richmond. At most places, except Richmond, we had to, or made it a definite point, to get out of town before Dark. These towns loved to have us come to town, loved to watch us play, but everyone knew that was as far as the love affair went. We were still "colored boys." The usual ten to 12 carloads of Black followers would leave quickly, without causing a scene, as soon as the game was over. We left town shortly after. We all had to be out of town before dark. No Blacks were allowed in these towns after dark." It was sad to see his countenance darken as he thought about this aspect of those years long ago.

As a final tribute to the "Baby Lincolns", "Uncle Pete" told me with pride that one of his teammates went on to play in the Major leagues. It was Sad Sam Jones, who played with the Cleveland Indians in the American League.

THE BROWN BOMBER INVADES LEBANON

I don't know who among the city fathers was able to pull of the great feat of bringing Joe Louis to Ulen Country Club to play an exhibition round of golf with some of the local businessmen. All I know is that one Saturday in mid summer, Joe came to town amid plenty of advance publicity rightly accorded a heavyweight champion of the world. Among the Ulen club members selected to play in his foursome that day was "Sonny "Shelby the person I usually caddied for during the regular golfing season. Gratefully, I was to caddie for him again that day.

When Saturday morning arrived, I was totally shocked to see hundreds and hundreds of locals and folks from the surrounding farms and small hamlets gathered around the first tee. Joe looked splendid in white golf shoes, dark blue knicker trousers, white polo shirt and dark blue tam hat.

Joe was first to tee off. All eyes were on this splendid, physical giant of a man. He drew the club back with his huge, highly toned muscled arms that made the golf club look like a tootpick. The club flashed down in an arch toward the ball with awesome power. It seemed as if the birds stopped chirping, leaves stopped rustling, men sucked in their breaths as one. Then, an earsplitting "THWACK" as the club made contact with the ball. The spectators shaded their eyes and looked far in the distance down fairway. "OH! NO! I said uncontrollably. "He's nearly missed the ball completely, as my well trained caddy's eye saw the ball bonding to a stop not seventy five yards away. Even at my age of thirteen, I could hit a pitching wedge that far, with little effort. The crowd groaned in disappointment and despair. However, Joe merely smiled a crooked smile. He must have known something the rest of us did not know. On his next swing he rewarded the crowd by hitting his next shot on to the green some 300 yards away. "Way-to-go Joe," I said to him as he came near me to return his club to his caddy.

Joe proceeded to play well for the remainder of the round, shooting a very respectable for the day. It was quite a day for me personally, as well as the local citizens. The Brown Bomber had made a spectacular comeback, just as he had done by defeating Max Schmelling.

A DAY AT THE FAIR

Boone county farmers sought diversions in the summertime, especially on weekends. It was then that they came to downtown Lebanon to shop, go to movies, drive endlessly around the courthouse square or just sit on the steps of the courthouse. The fields were planted with corn, wheat, tomatoes, and soybeans. The city folk worked hard in the factories and small businesses. So when the circus came to town, everyone would make a break for it. To those not sophisticated in the ways of the world, the circus provided a window on the world.

The local farmers and city folks alike stood in absolute awe of the lions, tigers and elephants. It was nearly as much fun to watch the carnival folk put up their tents, as to see the circus at night when all of the multicolored lights cast everything and everybody in a surrealistic atmosphere. The hawkers out front of the side show, the strongmen, boxers, wrestlers, the tall people and short people filled their pockets with nickels, dimes and quarters as we gazed upon them with endless curiosity. The favorite money maker for the hawkers was the selling of snake oil. They promised the invigorating elixir of the gods would heighten sexual powers and others that would relieve boils, bunions, get rid of spells, you name it. But the grandaddy of them all was the Hadachol. It would cure anything – even bad marriages. The dark brown bottle contained amazing power. As most of us learned later, after millions of bottles were sold, Hadachol was mostly alcohol!

The same allure was true of the county fairs. The men farmers would vie for blue ribbons by proudly displaying their ears of corn, baskets of beans, tomatoes and their farm animals. The women displayed their blankets, quilts, dresses and other handiwork. At one particular county fair, the <u>Lebanon Reporter</u> ran an advertisement stating that fair sponsors would be awarding a special prize of $50 and a dressed hog to the largest family in Boone County. To be declared the winner, all family members had to be present. That evening, Dad brought the matter up for family discussion. I was dumbfounded. I said something to the effect that, "No amount of money or meat is going to get me to parade on some stage in front of a group of gawking faceless white spectators." To me it would be a humiliation of the highest order, and conjured up visions of a slave auction. Family pride was at stake. We were who we were and we were proud of it. We couldn't be anything else. We might be ragged and poor, but we could not be bought for someone else's pleasure. The matter was quickly dropped. And do you know what? We wouldn't have won the prize anyway. The O'Brien family chose to participate and they won the prize. They had sixteen people in their family and the Scotts, of course, had but fourteen.

THE GOOD SAMARITAN

The early summer evenings after supper were very special for the families living on Pearl Street. It was the social hour for adults and playtime for the children. Most of the houses had swings or rocking chairs on the front porches, enabling the curious to observe all the other's comings and goings. Some might call it meddling in the affairs of their neighbors. It was a curious thing, but the men would reach the swing or rocking chair first, and their wives would arrive in their cotton house dresses and aprons forty-five minutes later. One would suppose that the husbands never helped their wives clear the dishes, mop the floors or carry out the trash.

Some neighbors used this time to just relax and reflect, perhaps dreaming dreams of what could, or should have been more important in their lives. Wilbur Padgett, however, who lived directly across the street, could be spotted lying prone on the porch swing, spitting tobacco juice into a brass spittoon, or drinking "home brew," with great liberality. This whole scene was greatly reminiscent of Jethro and his wife from the Tennessee Williams classic, Tobacco Road. While the adults were content to be content, all the neighborhood kids would be at play -girls skipping rope or playing hopscotch, boys playing catch or shooting baskets. Any children reading or doing homework? Not on your life.

One particular evening, regrettably as it turned out, I asked Barbara Saltsman if I could use her bicycle to take a little ride to the Big Four train station several blocks away. Barbara lived three houses west of us. She was very attractive, with long brunette hair that cascaded to her shoulders. She had perfect teeth that were obscured too often by full red lips. She also turned many a fella's head when she wore tight dresses. My sisters played at her house all the time and she welcomed their visits, since she was an only child. Barbara's parents were of modest income but she did have many things other children on the block did not have, including a western guitar. She often came to our house and we would all sit around in a circle in front of her while she sang and played her guitar. I marveled at her skill in using a finger pick and a four inch, solid steel round bar that whizzed over the strings. But I liked to ride her blue and silver girl's bike best. It was easier to pilot than a boy's bike.

After being granted permission to ride her bike and given final admonishing to return in thirty minutes, I gleefully rode toward the railroad station, all the while practicing my one-hand handle bar grip and the astounding maneuvers of "Look, Mom, no hands!" riding skills. You know – hands on top of the head or both hands behind the back. It was the favorite skill to perform in front of the girls. Some might call it showing off. I should not have been doing that. Suddenly, while I prided myself on my technique with the "no hands" style, the chain slipped off the rear sprocket, locking the rear wheel and tossing me over the handle bars. The hard pavement broke my fall. I went one way, and the bike went the other. Luckily I wasn't hurt too badly, nothing broken, just a few cuts on my forehead and bruises on my arms, legs and thighs. But I felt a large bump on my forehead, that was now starting to ache and get larger and larger. I also noticed a huge gash that was taken out of my pants leg, and I was suffering calamitous sensations of light-headedness. The air seemed to shimmer at the edges of my vision and was full of dancing lights that appeared and disappeared instantly. I was not in very good shape.

In times like these, I did what everyone does under such circumstances – I began to cry. At the same time my eyes darted in all directions, trying to focus in on anyone that might have witnessed this disaster. Secure in the knowledge that no one had seen me, I turned my attention to the condition of Barbara's bike. I painfully walked the ten feet to where the bike lay on its side, curled up and still, as if it were sleeping. With my aching arms, I lifted it up for inspection. Not a scratch on it. Allah be praised, and his best goat herder given a thousand gifts of his choosing! I tried to roll it forward in order to mount it and get it back into Barbara's possession. Oh no! The back wheel wouldn't move! Maybe the wheel was rubbing the frame. "If so, a quick kick would free it," I thought to myself. Wrong! The chain had come off the rear sprocket and was wedged tight as it could be against the bike frame. I needed help and fast. Looking all around again, in all directions, I saw no one. I had now exceeded the thirty minutes Barbara had allowed me. Panic began to creep up my spine like a dangerous, writhing snake. More tears began to well up in the corners of my eyes from pain and distress. Wait a minute! What, or who, was that rounding the corner of a building? I asked myself. It was a man! It was an elderly man who was walking crazily like a drunk. As a matter of fact, he was drunk! I watched him spin dizzily into view. It was Zeb Ellis. Zeb Ellis, the town drunk! "My God," I thought to myself, "Is Zeb Ellis going to be my good Samaritan?"

Zeb Ellis had the appearance of a mountain man who had just come out of the wilderness from winter hibernation, seeking to replenish his provisions. He was more than sixty-five years old. His flowing white hair was curled and matted. It matched his skin color. His steel gray eyes were now cloudy and vacant and they, too, matched his skin color. He wore a faded blue shirt and bib overalls that were yellow-stained, in the wrong places! He wreaked of alcohol and failure. Rumor had it that Zeb was a civil engineer and was the only person in the city who knew where all the sewers and water mains were. He still carried that knowledge and, when he wasn't drunk, which was not very often, was called upon to find underground mains by the local utility. Now, I needed his help too!

"Mr. Ellis, can you help me fix my bike? The chain is off the rear sprocket and I can't repair it by myself." Zeb said something unintelligible and bent down to take a look. It proved to be a big mistake on his part. The simple act of bending over proved to be his undoing. It disrupted his already unstable equilibrium. With arms flailing like a windmill, he went sprawling backward, collapsing in a ragged heap. Two attempts to struggle to his feet gained him nothing. He crawled ten feet to the wall of a building, barred his teeth into a maniacal, frozen grin, and with eyes fixed on the heavens, he passed into another time and place, perhaps even another reality. The only possible solution to my problem came to me, unbridled and unwelcome. I would have to hoist the rear end of the bike with one hand, and guide the handlebars with the other. This proved to be a tiring, unwieldy and embarrassing solution, but it would have to do.

What a sight I must have been to the neighbors sitting on their porch swings and rockers. They needed something to break their monotonous reverie, and I was it! No one offered to help. I thought I heard muted laughter as I staggered crazily, like Zeb Ellis, down the street, aching from my bruises, tears falling, unwiped, from my face. Barbara on the other hand was a dear. I was braced for more humiliation from her, but she only said, "It's okay, Steve, my dad will fix it tomorrow. Go on home and get cleaned up."

Shakespeare was right – "Never a lender nor borrower be."

"Work is not a curse, it is
the prerogative of intelligence, the
only means to manhood and the
measure of civilization . . .
Savages do not work"

WORK IS NOT A CURSE

Calvin Coolidge

One of the drawbacks of human development is the long period of infancy. A child, until fifteen or so, depends on parents. As Joseph Campbell, Master of Mythology, states, "This attitude of dependency, the attitude of submission to authority, expecting approval, fearing discipline, is the prime condition of the psyche of the young." But work outside the home can lessen the dependency and hasten the arrival of early manhood. For this reason and many more, I worked!

All children in the Scott house, like children in all of the poor families along Pearl Street, worked. Some were expected to work, others did it because it seemed the thing to do if they wanted certain necessities, food and clothing for instance. I do not remember how old I was when I first began performing odd jobs for pay. A reasonably good guess would be seven years old. During the next ten years, I had a number of menial, low paying jobs.

First, there was hauling coal ash for neighborhood residents. Coal ashes were the remnants of coal used for cooking stoves and fires for heating the home. As curious as this may seem to the modern day reader and those environmentalists of different stripes, the answer to the question of what to do with the coal ashes loomed large in the eyes of home owners during this period.

Somehow, my brothers and I were able to get our hands on a rickety old cart. You know the kind? It was similar to those used in Europe during the days of the

Black Plague and described in Charles Dickens' book, A Tale of Two Cities. He wrote of a miserable excuse of a man who would walk the cobblestone streets at dawn, crying out, "Bring out your dead! Bring out your dead!" We would do the same, and probably looked just as miserable, as we walked the streets in the fall and winter months. We would yell out at the tops of our tiny voices. "Haul Your ashes! Haul Your Ashes, today!" If that didn't work, we would walk through the alleys looking for the telltale unsightly mounds of ashes hidden behind their garages. Most families wanted to get rid of them properly, especially older folks and widows. For a medium-size pile, up to three feet high and four feet wide, we would get fifty or sixty cents to cart the debris away.

These odd jobs were not scheduled as steady customers. On a particular day when my brothers and I sat around doing nothing, perhaps tired of playing basketball, we would say, "Let's go make some money hauling ashes!" Usually, one or two of us would agree, and away we would go. There was one aspect of this job that I never could understand at the time. If the piles were so small, why did it take so long to shovel them onto the cart? It was compacted, of course, and therefore the actual mass was usually twice as high as perceived. During the winter, the pile would be nearly frozen. The job was never as simple or as easy as one might expect, but it was honest work for honest pay. We found other uses for the cart, hauling garbage!

Throughout most of human history, there was no commercial market in disposing of garbage at all. People merely tossed it outside their homes or farms for pigs, goats and other domesticated beasts to eat. But things changed and at the turn of the century families had to dispose of their raw garbage beyond the city gates. Hence the need for the garbage man who would haul it away for a dollar or so. On occasion, my brothers and I would perform that service. If I ever find out which brother came up with that bright idea, he'll get a punch in the schnoz. I suppose there is something to be learned from every form of toil, but my final word on the matter is, bless the man or woman who came up with the idea for the garbage bag and for landfills.

After a couple of years of doing my share of this type of miserable work, I moved up the career ladder. The neighborhood guys found out that summer money could be made picking tomatoes. The going rate of 10 cents per hamper was the enticement. It was easier than hauling ashes and garbage, so we decided to give it a try. If we filled twenty or thirty hampers a day, which were really a lot of tomatoes, we could earn a lot of money. I was twelve years old at the time and 10 to 12 hampers a day was a great deal of production for me. I simply quit for the day after achieving that meager amount. The humbling, back breaking work of picking tomatoes, to some degree, was no different from picking cotton in the South. As a matter of fact, in college, when my black friends chided me for never having experienced the drudgery of picking cotton, and for having such a good job as a professional broadcasting student, I could empathize, thus preserving my blackness within the group. The Gods continued to smile on me and I made further advancements up the job ladder.

The next step up was mowing lawns. Now that was a very honorable pursuit. Any yard that needed mowing my brothers and I would do. We would knock on some prospect's door, and borrowing from our garbage and ash hauling days would say, "Lady, I will cut your grass for fifty cents." Or, "Lady, I will cut your grass for two dollars and fifty cents. I enjoyed this work. I tried to make the lawns as manicured as I could. It was enjoyable because I knew what I had accomplished at the end of the day and my work looked great.

From age fifteen to sixteen, I had three steady jobs, cleaning the home of two older women. They were Mrs. Ward, a teacher at Lebanon High School who would one day be my speech teacher and Mrs. Mac Daniel who was an executive secretary of Ulen Country Club. They both were very nice to me and I never got into any trouble with them. That is until the episode with Mrs. Winfield.

When I was seventeen, I landed the summer job most young men my age yearned to have: construction work. It paid very handsomely. Looking back, I think the reason summer work gave such pride was two fold. First, the money earned was two or three times what could be earned doing odd jobs. And it was an eight-hour a day job. Secondly, it satisfied the hunger a young man has to build, get dirty, carry a lunch pail, emulate older men, and hear swearing and dirty jokes. Construction work had all of that and more. It was dangerous.

I didn't have any thoughts of the latter reason, as my best friend and basketball teammate Bill Llewellyn and I were offered summer jobs by the Lebanon Tigers Alumni Association. The association was a group of local businessmen who were boosters for the team. We would meet at my house and then walk the quarter mile to the work site on the west side of the city. A large manufacturing plant was under construction there and we felt very lucky to be a part of something so large. We would be builders!

The construction firm was from Oklahoma. They brought a cadre of raw boned men with them. All of them were very hard workers and they taught us "City Slickers" what teamwork and a strong work ethic was all about. The fact that Bill and I were high school students didn't exclude us from hard work. We dug ditches, carried stacks of lumber and mixed cement in a huge mixer.

The construction foreman was a jolly, bear of a man named "Big Red." He was rugged as a wolf. Big Red had bushy red hair that never seemed to do anything but stick straight up and fire off in all directions, and a face that looked like something you would see at a medical school in a jar! Big Red was always on the move, barking orders to the several hundred men on the job site. He reminded me of a torn kite caught in changing wind drafts. If we were standing around gossiping, he would approach us and yell in a thunderous voice, "Okay you men, spread out. . . If lightning would strike, it would kill half of my workforce with a single bolt." How prophetic this saying would turn out to be. In reality, though, he was really a harmless, likeable man, and Bill and I got along well with him.

Bill was a rather chunky kid, but he was a good athlete. We grew up together and he was part of the gang at the "ole swimming hole." He was rather dark complexioned, about five feet ten inches, and left-handed. Maybe that trait was what made him one of the leading pitchers on the Lebanon High baseball team. He was a good, hardworking guard on the basketball team. Bill had a wonderful, playful disposition, and he was a team leader. He laughed a lot, and his eyes danced about like fireflies when he grinned, which was a lot. Something really tragic happened to Bill the likes of which haunt me to this very day. It involved my first encounter with the specter of death.

One morning Bill met me at my house, as usual, for our brief trek to the construction site. It was going to be a hot day. It was mid summer and school would be starting soon. The sun was already beginning to make the air shimmer with heat, even though it was only seven thirty in the morning. But we were unusually happy that morning because it was pay day. Pay day meant a brief shopping spree after a hard days work and a refreshing bath, taking in a movie or perhaps a poker game.

We were pouring concrete into platforms for the wall around the superstructure of the building. We would place the freshly made concrete into a bucket, then in turn would hoist it up to men on platform scaffolding. The bucket had to be guided initially for a few feet because the derrick operator had to negotiate some power lines that were in the near vicinity. After guiding the bucket operation for about an hour I was called by Big Red to do another chore, and Bill was sent to relieve me. I was gone for more than forty-five minutes when, suddenly, I heard a loud Whoop! Then men began to shout alarmingly and run to the area where I had been working. I ran over to the site myself because there seemed to be an anxious urgency about the shouting and movement of the men.

When I arrived at the site, I was appalled. Lying on the ground next to the cement bucket was my friend Bill. I heard shouts for someone to call an ambulance. Others were told to turn off the power to the downed lines. I couldn't believe it. There was Bill lying on the ground, unconscious. The downed power line was draped over the cement bucket, still snapping and popping. "Give him first aid!" I shouted. "The same as you would give a drowning man!" I saw his body make a final spasmodic twitch. First aid wouldn't have helped. Bill was dead, electrocuted in the blink of an eye. I left work immediately with unwiped tears streaming down my face, unashamedly. My family did their best that day to console me, but it didn't help much. That night I dreamed dreams of the most sinister dimensions. They dealt with death.

Several of Bill's teammates, including me, were pallbearers at his funeral. I never really thought about the fact that it could have been me. As William Jennings Bryant said at the Scope Monkey trials, "I don't think about things . . . I don't think about." That was the best thing for me, not to think about what might have been. But I believe it can be fairly stated that we are irresistibly attracted by the thoughts and anxieties we find most terrifying; we are still drawn to them by the primitive excitement that arises from flirtations with danger and death. Moths to flames, mankind and death; there is little difference. What a sad day.

In those dim, backward years, there was no shame in working. Any kind of work, no matter how menial, was the accepted way. Everyone on Pearl Street, black and white, worked out of necessity for the petty annoyances of everyday life. Things like, food, clothing, and shelter. The quest for these basic needs crowded in on all of us. The Scott family was certainly no different. But there was another aspect of working which my father and mother had counseled us about. "We don't want a penny of your earnings, but whatever you do with it, don't waste or squander it. Buy your own clothes and pay for your own entertainment." Dad always said, "Pay yourself first, you earned it. Then, religiously, save a portion of it. The remainder of the money is for you to do with as you please."

> The mind is Its Own place,
> And in Itself Can Make Heaven of Hell,
> Or Hell of Heaven . . .
> Milton, Paradise Lost, 1667

BILLY THE BULLY

One of man's most basic instincts in a potentially dangerous situation is grappling with the prospect of fight or flight. Our primitive ancestors faced this dilemma on a daily basis. Should he stand his ground with a spear in hand and face the saber tooth tiger or make a dash for the cave. Luckily the young boys of my youth never had to face the saber tooth tiger, but there was something just as fearsome to us. The bully on the block! What was to be done when one was confronted by him?

We all know that sooner or later every young man, perhaps old ones too, must face his own terror, stare at destiny down a gun barrel. When what he sees as he looks down the barrel is a Bill Bates, he may begin to wonder if he will live to experience any future destiny at all. Indeed, Bill Bates was the worst nightmare of every kid on my block. Actually, Bill Bates did not meet many of the criteria for humanoids, the primitives we studied in biology or anthropology class. He was two years older than most of us in the third grade, for he had been detained in second and third grades for poor academic performance. Bill had bad breath and green teeth too! Blowing his breath in our faces was the least obtrusive trick he would play. It could have been something more unworldly for all I know. He was four or five inches taller than most of us with a sub orbital Tories that hid his large, sad, blue eyes. His head was too large for the rest of his body. But beyond all of these regrettable abnormalities, he had red hair that stood erect and seemed impossible to comb.

At most times Harney Grade School was a very placid place and conducive to learning. Lots of good old fashioned learning took place under stern, no nonsense teachers. Perhaps that is why we looked forward to the playground activities. Our playground was large, accommodating all third graders, some 60 girls and boys, with ease. Every student waited eagerly for the ringing of the recess bell. It signaled time to play games outside with our friends or just enjoy each other's company. But, Bill Bates had his own evil agenda. Bill would use the first five minutes of playground time stalking his prey for the day, Looking for some little kid he could walk up to and hit on the arm, just below the shoulder blade, where the outer muscles meet the bone. He knew it was just the spot to ensure a huge welt would rise or paralyze the whole arm for a half a minute or so. He would then laugh and dare the victim or anyone else to tell the teacher. Another favorite punishment he meted out was to grab a kid in a hammer lock hold around the neck and squeeze. This maneuver was guaranteed to elicit maximum pain. After satisfying his appetite for administering severe pain, he would saunter over to the softball diamond where a game was always in progress. He would walk up to the pitcher and snatch the ball away from him. Bill wanted to be the pitcher. And if Bill wanted to be the pitcher that is what he would be. The reason he wanted to be the pitcher is because he could hit the batter with the ball. Bill did not pitch the softball underhanded. He threw it overhand, hard ball style. More pain when he hit you, of course.

Fortunately for me, from the beginning of the fifth grade until about April of the second semester, I escaped Bill's attention. Alas! He must have exhausted his supply of uninjured arms and necks, because one day while playing ball with Bill pitching (remember Bill does what Bill wants to do), I committed an unpardonable sin. When Bill was the pitcher no one was to embarrass him by hitting the ball too long, too hard, or too often. I was not good at hitting the ball at the time, so I was generally safe on all three counts.

Bob Kincaid, my neighbor down the street, and the world's worst athlete, somehow delivered a sharp single down the first base line. Bill sneered in his direction. "But, have no fear Bill, I'm the next batter up." I said to myself. "If I hit a single no harm will be done and I can advance Bob Kincaid to second base. My team will still be very proud of me." I took ball one on his first pitch, which by the way, went whistling past my head. "Was he trying to hit me?" I wondered. The ball got away from the catcher and Bob Kincaid scooted to second base. Bill looked at me, his eyes narrowing to tiny slits. Bill wound up to pitch again. In retrospect, it appeared that Bill's arm, and the ball, came closer and closer. I swung the bat, hitting the ball solidly. It seemed to immediately rise over the third baseman's head. All time stopped. Birds stopped chirping! The earth seemed to slow in its revolution around the sun. Then my teammates let out a chorus of, "Yeah! Yeah! It's going to be a home run!" I groaned to myself. "Oh no! Come down a foul ball! Come back!" I said as I rounded first base, knowing that I had done the impossible. It was going to be a home run! We were going to win the game, and I was going to die at the hands of Bill Bates. I feigned a limp to slow down my trip around the bases. No Good! I was rounding second. Now third base. The ball was still being chased down by the outfielder. I was going to be dead meat.

Mercifully, just as I was crossing home plate, the bell began ringing, recess was over. I was in a fugue state, but with a feeling of elation at hitting a home run off Bill Bates. The feeling lasted only briefly. As I began to make my way to the "line up," where all students assembled for "head count" before entering the building, I heard over my shoulder, "Damn you, Scott, I'm going to get you after school today. Just you wait and see." There was no mistaking the voice. It sounded like thunder. It was Bill Bates.

I suddenly experienced the most indescribable sensation, lasting no more than seconds. It felt like a series of electrical shock waves searing the back of my head. Even a freshman psychologist would have described it as "acute anxiety." I looked neither left nor right, following the rest of the students into the building like a quarry slave heading for the dungeon. The next class following the recess was math. We were working on fractions. Mrs. Berkshire, the teacher, called on me to work a fraction at the blackboard, but my mind was mush. Forget the fractions. I was thinking about Bill Bates. After being scolded by Mrs. Berkshire and told to "Sit down and be more prepared tomorrow," I slumped into my chair. I thought about what it would feel like to die. What to do when in an hour school was out for the day? Bill Bates would be waiting for me. My survival was at stake. Suddenly, the answer came to me. It was so simple. "Run home as fast as you can," a tiny voice whispered to me. And I did.

This went on for more than two weeks. The plan remained simple. Avoid Bill Bates on the playground, and after school, run home as fast as I could run. But, the plan had its consequences. I couldn't sleep at night. My attention span was getting short at school and those panic sensations at the back of my head were constant. My life was now reduced to go to school, avoid Bill Bates and his constant threats, and run home. Something had to give! I needed another plan. I couldn't tell my dad or my mother. I couldn't tell my brothers, they would just laugh at me and call me chicken. I knew the solution was up to me. One afternoon after resting from running home, I developed a plan. A desperate plan born of frustration that I couldn't go on avoiding Bill Bates.

Anyone who had been a witness to what happened next would have thought I had gone stark raving mad. In reality, I had. I secretly returned to school looking for an ideal spot to ambush Bill Bates. I found a clump of bushes, just south of the baseball diamond. It was nearly secluded, but contained a path where students took a short cut going home. There, I stashed three bricks and a baseball bat (just like the one I used to hit a home run). There would be no plan B. Running home again was not an option.

The plan was for me to get Bill Bates "hopping mad" during the afternoon recess period and challenge him to meet me in the thicket. It was there that we would settle the matter once and for all. Everything was in place and ready for the next day after school. There was to be no more flunking math, avoiding Bill Bates at recess, or running home. I slept like a baby that night. My headache was gone.

To this day I shudder at what I did the next day at the afternoon recess. I strategically waited until about two minutes before the bell would ring to end recess. Then, with the other kids watching, I walked up to Bill Bates, put one foot behind his leg, and with all my might, shoved him to the ground. He took a mighty fall on his right shoulder and side of his face. The kids groaned. Remember, you don't laugh at or hit Bill Bates. Then I did another extraordinary thing. I stood over him as he lay prostrate on the ground and yelled defiantly, "I'll see you after school, over there by that clump of bushes, next to third base. And you had better be there." The kids groaned again.

I felt wonderful, as I walked away, knowing the bell would ring any second, ending recess. I even paid attention to Mrs. Brookshire in math class. As soon as school was out, I raced to the clump of bushes by third base, crouching low and unseen. I waited for Bill Bates with baseball bat in hand. Through the leaves and branches I saw a couple of kids coming near the appointed battleground side. They couldn't see me. They waited. And I waited. No sign of Bill Bates! Thirty minutes went by and still no Bill Bates. Could it possibly be he wouldn't show up? Well, I wasn't waiting around any longer to find out. I came out of hiding, after picking up my bricks and bat. I made sure three or four kids who had gathered near my hiding place, saw me, verifying I was there. After turning the corner near a group of small trees I drifted out of sight.

Out of sight of Harney School, out of sight of my peers, and you guessed it. Out of sight of, Bill Bates!

I whistled a merry tune as I lightly skipped home (notice I didn't run!). The world had suddenly become a wonderful place. Again! You may wonder what the final resolution to this episode was? Well, it may not surprise you to know Bill Bates never, ever mentioned the episode or did anything untoward to me again. We actually became very good friends. All is well that ends.

No man is born into
this world whose
work is not born with him.
There is always work
and tools to work with
for those who will.
And blessed are
the horny hands of toil
James R. Lowell;

"A Glance Behind the Curtain"

THE HORNY HANDS OF TOIL

As a young child, I, like my brothers and sisters, had chores to perform at home. and as time went on they became more onerous. The responsibility I dreaded most was taking out cinder ashes and then bringing in the coal from the shed. Most of these assignments lasted a week and were then given to another brother.

Carrying the ashes involved more than just carrying a "skittle bucket" to the backyard ash pile. First, one had to wait until the fire dwindled to a low temperature value. At the bottom of the stove was a large heavy iron grate that the hot coals rested on. Below the grate was a heavy flat receptacle that caught the ashes. One pulled this receptacle out of the stove to the degree that he could reach in with the shovel and draw the ashes out, put them in the bucket without burning himself, the floor or anyone around him. This process usually produced two buckets full of ashes at a single clean up. The final process was to then shake the warm coals enough to get all of the waste debris out. We accomplished this by shaking violently. A sturdy iron device attached to the bottom of the stove. This permitted maximum air to flow from the bottom of the stove to the bed of hot coals above.

Ashes, if they are cold, are like snowflakes and they will scatter, mostly over the furniture and the floor! I would leave a trail of ashes leading from the pot bellied stove in the living room, through the dining room and kitchen. So, this chore was not completed until I had cleaned up my dusty trail.

Another chore I had to do, again in rotation with my brothers, was to carry in coal from the shed behind our house. Ironically, I would love and dread this job at the same time. I would stand in awe as the coal delivery man arrived in his truck to deliver the coal. The driver had a backbreaking job. It was something to witness. With a wide, heavy shovel he would toss the coal over his shoulder, down a coal chute. Dad would usually order a half ton or ton of coal at a time. Can you imagine doing that job all day, five days a week? Talk about hernias and an aching back!

Nevertheless, when he finished his job, I had mine to do, which was to deliver it to the back porch for ready access to the pot bellied stove. With coal bucket or "skittle" in hand I would take two or three buckets full to the back porch. Lumps of coal had to fit though the pot bellied stove door, which was a foot wide and a foot high. If the lumps of coal were too large for the door, it was necessary to use a sledge hammer to break them into a usable size.

What was more daunting were the times when I played too late into the evening and was caught by darkness. Then it was necessary to go into the dark coal bin. There were no lights there. Trust me, it was "black as a thousand midnights down by a Cyprus swamp." As I opened the shed door, I shivered. It was fear, fear of the dark! It was that carefully controlled fear, refined and hardened to a razor's edge as I groped my way inside. I feared the imaginary demons that waited for little boys in the dark abyss of the shed. A job that would normally take just a few minutes during daylight seemed to take hours in a young terrified mind, mainly because I thought I saw and heard the demonic archetypes of my buried nightmares in the inky blackness. Trust me, I tried to hold such misadventure to a minimum.

Another chore that none of us rushed to do was beating the dust out of the rugs. Dad, in his meticulous way, constructed a clothesline in the back yard for Mom to hang out the day's wash in the gentle summer breezes. Three- inch cast iron pipes were placed in holes 30 feet apart, which were then placed in cement. They were very sturdy. Then a quarter inch steel wire was strung taut between the poles. I watched him when he built it and it was sturdy as a bridge.

The living room rug, 9 feet by 12 feet, was draped over the clothesline. The fun would then begin. Mom would hand me [or whatever child had drawn this task this time] a straw broom and simply say, "Beat the rug on both sides until you no longer see any dust." That was an all day job. I could never get all, or even most, of the dust and dirt out of the rug. I suppose if ours was a normal household with four or five people it could be done in minutes. However, with 12 kids running through the house all the time, keeping that rug clean was hopeless.

Unfortunately, the clothesline was known to have other things draped over it, including a couple of my brothers and sisters as they ran into it while being chased during "hide and seek" games. I recall my brother Charles had to be taken to the hospital one afternoon when an errant pole vault effort fell short and he ended up straddled on the clothes line. He jumped as smiling Jack and nearly landed as Brenda Lee. Running through our backyard at night was not the safest thing to do!

CHAPTER 4

WINDS OF CHANGE

As I reached my ninth year, the bone-crushing poverty began to ease its stranglehold on our family. The year was 1941, and women were beginning to join the labor force in large numbers. Mom was no different. World War II was just beginning its deadly fury in Europe and Japan. Mom joined other housewives who secured work at the U.S. Machine Corporation, just four blocks from our home. The factory had three shifts working 24-hours-a-day, seven-days-a-week, making artillery shells. She worked on one of the assembly lines inspecting the shells.

Although it was difficult and demanding work for Mom, the additional income had an immediate impact on our standard of living. Suddenly extra food began to appear in the cupboard, along with new labor-saving devices for our home. A new gas range and oven, a new washing machine, a new heating stove, new carpets, rugs, even a sofa adorned the living room. Bunk beds were purchased to ease the overcrowded sleeping quarters. All of the above blessings were welcome indicators that the Scotts were finally crawling out of the miseries of abject poverty.

It seems sad, in a way, that it would take a world war, with men dying by the millions, to rescue our family, as it did desperate families all over the country. With the cream of America's men engaged in the war, women and black men, previously in second class roles, were now asked to step forward. The crisis of the war changed the way Americans perceived women and blacks. When the war ended in 1945,

Mom left her job and returned home to the equally difficult job of rearing her children. By then, however, our family had received the jump start it needed to escape the bleakness of poverty. Such is the strangeness of war: that someone always benefits from the sorrow of others? I suppose it has been that way down through the ages. It just happened to be our turn this time.

Dad's fortunes changed during the war period as well. He went from his job of working for the wealthy Stanworth family as their handyman, with a salary of $15 per week, to a tool and dye machinist, making nearly four times his previous salary. As fortune would have it, the Stanworth family owned the tool and dye factory located at the end of Pearl Street, and with Dad's prior knowledge and skill at making things, it was easy for Mr. Stanworth to ease Dad in as a machinist. He was the only black man working in the factory. It was indeed fortunate that he was held in such high regard by all of the townspeople, and I never heard him speak of any problems of jealousy and hatred.

Dad loved his new job. He had a tool shed full of hand-held and power tools, and he knew how to use them too. Dad devoured books and manuals on how to read blueprints. He quickly advanced beyond the journeyman phase, becoming one of the company's more valued tradesmen. He told us many times how proud he was to turn a piece of metal into a precise tolerance, enabling it to fit precisely into the next stage of assemblage.

It didn't take long for workers all across the land to lose that pride in workmanship along with the pride in the skills they had acquired. The pent-up demand for goods and services by servicemen returning home to their families was enormous. America needed new homes, cars, and appliances, and they needed them fast. They got them, but quality suffered. If a product worked for a little while that was good enough. Dad told me one day, with sorrow in his voice, his supervisor told him the parts he made did not have to be made exactly to "specs" because it took too long. Industry decided that if something worked for a little while, that was good enough. Americans became conditioned to shoddy products and workmanship.

110

Economic times were good, and if something didn't work right we disposed of it and bought another to replace it. The nation would pay dearly for this apathy in the coming decades as the Japanese would produce superior products and sell them to the eager Americans, causing enormous trade deficits and millions of Americans to lose their jobs. Nevertheless, the Scott household benefited from the national prosperity and a welcomed change in our economic circumstances was ushered in as I entered a new phase of my life, middle school.

FLEECY LOCKS AND BLACK
COMPLEXIONS CANNOT FORFEIT
NATURES CLAIM; SKIN MAY DIFFER,
BUT AFFECTION DWELLS IN BLACK
AND WHITE THE SAME
AUTHOR UNKNOWN

PREADOLESCENCE [IDENTITY CRISIS]

Euphoria, optimism, and a dash or dread, contrasted the hardship years of my early childhood. I was now entering pre-adolescence. Much excitement came from the realization that I might make the junior high school basketball team, which was an absolute prerequisite to any player wanting to play varsity basketball for the vaunted "LHS, Tigers." The dash of dread was the apprehension that I might not be good enough to make the team.

In the city of Lebanon, the three elementary feeder schools: Harney, Stokes, and Central, were combined into one junior high school for students of the sixth, seventh, and eighth grades. The junior high was a two-story building with basement, made of dark yellow brick, adorned in limestone. A small, well-trimmed landscape surrounded the building which fronted on Lebanon Street. Curiously enough, the small gymnasium used for gym classes, Mayday festivities and other extra curriculum activities, was right next to the high school gymnasium, only a wide alleyway separating the two. However, we didn't mix with the high school students.

As far as my physical maturation was concerned, I was beginning to start a growth spurt during this period. But, it was really a false alarm. I was five foot six and weighed 130 pounds as a twelve-year-old child. Neither height nor weight met my expectations then or in future years, as I finished high school stretching to reach six feet tall.

As one well knows, this period is generally regarded as a time of identity acquisition and some liberation from parental control. Although I did work at odd jobs, the time had not yet come when my being Black played a material difference in my thinking or my lifestyle. Again, all my friends were white and my father and mother were accepted as equal to whites of their socio-economic classes. But his was a period in my life that I began to develop nagging thoughts about my Blackness.

I had never thought much about racism or even about Blackness up to this point in my life. We had read the history books that described the horrors of slavery, and the Chicago riots, and we knew about Little Black Sambo. But, somehow, in my tiny enclave in Lebanon, such events seemed remote from my existence. Admittedly, I would get a certain twinge of discomfort at certain times. However none of these incidents could have any relevance to me and my family, could they? After all, whites seemed to love us, didn't they? No separate drinking fountains. No restrictions at lunch counters or movies. No Black ghettos. No denigrating, derogatory racial graffiti on shops or in windows. And no signs in the parks or the swimming pool, despite the fact I couldn't swim there. But I was beginning to feel I was an invisible Black boy, without an accurate reflection of myself in my immediate surroundings. The few times I was called a "nigger" [to my face] someone paid for the remark with a punch in the nose. And that was that.

I have already described my vexatious feelings at not being able to swim at the park, but that worked in my favor. It was more fun to swim in the gravel pit with my poor white friends. All in all, there were no anxious, racial times for me. And as far as I knew, my brothers and sisters suffered no dissimilar indignities. At no time did I really feel inferior to any white person. As a matter of fact, their values were my values. My older sisters, Arthelma and Valada, were very popular in high school. The same could be said for my two younger sisters, Vera and Teya and younger brothers Don, Gary, Charles, Larry and Jon. My older brothers,

Sonny and Marlon were great athletes. As a matter of fact, all of my brothers were good athletes and participated in numerous school activities. Sonny was a stellar track star, and Marlon was the first Black to play varsity basketball and baseball for Lebanon High School. On the same basketball team with Marlon was a lad named Benny Campbell who, I believe, was of American Indian heritage. He was strikingly handsome, and possessed a bronze physique of a Greek God. He openly dated white girls. To my knowledge, the Scott boys never did, but that is not to say we couldn't. Many white females invited us to their house parties and attended community center dances.

I am not saying racism was not lurking in a subterranean current in some of the town's residents, but it was not overtly manifested by anyone I came into contact with, which was most of the city's residents. Paradoxically I probably developed the same prejudices toward Blacks as the whites had.

For example, when I was in the seventh grade, the "town fathers" decided that if my brother Marlon and I could advance into high school faster, the immediate fortunes of the Lebanon "Tiger" varsity basketball team would be enhanced. So, they decided to send us to summer school in Indianapolis. We had represented our middle school very well in basketball competition and had unblemished win records against the local and surrounding area schools. Both of us were anxious to begin our high school basketball careers. Mom and Dad went along with the proposal, but made it clear it would be our decision. The deed was done. All summer long we rode the bus to Indianapolis and attended School #17, an all Black middle school physically located adjacent to Crispus Attucks High School. This adventure was our first introduction to large numbers of Blacks, and the "big city" cultural environment. And the word adventure is the operative word.

The first eye opener was the bus ride down Indiana Avenue. Blacks were everywhere! I marveled at the brightly colored suites, hats, long golden chains hanging from the men's trousers. I envied the carefree ease of motion of the men who moved up and down the crowded streets. I noticed "tiny knots" of Black men openly drinking from whiskey bottles, talking to beautiful young black ladies, adorned in revealing dresses. I would look out of the bus window in total fascination, mentally wrestling with the juxtaposition white society had taught me. I was one of them, yet it appeared to be true. Blacks were shiftless, lazy and low in moral character. I cringe at that "brainwashing" as I write these pages. But, at the time, I didn't know any better. Such was my view of reality at that time.

I did enjoy the fellowship of the students in my classes that summer, moreover, one myth was soon dispelled. Many of them were much brighter than I was. But, again, something was wrong with the picture. In Lebanon, I was being taught the same subjects the other [white] students were being taught, and my white teachers could not discriminate in that regard. I was taught that Black schools were inferior. So much for that reality check. To expand further on the point of my first awakening to an identity crisis, I must tell of an incident that could scarcely have taken place any where in the country at the time except Lebanon, Indiana.

My uncle Charlie Sweeny was a brute of a man. He worked for the Boone County Highway Maintenance Department. Heavy lifting was a part of his every day grind, and iron-hard muscles framed his short, stocky body. But, deep down, he was a great big teddy bear. He and his wife, Inella, raised two sons, Adrian and Jack. Although the Sweeny boys were eight or nine years older than I was, it just so happened that Aunt Inella enjoyed having me and my older brothers over to their house frequently for Sunday dinner. Aunt Inella made the most sumptuous meals I had ever seen or eaten.

I was particularly fond of her homemade corn bread, golden light and fluffy biscuits, chicken and dumplings, and mixed greens that melted in my mouth. Also adorning her table would be a platter of freshly picked, red ripened tomatoes, cucumbers and green onions, from the garden in the rear of their house. She had to be good cook because Uncle Charlie, Jack and Adrian were all mountain men, and quite frankly behaved like them as well at the table. I was frightened to death by all three of them because of their size and their unpredictable behavior. They would fight each other like cats and dogs. No! More like giant buffalo fighting over females at the height of the mating season. Many times, my wonderful Sunday dinner was interrupted by fighting among the three of them. They chased each other about the house, roaring like elephants in full rush. This would go on until Aunt Inella would grab a broom, or rolling pin, and scream like a banshee, "Ok! Ok! Take it outside you guys! Or, you will get no more supper!" Usually they would take their squabbling outside. They would return shortly, battered, bruised, but hugging one another. Perhaps their antics were a calculated ritual to whet their appetites. But, nothing like that scene would ever take place in my house. I loved my aunt's cooking, but I could have done without the preliminaries.

They would not hesitate to get into scrapes with white men in the city either. One Saturday morning, my uncle came to get me for late breakfast at his home. On our return trip he had to stop at the Hagg drugstore downtown, to pick up some medicine and other first aid items. Probably to bind and repair physical damages someone might incur prior to eating breakfast, I thought. I remained alone in the car for about 10 minutes. When he returned, we continued along our route around the town square.

Suddenly, without warning, a young white man, about 23 years old, darted in front of our car. Uncle Charlie slammed on the brakes, barely missing the man. I barely missed hitting my head on the windshield. If it had not been for my lightening like reflexes of putting my arms and elbows in front of my head, I would have been a basket case. For a moment Uncle Charlie's mouth was frozen in a hellish sneer. He jumped out of the car and within seconds, he had tackled the poor guy and began to flail away at him with both fists. All the while saying something like, "You white b-----d! I could have run over you and killed you! And you could have made me hurt my little nephew." It appeared to me that Uncle Charlie was going to kill him anyway. People started to gather around the ugly scene, as spectators to the fight rather than to intervene. I got out of the car and ran to my uncle screaming, "Uncle Charlie! Uncle Charlie! That's enough!" The entire scene was just like the fighting at Aunt Inelle's dinner table. Uncle Charlie stopped beating the poor guy who wisely, but awkwardly, got to his feet and ran across the courthouse lawn, nursing bruises from head to toe. Do you know what happened next? Nothing! The whole sordid affair was witnessed by several white male spectators...and they did nothing! The point of relating this miserable episode is that it occurred nearly sixty years ago. A Black man beating a white man on the town square court house, in Lebanon, Indiana, without reprisals, or a lynching! Lynching of Black men did occur in Indiana in the early I900's.

To my knowledge, my family dealt only with the more subtle forms of racism. Dad often told us the story about the time he went to one of the local filling stations for gasoline. In those days gas stations had attendants who checked all vital elements of a car when a motorist stopped for gasoline. They checked the oil, tires, and they even washed your windshield...for free! Dad said he was clearly the next car to be serviced. A white man arrived soon after Dad, and stopped at a pump across from him. The attendant went to service the white mans vehicle first. Dad was furious. He jumped into his car, spun the wheels in disgust, and drove on to another station. He didn't get far. He ran out of gas! Meekly, he had to return on foot to the original filling station and ask the attendant for a gas can to be filled with gas. Thinking the attendant might have realized he was angered by the fact he was not served first, as was his rightful due, he said," I was in a hurry a minute ago and had to leave, but I ran out of gas. Can you fill up the gas can for me?" The attendant gave Dad a toothless grin, and went to get a gas can for him.

One can see that my Uncle Charlie reacted to the white environment in an entirely different manner. However, Dad told me never to forget such insults and try to make the world a better place when I got older.

I must have pulled the incidents related above from my brain the day Dad sat me and my brothers down at the dining room table to discuss a proposition someone had made to him that day. It seems one of his friends, a white small-business man who operated a barber shop, offered to rent Dad space in his shop to open a shoe shine parlor. I vividly remember that he quietly stated the proposition to us. Essential to the point, it was an opportunity to earn extra money. Each of us could keep what we earned, after paying for the space in the barber shop. He never for a moment tried to persuade us, one way or the other. To this day I admire him for that. I was approaching 11 years old at the time. I don't know why, but I quickly cast a negative vote. Our household could use the extra money, but I was not about to shine shoes. For me it was an admission that I was not as good as my contemporaries. Poverty is no disgrace to a man, but I felt I didn't have to lose my dignity along with it. Perhaps it makes little sense, knowing the other jobs I have described, but for me it was a matter of the freedom to make choices and the freedom to live by the consequence of the ones we make. This point was brought home to me a few years later when I was in high school.

In the early morning hours, when my brothers and sisters were preparing for school, we enjoyed listening to Earl Nightingale. He had a five minute program wherein he related inspirational themes that one might choose to follow to broaden and bring meaning and happiness to life. I have always treasured his tale of the "Man in a Cage."

Once upon a time there was a King of a small European country who ran an interesting, but terrible experiment. He was looking out of the window of his castle one day, when he saw a man, an ordinary appearing man, walking along a street. He suddenly got an interesting idea, and he ordered the palace guards to capture the man and bring him to the castle. The man was held in captivity until a large, comfortable cage had been constructed in the castle's great drawing room. The man was then put into the cage. He was provided with a warm bed, three good meals every day...just about anything he wanted.

At first the man shouted, ranted, and raved. He banged his head on the bars of his cage. "Let me out," he screamed. "Why have you locked me in this cage? I've done nothing wrong."

Every morning at about the same time, the King would appear before the cage and listen to the man raving to be turned loose. The King would say something like this, "Why do you want to get out? Here you have everything. You're warm in winter, you have no problems, you are given three good meals every day, and a comfortable bed. You have everything you want. You no longer have to work hard all day and take your chances in the cruel world. You don't realize how well off you are."

The King would say something like that every day to the man and gradually his cries to be free lessened. He no longer shouted and raved.

One day several months later, a group of tourists being conducted through the castle, happened upon the man in the cage. One of them said..."Why you poor man...locked up in a cage like this...it must be terrible."

They were amazed to hear the man say to them that it wasn't terrible at all. "I have everything I want...three good meals every day. I no longer have to work. I'm safe and protected with absolute security." he said in a robot-like voice. One of the group looked more closely at the man and, looking into his eyes, saw that he was quite mad!

Our awareness of our freedom of choice and thought is something we should think about and review in our minds every day; otherwise we to could find ourselves in a similar position as the "Man in the Cage."

As it is known by now, nothing was made easy for our family during my early years; our life was happy but certainly not easy. However, I was now about to enter one of the great periods of my life, Lebanon High School.

HIGH SCHOOL DAYS

The high school years are generally regarded as the times in ones life that are most pleasantly remembered. They are the years where one weighs anchor and sets sail into unchartered waters, alone. Ordinary events of the past are no longer ordinary, or secure, or comfortable. Physical and mental growth come in a flash, and unheralded. It is a time when ones family values are tested at home, and the world at large presents itself as contradictory and full of half truths. It is a time when life speeds up to never slow down again until death itself becomes ones ultimate timekeeper. So, I intend to languidly walk through several significant events that shaped my high school years.

Lebanon High School was situated just a few blocks north of the downtown square. Lovely Dutch elm trees lined the long sidewalk approach to the school entrance. There were two buildings principally - the high school proper and an awkward attached section which led to the gymnasium at the far end of the block. The high school itself was made of red brick and was trimmed in the famous southern Indiana limestone. The interior was immaculately cleaned and maintained by three janitors. One was "Slim" Watson and the other two were brothers, Bill and Alva Hudson. The floors were dark maple hardwood that always glistened. The halls were wide and easily accommodated the comings and goings of the students. Personal lockers lined the walls. A huge trophy case was located near the principal's office wherein the honor and glory in the form of trophies and pictures of past years was prominently displayed. Lebanon Junior and Senior High Schools had a combined student and faculty of over 700. There were 87 seniors in my graduating class.

The principal of LHS during my tenure there was Paul "Butch" Newman. He apparently loved the name Butch, as it was okay to call him by that nickname. Butch was a tall, spindly man, with hawkish eyes that peered at us from a pointed head nearly bereft of hair. He never smiled, so no one knew whether he had teeth at all. He ran the school and there was never any doubt or debate about that. He led a cadre of excellent, dedicated, no-nonsense educators, with all the diplomacy of a general guiding his troops. Butch Newman was a former basketball standout at Purdue University, playing for their celebrated coach, Ward "Piggy" Lambert. This athletic background of the principal assured that sports would dominate the atmosphere of the school. This is certainly not to imply that academics was not the school's number one priority, because it was. The traditional curriculum of courses was offered for entrance to a liberal arts college. I can't say most students planned to go on to college, but many did and went on to successful professional careers.

The school superintendent was TT Christian. As superintendent of the LHS system, Mr. Christian had the job of coordinating all of the schools in the city, including recommending the selection of teaching personnel. Mr. Newman, as principal, was in charge of keeping the high school running smoothly and seeing that the senior and junior high school worked effectively. Overseeing all of the above administrative personnel was the school Board of Education, which was chosen by the City County Council. Its job was to determine and set the policies for the efficient operation of the city school system and to administer school funds and property. At the time I was in high school, the board members were city businessmen Harry Harlow, William Parr and Clyde Perkins. I knew them well.

TEACHERS PET

In spite of the fact that I was only marginally successful in the classroom. However, I did enjoy learning and did all the required work. It was important for me to do homework during the school library period because I was involved in many extracurricular activities that occupied all of my spare time. Studying at home was pretty much out of the question because of the beehive of activity around our house, besides the mandatory chores! I'm sure this conclusion would equally apply to my brothers and sisters.

Some family members will not like this statement but it was always my view that Don, Gary and my sister Vera were the real "brains" in the Scott house. They seemed to soak up any and all classwork with ease. For me, all course work was hard. I was pretty much a plodder!

I struggled along with C's in Chemistry, Math, Biology and Bookkeeping. I took one year each of Spanish and Algebra. Although I made C's in both, I was advised by my counselor, Mrs. Drubelle Stephenson, and my teachers, Mrs. Ruth Brookshire and Mrs. Helen Wilson, that my energies should be otherwise directed. Their advice was well founded, and not regrettably, I took it.

There were other teachers that I took a liking to and made mostly B's in their classes. These subjects and teachers were Miss Lillian Witt — Social Studies, Glen Neeves — Social Studies and Economics, Mrs. Lila Bowman — English, Mary Ann Tower — English Literature and Mrs. Jane Ward, Speech.

Miss Witt dearly and passionately loved history and social studies. She was a short, middle-aged woman, whose face was accented with prominent cheek bones and wide-set intelligent, dark, sad eyes. She had a crooked smile that seemed to be worn thin by the weight of her own abandoned dreams. Her control over her situation was an illusion, and she knew it. She was strictly business, with no horsing around in her class. I quickly learned of a peculiar quirk she had toward her subject matter. If students were ill-prepared with their lessons, she would burst into tears and leave the classroom. Little did she know that after being exposed to this aberrant behavior, I buckled down and worked twice as hard so that I could hold up my hand, signaling I knew the answer to her questions. I didn't want to see her cry, because for some strange reason she reminded me of my mom. Even today, American and World History are among my favorite reading pastimes.

Mr. Glen Nerves was liked by most students. He had so much fun teaching Economics that students were eager to take his classes. He made this boring subject come alive. We called him "General Neeves," [behind his back, of course] for he looked the part, with graying hair that had not one strand out of place, and a face carrying a sly grin. In the classroom he was a tornado, hurricane and whirlwind all rolled into one. I personally marveled at the way he addressed his students – "Mr." for the young men and "Miss" for the young ladies. This doesn't appear to be such a big deal, but for me, it was the first time I was accorded the respect due to much older people. Normally, it was I who called my elders, "Mr," "Mrs," or "Miss." In discussions of supply and demand theory, Mr. Neeves would be doubled over with laughter as he played his usual tricks on students, catching them off guard. Speaking with lightning quick speed, he would say something like, "Now, Mr. Scott, if there were more beans in circulation, the price of the beans would go . . . ."

Trying to respond just as quickly as he spoke, I would say "up."

"Oh no, Mr. Scott, you'll never feed a family with that kind of knowledge." I would laugh along with my classmates, but he got his point across as well.

Miss Mary Ann Tower was a world class storyteller. She made European and American Literature come alive for her students. She was a grand, elderly woman, full of memories good and bad that with the passing of time she couldn't quite grasp, or lose them. Her classes were always in the afternoon when my mind would have a tendency to drift into the netherworld. What could be a better time to let one's mind drift far away – to Beowulf's castle, or to Chaucer's England, through the *Canterbury Tales*, even to the dark broodings of Shakespeare's *Othello*. If the boys got out of hand, laughing too much or in general being boisterous, Miss Tower would reach in her desk drawer and bring out a mysterious, pink silken cloth which she would threaten to tie around the offender's mouth. Legend and myths from her previous students had it that it was a remnant from one of her most private undergarments. She would reach for the drawer and ominous, grim silence, like before a rainstorm, would descend on the room. It was an effective "attention getter."

It was a joy to listen to Miss Jane Ward, the Speech teacher. She spoke elegantly and with lots of flair. She taught drama as well. Several of her students did remarkably well in debate and speech contests. Bob Shanks won the national "I Speak For Democracy" oratorical speech contest. Charlene Kincaid won first place in the state in oratorical declamation as well. Both were a couple of years ahead of me in high school. Believe it or not, I was one of her promising students.

Now I want to turn to the king of sports, Hoosier Hysteria – Indiana Basketball. One of the most important phases in the life of any male student at Lebanon High School, next to academics, was the sports program. Baseball, basketball and track meets gave us a chance to learn about competition-how to win and how to lose. Just as important, sports afforded opportunities to work off excess energy – if not in direct participation, then in rooting for the home team. Competition with other schools built spirit and pride in our hometown. There seemed little else to cling to. Certainly sports played an important part in my younger life.

Just how far back in history organized athletic contests were first held remains a matter of speculation, but it is reasonably certain that they occurred in Greece at least some 3,500 years ago. However ancient in origin, we know that visiting the Circus Maximus and thinking about the ancient Greek and Roman athletics gives one a perspective of scale the enthusiasm for sports that existed in Lebanon, particularly basketball. The Lebanon High School basketball gymnasium had a spectator capacity of 4,560 persons, this in a city whose entire population was slightly fewer than 5,000 people. Albeit, many local farmers came into town for the basketball games and to see baseball on weekends, it would be fair to say that the whole town showed up for games. Naturally, this meant the players received a lot of attention and adoration by the fans. As a matter of fact, most of the local businessmen were tremendous boosters of the team and many would even come to the practices.

This kind of community and business support created considerable pressure on coaches and players alike. Well-meaning businessmen would try to tell the coaches whom to play and whom not to play. There was also plenty of advice and critique of why games were won or lost. This dialogue took place around the city's square, in barber shops and pool halls, and among the frequenters of the one and only bar.

If a man be lucky, there is no foretelling
The possible extent of his good fortune.
Pitch him into the Euphrates
And like as not he will swim out
With a pearl in his hand.

Babylonian Proverb

THE GODDESS OF GOOD LUCK

The desire to be lucky is universal. It beat just as strongly in the breasts of men four thousand years ago in Sparta as it did during my adolescence years, in Lebanon, Indiana. We all hope to be favored by this whimsical, but fickle Goddess. Is there some way we can attract not only her favorable attention, but also her generous favors?

We were not searching for such answers during my younger days at the rotating poker games held at my home, at my Aunt Harriet's, at my Aunt Lois', or at the Levi home. To us, it was a way to spend a Friday or Saturday night in the fellowship of each other's good company. Most times, in concert with huge pots of steaming chili, toasted cheese sandwiches, or saltine crackers, laughter would abound, win or lose. We also discussed affairs of the day, gossiped, and shared our future hopes and dreams. The poker games were the black folks' town meeting.

Here is how the games ensued. With very few extracurricular activities for blacks in the city, and everyone tired of the everyday grind, we sought excitement as we tempted the Goddess of Good Luck. Perhaps she could save us from our dreary existence by dealing us three aces, a full house, or a royal flush. "Let's gamble tonight," was a call that would go out to the regular players, and the game was on. Anyone with a few dollars could play, provided they were at least teenagers. The games were not high stake affairs. Normally, we played a quarter maximum bet. Five card stud was the favorite, but six and seven cards were allowed, and wild cards were allowed when dealers' choice was agreed upon.

It is strange, but I can't remember when anyone was accused of cheating or currying favor with one person or another. No one was given special treatment. Each would play the others with vigor and aggressiveness. Young or old, immediate family or not, everyone at the table was equal. I would wager against my father, mother, brothers, and sisters as aggressively as I would against my older aunts, uncles, and others invited to the game.

The games would begin around eight o'clock. It would not be unusual for them to continue until two or three o'clock in the morning. One can imagine that many times a person would go broke during the course of this extended time period. If someone went broke early, someone else who was winning would give the loser two or three dollars and he could continue in the game. Ultimately, as time went on, if this "loser" continued in his losing ways, no one would lend him any more money. He or she was smitten low by the Goddess. Whoever endured these long hours and had money at the end was the undisputed winner. He or she would gather their winnings, without boasting of course, and the game would end of its own lack of energy and money.

To those whom the Goddess did not favor, ten or fifteen dollars was the most I ever saw anyone lose in those early days, albeit that was a lot of money in the late 1940's and early 1950's. The games continue to this day, especially when the Scotts get together for holidays and reunions. And they are played with the same gusto.

Some who read these pages might disagree with this form of recreation. Yes, gambling is morally wrong and in some cases, it is against the law. But, in the context of how and why we played, perhaps they will be less harsh on all of us for turning to such a sport for recreation. At any rate, I enjoyed those evenings and so did everyone else. To remember the laughter, the camaraderie and the fellowship we shared were worth the several dollars that any of us might lose on those evenings when the word went out, "Let's gamble!"

In later years I played poker in the Air Force with my friends, where a considerable amount of money was at stake. I fared very well, even making a sizeable down payment on my first car with my winnings in a game at Stewart Air Force Base in Newburgh, New York. I'm not sure I'm proud of that fact but, as I said at the beginning of this chapter, learning about the fickleness of the Goddess of Good Luck has helped me meet life head on in the intervening years.

I enjoyed the status of an athlete. We were pampered, given summer jobs and a degree of self respect for my parents and siblings. My Dad and Mom attended every local basketball game we played. They also traveled to many of the games played at Crawfordsville, Frankfort, and Lafayette. Regardless of the "Tiger Team" on any given night, we never failed to receive praise from them for the effort. I must be quick to add however, that we received no favoritism at home. We still had our chores to do.

My brother Marlon was a year older than me and had made the Lebanon Varsity club a year ahead of me. In fact, I believe he was the first black ever to play varsity basketball for Lebanon High School. The local towns people loved him as a person and a player. Every time he entered a game, it was to thunderous applause. This made Mom and Dad very happy and proud. The varsity coach at the time was Forrest Whitman, and he deserves to be recognized for this breakthrough.

I believe my first game as a freshman was with the always tough Frankfort "Hot Dogs." "Doc" Heath, as he was called by all of his players, was my freshman coach. He also was the assistant varsity. "Doc" was literally too handsome to be a coach. He was tall, athletic, with curly black hair that framed a large head. His cherubic smile reflected a childlike sense of humor. But, make no mistake about, "Doc" was a no nonsense person. His demeanor was such that when he barked out orders, or chewed a player out for poor performance, it rarely happened again.

"Doc" was plagued by a left arm that was "frozen" to such a degree that it was nearly nonfunctional. No one seemed to know or care how it got that way, especially his players. "Doc" was a superb shooter of the basketball. No player could out shoot him during the shoot around practice sessions. Any shot he took from 20 to 25 feet was nearly a sure bet to ripple the net. I mean literally touch nothing but net. Those of us who dared challenge him had to fudge our bets by saying that if his shot hit the rim while entering the hoop, it was to be canceled. But, his main job, as a coach, was to teach his players to be fundamentally sound, including our mental approach to the game. I was soon to come under heavy fire from "Doc" for ignoring these precepts.

As the leading point producer on the freshman squad I was given the rare privilege of joining the varsity squad during their warmups before the start of their games.

In my first game as a freshman, I think I scored nearly twenty points, over half of the teams output. I was so overjoyed by my performance that I got on the referees Every time a foul was called on me, mostly gesticulating wildly and muttering nonsensical oaths. The game was on a Friday a night and I had all weekend to anticipate the accolades I would receive Monday morning from my classmates, to say nothing of "Doc" Heath and my teammates at the team practice.

At the Monday afternoon practice, and following his normal chewing out of the team for lack luster defense and other fundamentals, he suddenly called out, "Steve, come here on the double." A self-assured smile played gently across my face, along with an extra jaunt to my legs, I bounded down the court to where the players had gathered.

"Doc" began speaking very firmly, his face turning a burnish orange as he spoke. "Friday evening I witnessed, [Here it comes I thought to myself as my teeth began to show through my broadening grin] . . . I witnessed the greatest display of poor sportsmanship any athlete has every exhibited in a "Tiger" uniform." He continued with his eyes locked on mine like a laser beam. "Steve here, is the epitome of the type of athlete we don't want representing the proud tradition of this school. Sportsmanship is what is expected, first and foremost out of our athletes. I anyone is going to get on the referees, it will be me! Is that clear Mr. Scott?"

I was too dumfounded at my sudden decent from my lofty perch as a budding "superstar," to the depths of lessor ordinary men, that I was speechless. His directive must have been the same kind of ultimatum the Gods gave Achilles, "A brief life of glory, or a long life in ordinary, uneventful mortaldum."

"Ohh . . . Ahh! I mumbled, along with something else just as incomprehensible, in his direction.

"What did you say? I can't hear you!"

"Yes Sir." I said. "I understand you . . . Sir!" His voice came back loud and clear as bell tones.

"That's more like it. Now get back to your foul shooting practice and let's see if you can get ready to play next week . . . and without all of the "show boating."

I must have looked like a Wombat instead of a "Tiger" as I slunk out of his presence. For the rest of my basketball playing days I never again questioned officials, nor did I extoll the virtues of any success that came my way during the coming years.

DIAMONDS ARE A MANS WORST FRIEND

There was plenty of talk in the school halls, around the courthouse, and all other places where towns folk gather to engage in small talk and spread rumors. These gentle folk had plenty to talk about the day the highly vaunted Gary Froebel "Blue Devils" basketball team blew into town on a cold winter day in February, 1951. The "Blue Devils" were rated one of the top five teams in the state. But, the "Tigers" were a good team as well. Many people young people remembered, along with their parents and grandparents, the three times the "Tigers" were crowned State basketball Champions. Could this possible be the year for a repeat?

In looking over countless faded yellow clippings Dad had saved will give some indication of the exploits of the "Tigers" and my own involvement of that game. Despite the faded years and my equally fading memory I will, with some dread, reconstruct that game.

I recall coach Overman driving home the point in the locker room prior to the game that "We have a proud history of basketball at the school, and despite the "Blue Devils" impressive team, we were not expected to give them the game just for the taking. After All, aren't "Tigers" among the most feared animals in the jungle?" The pep talk settled us down for the moment. He continued to give us a briefing of the team, stating they would be the tallest players we would likely face in our high school careers. In fact, he stated they were the tallest team in the state. They averaged over well over six feet tall. Our tallest players were six foot two, or so. Coach reminded us that we had the advantage of speed and size should not be a factor. "Yeah! Right!", we said, as we sucked in massive amounts of air just thinking about the prospect of guarding any of them. But, we felt we had a good shooting team comprised of Gerald Padgett, Jim Schulmire, Jim Hendrix, Bob

Voorhis, Loren Walker, Bill Llewellyn, and myself. Rumors had circulated the day of the game that one of their starters Johnny Moore, was injured the previous Friday, and would not play. Did we now dare to smell victory?

During the pregame warm up, I could smell the tension . . . No fear! Fear in the hearts of the Lebanon faithful, as well as some of my fellow "Tigers," as we looked as one across the time line at the "giants" taking their warmups. It was then I noticed a vary curious thing. Gastovich was wearing <u>low cut sneakers!</u> I had never seen a player wearing low cut sneakers before. All players of the day wore ankle length "high top" Converse All Star playing shoes. The low top shoes made him look even taller. They returned our stares of awe with plastered sneers. I turned away in disdain. I never did like the idea of David going up against Goliath. I told myself that "action speaks louder than words . . . doesn't it! I returned to the serious business of the warm-ups.

The game began slowly. The score was tied three times in the first period. The "Tigers" trailed at halftime 23 - 20. I had hit five baskets from deep in both corners of the court. The second half opened as I hit another fifteen footer from the corner. I was in a "Zone." Too much so for my own good, as it turned out. The "Blue Devils" decided to come after me.

I had been beating Valdimir to my favorite shooting spot of the court. "Why not fake this Goliath the next time and drive to the basket for an easy lay up?" I thought. "Let's really show this guy up." Wrong! Well, not totally wrong. I faked the corner shot and streaked for the hoop. Time seemed to stand still as I floated gracefully, like a ballet dancer in Swan Lake. I was liquid motion. Suddenly, from nowhere, the gym lights appeared to darken. It was from another form that was floating much higher and whose face was framed by a white toothed grin. It was . . . The last thing I remember was flying, ungracefully this time, and totally out of control into a sea of anxious spectator faces, their arms flaying, as I landed four rows up into the stands.

Gentle hands began to assist my reentry onto the court. For about a minute I had no idea what a court was. Mainly because I was too busy watching beautiful, brilliant, floating diamonds in the air about me. They quickly dematerialized, only to be followed by two basketball goals, as I stood wobbly legged at the foul line. I shook my head to see what was reality and what was not. I shot the first of two foul shots at the one goal that was shimmering the least. It was the wrong one, as I heard groans from the crowd. And I missed the second shot as well, because the goal seemed to move, involuntarily out of my view. I was taken out of the game. I returned later in the early part of the fourth stanza. But, I was woefully ineffective, suffering from a dizzying headache. According to the box score in the faded yellow newspaper account of the game, I must have had another foul shot, or two, but missed them as well. I was doomed.

The "Tigers" went on to lose the contest, 56 to 41. We had missed our one chance to slay "Goliath" all because I wanted to "show off" against the "Blue Devils" from the North.

I continued my merry way through high school, "tilting at windmills," and I can feel the memories coming back, fresh and strong. But, I also feel a twinge of dread as more misfirings of judgement lie ahead.

THE MOONLIGHT SKATE

Perhaps you would not find it shocking to learn that one tool the white majority used to appease Blacks and keep the races separate at white facilities was to designate one day for Blacks to utilize such facilities. That would be the day <u>no whites were aloud</u>.

I've told you about the community swimming pool in Lebanon that excluded blacks, period. This curious act of segregation was the only community facility where we did not have complete access to. All others, boy clubs, community centers for games and dancing, parks, movies, were fully open to us. But the Blacks, loved to roller skate too. However, the city did not have a skating rink. In order to participate in this exhilarating sport, my older bothers and sisters, and my other aunts, uncles, and cousins living in the city, had to go to Crawfordsville. It seems the city fathers' there, would graciously, magnanimously, and with plenty of forethought, allowed their Black citizenry, Monday nights to enjoy themselves at the local skating rink. Young people from the surrounding cities of Frankfort, Lafayette, Brazil, Greencastle, and Lebanon would gather there on Monday nights for fun, social entertainment, and skating. It was great to witness the skill and airing of the young male and females as they cavorted around the rink. Usually a music master would be playing the latest popular records. Psychedelic lights would be shimmering in an eerie glow from the ceiling, casting the skaters in unnatural forms, as perspiration glistened like liquid silver from their smiling faces.

I was sixteen years old before my older brothers and sisters would permit me to accompany them on these magical Monday night soirees. There was only one monumental problem. I didn't know how to skate. This was a terrible blow to my ego and placed me in a very awkward position as a "big time athlete." I was beginning to receive a great deal of recognition from the ladies because I played basketball in their respective hometown schools. "Come on Steve," the young ladies would gleefully implore me. "Let's skate together at the next "moonlight skate." These segmented parts of the evening were the greatly anticipated moments when romance beckoned. As I stood by the guard rail, all I could do was smile broadly, square my shoulders and jaw, and say something stupid like, " I think I'll watch." Or, "Maybe after a while." This charade went on for months. Finally, a plan came to me. It was beautiful in its simplicity. I would learn how to skate. Remember I said we would revisit the canning factory? Well, come with me now as I attack this ultimate challenge.

One Tuesday morning in mid summer, following another night of excuses at the Monday night skate, in Crawfordsville, I decided I had had enough. I went to the sporting goods section of the local department store, and purchased a pair of plain, all metal skates. Not the ankle shoe skates you are familiar with, but just plain ole skates you snapped on over your shoes. I wanted no coaching from others. I would conquer this demon, alone.

I knew just the place for my training lessons as I began my tortuous first steps. The "Canning Factory." I was well aware of a large cement platform some forty by forty feet wide. Actually, it was a flat revetment that protected a deep well of cleansing material for the canning process. "This can't be that difficult," I told myself, as I strapped on the skates. Standing erect, and with a determined game face and halting steps, I swayed back and forth, sideways, sometimes I would advance forward. This is, when I wasn't picking myself up. Remember Zeb Ellis, the Good Samaritan? He and I would have been mistaken for twins. But, my spirit and determination to see the ordeal through to the end was of Homeric proportions.

Every evening after supper, I would head for the practice ground. It was a real challenge to explain the scrapes and bruises to my Mom. But, I continued to press on. Cursing softly as I would fall, I staggered to my meet and began again. Weeks passed that way. However, I was making steady progress. Suddenly I was skating backwards, hands behind my back, and I was thunderstruck when I successfully learned the moving 360 degree spin maneuvers. I was exhilarating to experience the freedom of balance and blinding speed. I would drift into a definite fugue state as I made the appropriate moves I had watched other talented skaters execute. I even mimicked the moves the male partner would make when skating with a young lady during the "Moonlight skate."

Just before school started in September, I made my much anticipated trip to the Monday night skate. I took my usual spot by the guard rails, talking causally with the guys. To my astonishment a gorgeous, freckled faced girl named Rita, from Brazil, Indiana tugged at my sleeve and asked me to be her partner for the next "Moonlight Skate." I hurried, no floated, to purchase a pair of rental skates, the high top version, of course. Suddenly, the lights dimmed. The rink was plunged into near darkness with only the pulsating, psychedelic lights bathing the arena. Palms sweating, heart pounding and eyes tiny slits, and filled with purpose, I skated up to the lovely Rita.

"It would be my pleasure, my dear, if you would join me in this dance . . . I mean skate," I said bowing low and extending my hand. She beamed at my awkward approach, but drew closer. "But Steve you can't. I mean I . . . Well of course I would. I have been waiting for a long time for you to ask me."

With my arm around her tiny waist, enveloped in the wisp of her elegant perfume, and the lilting strings of a Strauss waltz, we glided off into the kaleidoscope of dim, swirling lights. Other skaters and onlookers gasped as their mouths flew open, fingers pointing in our direction. But the lovely Rita and I were nonplussed. Such was the magic of the "Moonlight Skate."

And Yahweh said unto Abraham
Get thee out of thy country
and out of thy birthplace
and from thy father's house
unto the land which I will show

Genesis Chapter 12

THE "BURNING BUSH" ENCOUNTER

Sometimes in the course of life, a boy may get a nudge from a strange source external to him. A time in life may come when he reaches a "fork-in-the-road," where there is much at stake riding on the path he takes. In my case, I was approaching 17 years old and needed to give serious thought to what I was going to do with my life. Amazingly, I received help from an unusual source, a very unusual one indeed. In fact my hand trembles as I write this episode. Therefore, I will take my time as I go . . . Down by The Railroad Track.

The railroad that ran directly behind the Scott house was a slow-moving one that hauled only freight cars that serviced small commercial and industrial business along its route. The tracks passed less than 200 yards from our home. The book The Iron Horses states that the Midland Hauling Company was organized in 1871. It reached Noblesville, Indiana in 1876, Brazil in 1892. In 1922 all passenger trains were discontinued, and in 1943, the road was abandoned between Advance, Indiana, and Lebanon. Midland was the only line left between Lebanon and Anderson. Today, the tracks are gone. When I visit the family home today, only fond memories about the railroad creep across my mind.

Evenings, just before sundown, were fun times at the rail yard. Sundown meant the trains would be coming soon. All of the Scott boys enjoyed watching the monster train engines pull into the rail yard, directly behind our house. As night fell and the trains rolled into the rail yard, spewing white, billowing clouds of steam as they came to a stop, we would race to the tracks and disappear into the steam clouds for a poor man's bath. We could have been injured by steam water or run over by the steam engine if it moved unexpectedly. But we thought ourselves immortal when we were young. We made it a point to greet the engineers. Many times they would share the remnants of their lunch buckets with us. I believe they knew we didn't have much to eat and they purposely didn't eat all of their lunch in order to save some for us. The engineers were great guys and would delight in telling about the adventures of their day's run.

After maintenance was pulled on the trains and everyone had gone home, we would scamper up into the cab and pretend that <u>we</u> were the engineers, leaning out the cab window and imitating the hand signals we had observed them making. We pulled braking levers. We pulled the chain for the whistle and we pushed on countless buttons and other unknown devices, not having the slightest idea of their purpose. Of course, there was always the game of seeing who could walk for the longest period of time down the tracks without falling. Sometimes we could walk for several blocks without falling off. It was especially fun to walk the tracks west where the elevated Pennsylvania Railroad overpass and train trestles ran.

Often we would come upon hobos camped under the bridge for the night. They looked simply dreadful to us with their long hair, tattered clothes and huge knapsacks with leather arm straps to hold all of their earthly possessions. Come to think of it, we probably looked just as dreadful to them. One thing for sure, they never seemed to bother anyone. But what I remember vividly is how slowly and deliberately they moved. I guess they felt no need to hurry. Where were they going? When they wanted to catch a train, they just did it. To my recollection, none of us ever talked with any of them. I'm sure we were admonished by our parents not to. What stories of adventure they could have told us! I'm sorry we missed out on that slice of Americana that presented itself to us daily.

Many of the Scotts, I especially, used the elevated train tracks for escape, just like the hobos. We escaped from a house full of brothers and sisters, escaped from parents, escaped from whatever demons hounded us as we struggled through the early years. What the hobos were escaping from only God knows.

It was in just such a place, sitting by the railroad tracks, that I had one of the greatest experiences of my life, albeit one I have had difficulty in rationalizing even today. Was it a real experience or one of delusion? I hope you will not abandon me at the end of this episode.

It all happened in a late summer, following a heavy rain that had lasted most of the morning. Heavy rains in summer were really bummers for the Scotts because it meant no one could go outside to play. As a result, we were thrust upon one another, competing space. Remember, all members of the animal kingdom are "territorial" by nature and must have ample space for themselves, which space they ferociously defend against intruders. Unfortunately, there just wasn't that much space in our house to defend. So we would either pick a fight, get on one another's nerves, or seek sanctuary or isolation elsewhere.

When the sun finally came out that early afternoon, all of the Scotts immediately went scurrying like mice to their own safe havens. Some ran to Ulen to caddie at the golf course, some to the baseball diamond, some to the basketball court. On this particular occasion, I decided to go up to the train trestle to wrestle with a personal dilemma.

I recall I had been troubled for some time, perhaps a year or more, about what I was going to do when I graduated from high school. I knew one thing for sure. I had to get out of Lebanon. But to go where? To do what? I had watched my white friends and, my uncles and aunts,

140

most of whom were very bright, much brighter than I was in school, settle for less ambitious jobs or, very ordinary career paths. Most who preceded me found decent jobs in Indianapolis at the huge Finance Center at Fort Harrison. My eldest brother, Sonny, went to college at Indiana University. He spent two years there, before being involved in a serious automobile accident that caused him to drop out of school. Nevertheless, he was the first of the Scotts to go to college, and I am eternally grateful to him for setting an example for the rest of his brothers to follow.

I remember driving down to Bloomington with Dad one day to see him during his first semester there. Dad was extremely proud, in his quiet way, of his first- born son, who was going to college, something he was never able to do as a young man, go to college. I was proud of Sonny, too, and walked a little taller as I followed them on a tour of the campus. He had just been selected to ride in the first "Little 500" bicycle race and was the first black to do so. The race now receives national attention. A movie called "Breaking Away," made several years ago has Indiana University as its setting and the "Little 500" as its exposition. I will never forget that day, a special frozen moment in time for our dad.

Subsequently, seven of the eight Scott boys went to college for at least two years, an achievement indeed for those days and for a very poor family. Marlon, the only one not to attend, would have gone to some college, I'm sure, if not for his unfortunate and untimely death while serving in the United States Air Force.

I was nearing the age of 17, and I really wasn't much different from most young men and women who sooner or later had to consider their future after high school. Modern man has always been intrigued and compelled to think about the future. It is, after all, where we all hope to go. We think about it daily, monthly, yearly. Why else are we drowning in books, television documentaries, mind readers, prophecy gurus, ad infinitum. We stagger toward the future alone and afraid. The future is, all too often, the source of most of our fears.

Anyway, I was sitting alone by the railroad tracks of the Penn Central, looking out over the farmlands of corn and wheat and tossing gravel rocks at nothing in particular. Suddenly, without warning, out of the corner of my eye I noticed a bush that seemed to be wavering, or "shimmering" in an unusual and extraordinary way. The "shimmering" or glow of the bush was changing from silver to gold like millions of butterflies caught in brilliant sunlight. I could do nothing but stare at it, transfixed. Nothing seemed to move but the "shimmering bush." The air became heavy to breathe. My eyes became void of moisture and focusing was difficult. All known reality was gone. My skin began to crawl and I felt chilled all over. I was terribly afraid. But, I could not take my eyes off of the "shimmering bush."

I became aware of someone or something tugging at me, then groping for my mind. It felt like electric fingers gently caressing me with a warm, compassionate embrace. I became aware of a voice. I could not be sure it was external to me, but somehow it entered my mind, soothing like a velvet fog. It was saying something puzzling like, "Do not be afraid . . . nothing will harm you . . . I am you . . . or you as you remain in this time frame . . . I am with you as you are . . . as you will be . . . now and into the future. Pay heed for this is how it will be." I nearly fainted, but somehow remained frozen to the spot. The feathery voice continued its mind touch . . . "You will join the United States Air Force and serve your allotted time, four years. It is there that you will embark on a unique career. But Indiana University is where you will be trained for two unique careers. The first is communications. The second career will begin before you are forty years old. It will be your 28th year when you marry and eventually have two children: first a boy, and then a girl much later. You will build your first home before your 38th birthday. Have nothing to fear during these years. I will be with you." And

142

that was it . . . that was all! With a perceptible swoosh, the "shimmering bush" stopped its dance. At that very instant I found myself coming out of the experience with a consciousness radically different from anything I had ever before encountered. I felt giddy and dizzy, and for a moment I could hardly recognize even the most familiar of objects; the steep hill and path leading down to ground level, the farms, the fields. I just sat there for a long while. I didn't know or understand what had just happened. But I do know that I felt a new sense of oneness with everything. Birds, trees, sky, sun, moon, people – everything. I felt wonder and at ease with my self and my future. Old fears were gone.

I surely looked like a wretched soul as I slowly walked down the hill and trudged home. I never said a word to anyone, my Mom, my Dad, or any of my brothers or sisters. After all who would believe me anyway. Even I was <u>suspicious</u>. First of all, what could I say . . . for sure. And who would believe me in any case. All I know is that it happened and I have told no one to this day.

Initially, I wanted to treat the whole affair as a "non-event." At times over the years my mind would flash back to that summer day and I would recall the event as if it were an old black and white movie. Was this experience analogous to the biblical episode of Saul on the way to Damascus? My own premise was and is that a superior current of consciousness of an angelic or mystical nature or origin took place. Nevertheless, I claim nothing more nor less than what I have stated. But I have a hidden agenda in telling of this experience. I would truly like to continue throughout life to stimulate my own processes, quieting my soul in order to listen to internal and external thoughts. Perhaps my recounting this episode in my life will trigger someone else's consciousness and awaken another mind to higher dimensional sensitivity and possibilities. The continuation of this hegira reveals that every future event related on that day actually came to be exactly as it was <u>foretold</u>!

Not everything since my 17th birthday has proceeded well. I have made some damned elaborate plans in my life since then, and a few of them have even worked. I have a strong feeling that this Everyman's process of getting in tune with himself and his surroundings first will be the new wave of the future and that those who will come down this path later may have similar experiences in their lives. Perhaps it has already happened!

TRIMMING A TIGER'S CLAWS

Basketball was an abiding force in my life from the time I entered Harney Grade School. I have already related the story of how the "stellar" on-court performances of Marlon and me had caught the eye of the local town merchants. They sponsored our attendance at summer school in Indianapolis. That decision created problems during my senior year in high school by complicating my true class standing. I would take a course or two during the summers, not because I had to for the sake of remaining scholastically eligible, but because I wanted to take some of the more difficult courses during a less hectic period than during basketball season.

As these course hours mounted, a warp developed in my graduation time table. I had an extra half year of eligibility remaining that would carry me through another basketball season. I guess it would be called "red shirting" now. Indiana High School Athletic Association [IHSAA] rules permitted four years of eligibility on the varsity level. I had played one year on the junior varsity as a freshman and, two years first string as a varsity player. As I entered my senior year, some unwelcomed surprises confronted me.

When school was about to end my during my junior year, Coach Overman, called me into his office to discuss the eligibility matter with me. I felt no apprehension as I entered his office, just off the gym area. I was thinking of a thousand things other than what happened next.

The usual acrid smell of sweat wafted in from the gym. I knocked on "Coach's" office door. The "Tigers" had experienced a reasonably good year the previous season. I felt I had played an integral part in that success. The goal of every Tiger team was to reach the State Finals. But the stark reality was that the path for us led through the Lafayette regional. There, waiting like a cheetah in the jungle, was the Lafayette Jeff Broncos, coached by the legendary Marion Crawled. It was virtually impossible to beat them at tourney time. The fate was pretty much the same for those unlucky teams facing the Lebanon Tigers in the sectional rounds. We perennially won our sectional, which was played in Lebanon. It was then that the Tiger growl was stifled when we journeyed on to Purdue Field House for the regional tournament.

Coach Overman was a thin, nervous, handsome man, nearly six feet tall, and approaching his fifties. His main distinguishing characteristic was his voice. It boomed even when he wasn't excited. One was immediately taken aback by his booming voice because it didn't seem as if it should be coming from such a mild mannered man. He came straight to the point and his tone was cold. "Steve, you have another season of eligibility left. I think you have enormous talent, but I've been thinking about bringing up Marshall Sheets. Our team needs more height and muscle. I can't promise that you will be a starter next year. As a matter of fact you are probably facing the sixth man role, coming off the bench." He continued. "If you stay, it will also mean you won't graduate at age 18 with your classmates, because the season spills over into the second semester. It wouldn't do us any good to have you for just the first part of the season. I want you to think it over, Steve. That's all." He leaned back in his chair, folded his hands behind his head and turned his back to me. There was no effort on his part to determine my immediate reaction. It was just as well.

I stood there, cringing inside, eyes full of questions. But, I knew it was of no use to pursue the matter further. My perspective shifted suddenly. I felt strange, too strange for my well being. I again became aware of the dirty sock smell and evaporating sweat smell of the gym. There being nothing left to say, I hauled my limp body and legs out of Coach Overman's office.

I talked the matter over with my father the next day. He listened quietly and said, not apologetically, that it was my decision to make. Dad and Mom never missed a home game at any point in my career. I thought he might have some scurrilous remarks to hurl toward the coach, anything to help me vent my grave disappointment. In retrospect, I know that it really instantly became clear what I intended to do, an internal nudge came from some unknown source. First, I had set a goal to win first place in the State Oratorical Declamation coming up in the spring. Preparation for that goal would help ease the pain. Once again, by dumb luck I had suddenly stumbled onto a simple, logical way out of my immediate suffering. I would play another year.

As it turned out, I was relegated to the sixth man, usually coming off the bench sometime late in the first quarter. Many times I played the rest of the game and acquitted myself very well. So, this Tiger's claws had been clipped, but he could have the potential to let out a might roar!

Be skilled in speech so that you will Succeed. The tongue of a man is his Sword and effective speech is stronger than all fighting
The Husia
Scared wisdom of Ancient Egypt
Translated by
Maulana Karenga

SPEAKING UNTO THEM

Man has almost certainly been, in some sense, a speaking animal. Most would agree that this has been true from his early emergence, as Homo Sapiens, or as a recognizable species. When individuals speak, they normally do not confine themselves to the mere utterance of speech sounds. Because speaking usually involves at least two parties, in sight of each other, a great deal of meaning is conveyed by facial expression, tone of voice, movements and postures of the whole body, but especially of the hands. These are collectively known as gestures. If all of this sounds like public speaking, or oratory . . . it is!

I had mentioned earlier that I was in a state of "post-traumatic syndrome" when I was not elected captain of the basketball team, and that I was relegated to the role of "sixth man" as well. It was a rough time for me. I felt I was nearing a dark abyss. I needed to have an emotional outlet to rid myself of these twin disappointments. Without prompting, or much forethought, I entered a public speaking class, taught by Mrs. Jane Ward.

Mrs. Ward was a tall, stately woman in her mid to late thirties when I first met her. She didn't demand respect, but one automatically conferred it upon her because of her bearing. She was always immaculately groomed, with perfumed brunette hair, finely sculptured facial features, and soft, alluring hazel eyes that spoke of long forgotten

148

hopes and dreams. She was a divorcee, with a daughter about my age. When I entered her speech class, I was void of technique as one could be. Her first words to me following my initial five minute speech were, "Steve, you've got to forget you are Negro. Effective delivery of a speech transcends race and culture. It is all about, Technique! Technique! And Technique! She also quoted Cicero saying, "The unpardonable sin in public speaking is the sin of inadequate preparation.

I plunged into the course work, diligently rehearsing the speeches I was given to write and deliver in class. I was getting straight A's for grades, [one of the few subjects I ever received that distinguishing mark in and loving it as well. Standing in front of an audience, delivering an effective speech fed the ego that had been badly bruised by the basketball episodes.

Mrs. Ward soon had me slated to enter speech competition. I placed first on the local level with what I thought was a pretty lack luster dramatic speech. It had to do with the burgeoning number of auto accidents and the sorrowful number of deaths that accompanied far too many of them. It was now on to the Regional level of competition. I won! Now I was on to the State Finals and I . . . But wait, I'm going too fast!

First, there was a great deal of stumbling before I became a reasonably effective speaker. For one thing correct word pronunciation is paramount to effective speaking. My vocabulary, although becoming more expansive, was riddled with slang and idiosyncrasies. Mrs. Ward spent a great deal of time teaching me phonetics. Anyone who had been an invisible witness to these sessions, would have been reminded of some scenes from "My Fair Lady." One would be where poor Eliza Doolittle was being tortured by Henry Higgins with these two sayings: "The rain in Spain falls mainly in the plain." And, "In Hartford Hetherington and Hampton, Hurricanes hardly Happen." I surely began as equally wretched as Eliza, as I stumbled over words. At the time, I honestly perceived myself as a very shy individual, and very slow to reveal my inner self to others. Perhaps self-centered, and a control freak, but shy.

Slowly, arduously, and with infinite patience on her part, Mrs. Ward transformed me from a street urchin into a thespian of some promise. In one year! . Now, don't get me wrong. I wasn't that bright, but she had worked so hard with me I didn't want to disappoint her.

One afternoon after her speech class, Mrs. Ward, in her usual silky, lilting voice, said to me, "Steve, I think you are ready for state competition. I am very impressed with the way you have progressed. in the presentation of dramatic material. I think I have the perfect speech for you. It's called [Enough of This.] It's about the senseless deaths of thousands of Americans in automobile accidents. What do you think?

I gave her a crooked smile. It was now time to decide what I was really made of. I flushed at her confidence in me. A thin voice spoke from somewhere saying something casual like, "If you think I can do it. Let's give it a try." The cracking voice was mine. Yes it was time to wade out into "white water." And I made myself ready. I took the speech home to read that night, and I liked it!

I had to memorize the ten minutes of material and deliver it with all of the techniques of a seasoned orator. I would practice every evening after coming home from basketball practice. But I would not practice it at home: too many people. I would go up onto the Pennsylvania Railroad depot and stand by the tracks and speak to the wind. Often my younger brother, Larry, would accompany me and help me immensely with the memorization. Larry was that way. He never chose to be an athletic, or follow in any of his brothers' footsteps. But, he was always there for us, offering encouragement in a quiet, sincere, and a cheerful manner. His deep blue eyes, yes blue eyes, sparkling with pride when success came to any of us. And success did reach out for me.

I must confess an unpardonable sin I committed during this episode, and it was one of galactic proportions. The incident happened just prior to the evening of the local contest, held in the Lebanon High School Auditorium. Dad and Mom told me they were coming to the auditorium to be a part of the audience and to wish me well. I told them I would rather they didn't attend because I was going to be very nervous, and a nervous speaker is a disaster to behold. In addition, the speech called for a great deal of gesticulation and emotional delivery and they had never seen me in that state. Only my brother Larry and Mrs. Ward had seen me in full oration. Dad's eyes fixed on mine, were fathomless and cold as an Arctic wind. He said nothing. I stood there cringing, shuddering like a groundhog just emerging from a long winter's nap, without casting a shadow. But Dad did, and over me!

The next evening, as I walked out on stage with the other five contestants, my eyes drifted out over the crowded auditorium. There, sitting proudly in the middle of the front row, were . . . Mom and Dad! I held their gaze for a moment. Dad's glance was enigmatic and he turned quickly from my gaze. Mom's smile was as bright as buttercups.

I won first place that evening and went on to win first place in the State Finals, held at Gary, Indiana. I also placed third in the finals in broadcast announcing. Dad and Mom did not accompany me.

Later that afternoon when I returned to Lebanon, I literally floated on air as I left the high school for home. When I turned the corner onto Pearl Street, and neared my house, I noticed that Dad was again "hoeing" in the garden. I ran to him, loudly announcing my success. "Dad! I won First place. I also won third place in the state in radio announcing." I proudly held up the large Whitmore, silver trophy, along with a chained necklace with an attached gold embossed medal in the shape of the State of Indiana. "My picture will now be placed in the halls of Lebanon High School forever!" I stood there, waiting for a hug of affection. Nothing! I got nothing! Only, "That's good son. I'm proud of you." His tone was not cold. It was . . . just emotionless. And he kept "hoeing" in the garden. I stood there, my eyes moist and full of questions, and blinking rapidly. I guess I got what I deserved for my earlier transgression. I slunk away.

There are two remaining bits of irony to this story. First, the judges for the finals were from the speech department of Butler, Purdue, and Indiana Universities. Jerry Chapman, an announcer from WIRE was a judge, and little did I know then that our paths would cross again years later and the meeting would transform my life. Secondly, you will recall my several misadventures at Ulen Country Club? Well, by virtue of my success at the finals, I was invited to be the principal speaker at a Rotary Club, monthly luncheon, where I presented the speech that had garnered me State honors. The event was even written up favorably in the Lebanon Reporter. My! How future events have a way of eclipsing all previous challenges, struggles, and heartaches.

The point on the time line for this chapter is the early 1950's. It was a period in our history that seemed benign on the surface, yet the world was lurching along in many dangerous and deadly directions, especially, in a far off place called Korea. Since my high school days were drawing to a close, I was about to enter that murky, apprehensive period.

In 1932, the year of my birth, America was eager to disarm itself of the tools of war. This enthusiasm for disarmament led Herbert Hoover to say, "The overwhelming burden of the armament which now lies upon the toilers of the world, all tanks, chemical warfare and large mobile guns. . . All bombing planes should be abolished." Six years later Hitler invaded the Sudetenland. Three additional years later the United States entered the fray with the advent of Pearl Harbor. And World War II, the most destructive war in human history, erupted. It ended in 1945 with the twin nightmarish atomic horrors of Hiroshima and Nagasaki. Less than half a decade later, in 1950, the Korean War was in its deadly fury. The Cold War followed and the nuclear stand-off began. For more than forty years, each succeeding generation lived with more than 50,000 nuclear warheads pointed at one another, awaiting the simple act of pushing a red button that would send cities around the world, and all their inhabitants, back to the Stone Age. Even though that did not happen, the torrents of blood spilled this century over issues now forgotten, has been horrendous. Naturally, one chooses not to think of the millions of noncombatants annihilated - charred or blown into nothingness. One chooses also to say nothing of the blind, battered bodies of soldiers returned to their homelands, mostly forgotten by all except their comrades. No one should forget that normal men have killed about 100 million of their fellows in this century alone.

This sad commentary shaped the world this century. Literature, paintings, sculptures, Armistice Day parades, the movies, all address these horrors and the egocentric overlords who started the wars. The heroism and moral dilemmas of brave men at war are mostly forgotten.

My purpose here is not to moralize about the hatefulness of war. Even the Bible says "There will always be war and rumors of war." Some readers may confuse the absence of moralizing for an absence of empathy with the victims. That thinking would be far from the truth. What I would offer instead is a simple statement. If, indeed, war is inevitable, we need to find alternative ways to keep it from spreading from nation to nation, and above all, to reduce the horrible losses and human suffering on all sides to the barest minimum. Total world confrontations would, and must, be prevented. We are beginning to see flickerings of that happening with the elevation of the role the nearly moribund United Nations in the conflict with most of the World and Iraq, as well as United Nations in its interdiction attempts to halt the horrors of ethnic cleansing in Bosnia. That is good!

Taking a pro-active peace-keeping role, all over the globe, President Harry Truman and the United Nations world body members saw wisdom in trying to halt the spread of conflict and communistic takeovers of defenseless countries in Korea. The line was drawn in the sand in that tiny far-flung place. To some degree he and the United Nations succeeded. For the first time in our history, the world acted upon the proposition that war is too important to be left up to the generals. You do remember President Truman firing General Douglas McArthur, one of the most popular, successful, and daring generals of this century? Regrettably, even he, at one point in the Korean war, considered invading China and dropping nuclear bombs on their cities. President Truman would have none of that.

The Korean war, coined a "police action," was conducted with limited objectives. The premise was simple, halt the spread of communism! At the time, nearly half the world was under the communist yoke. And they sought total world domination. Even though the premise was simple, the cost in human lives was again disastrous. America alone lost more than 50,000 brave young men and women. Our adversaries lost, God only knows, how many more of the same.

All of these issues were far from the minds of most Americans, including me, as we groped blindly through our daily lives. Korea was too far away. Even though during the fall of 1952, I had registered, as required, for the Armed Services draft. I had planned, or it was "planned for me," to enter the Air Force after high school graduation.

I could have been exempted under the "two or more members of one family," deferment. My brothers, Sonny and Marlon, were already in the military. College deferments that one could use to escape the draft were also available to young men, but that was not a viable option for me. There was no money in our household for college. It appeared I was destined after all to follow the murmurings of the "Shimmering Bush," whether I liked it or not. There was a brief detour which I had planned for the summer following high school graduation that would extend the time line for a few months before my entering the military.

THE PALE BLUE CONVERTIBLE

I met Harold Harris and his pale blue convertible during my junior year in high school. My parents knew his grandparents and several times during the course of the year, Dad and Mom would gather two or three of my brothers and sisters and we would make brief courtesy calls on my relatives in Crawfordsville and Lafayette. One summer, Harold appeared as if out of nowhere at his grandparents home in Lafayette. He and I became fast friends. He told me he was taking up official residence at their home in order to be eligible to play basketball for the Lafayette Broncos. When the school year ended he would return to his parents home in Chicago. Doubtless, this arrangement for his playing basketball at "Lafayette Jeff" barely skirted IHSAA rules.

We played against each other at least once during the regular season. If Lebanon won its sectional division, and we usually did, all roads to the state championship led through Lafayette. Then regional pairings were such that the strongest teams met for the regional championship in the final game. Normally, we would see each other twice a year, first during the regularly scheduled season and, as fate and the fortunes of our respective teams would have it, during the regional finals. Harold was an excellent basketball player; as a matter of fact, Harold was excellent at everything. He was tall for those days and stood about six feet two inches. His skin was light brown and he had a strong build and perfectly even white teeth that flashed brilliantly when he wanted to charm the young ladies. In addition to those invaluable attributes, he carried himself in such a manner that self confidence seemed to exude from every pore.

Harold and I became good friends. I am sure one of the reasons was the respect we had for each others' basketball abilities. Moreover, the "Jeff Broncos" always knocked Lebanon out of a trip to Butler Field House for the semi-state tournament, so I was no threat to his status among his peers. Among his other attributes were a premier singer and a jazz piano player. He actually ended up playing piano for Hugh Hefter, the famous <u>Playboy Magazine</u> owner, mostly for his private parties. No, I never got an invitation to one of them, but I did get several invitations to ride in his pale blue convertible."

During my senior year in high school, Harold asked me if I would like to spend the summer with him in Chicago as his house guest. I said I would be more than delighted. Having never been to a major city or anyplace else of note, how could I refuse? Both of our parents agreed to the arrangement. When summer came, I packed some meager belongings and headed for Harold's grandparent's home in Lafayette. That was the first time I saw the "Pale Blue Convertible." It was a dream machine. A possession beyond the dreams of any black person I knew at the time. It was low to the ground! It was sleek. It was powerful! Its side-walled tires and chrome fixtures literally sparkled with brilliance. Eagerly I jumped into his pale blue 1950 Pontiac convertible, and we headed for Chicago – top down!

One might pose this question – how did Harold, a young black man living in Lafayette, in 1950, have a great pale blue 1950 Pontiac convertible? I have no facts to back the following assumption, but I always suspected that the car was given to Harold by the Bronco Alumni. I do know that Harold and the Jeff Broncos had gone to the Final Four state basketball tournament two years in a row. I was jealous because he was being courted by several universities to play basketball. He chose Purdue.

At any rate, a warm sun was arcing toward its zenith and spying on us as we drove north on Highway 52, top down, passing one large cornfield after another. We laughed gaily as we plotted our strategies for finding jobs and having an exciting summer in Chicago! Finding jobs headed our priority list since we both needed money. With our pockets filled with coins, adventure could not be far behind, right? Well, maybe. I was also terrifically excited because this summer would mark the first time I would have been away from home by myself. Oh, I had overnight stays along with my mother or brothers in Crawfordsville with Mom's relatives, but no extended periods away from home, alone.

In many ways I envied Harold. He was going off to college in the fall. He radiated with his good looks and "big city" ways. He was going to play sports at a Big Ten university. He played jazz and blues and sang to his own accompaniment. And, of course, he had the pale blue 1950 Pontiac convertible. None of these attributes failed to be noticed by the young ladies.

The Harris home was a comfortable, spacious, well-kept four bedroom, red brick bungalow. The location was 69th and Prairie, which is on the south side of Chicago. It was a short street but lined beautifully with elm trees. All of the homes along their street were middle class by any standards white or black.

Harold's parents were wonderful people. Mrs. Harris was a nurse; Mr. Harris was the proprietor of a small short order restaurant, featuring thick and juicy hamburgers and cheeseburgers. Mrs. Harris was a rather stocky woman of medium height who moved with slow grace. She greeted no strangers and spoke with a slow Southern drawl and a charming smile. Mrs. Harris watched over me as if I were one of her own, prodding here, cajoling there, just as my mother would do. She loved to cook Southern style food - lots of golden fried chicken, mashed potatoes and gravy, green beans, and home made biscuits. Breakfast was a feast: eggs, bacon, fried potatoes, grits, sweet melons and orange juice. Since I normally ate little or no breakfast, I gained about eight pounds over the span of the three months I was their guest. Looking back over previous pictures of me, I think that I needed the eight pounds and a great deal more.

Mr. Harris was a handsome man of medium height and build. His face was finely chiseled, with an almost Indian or

Mexican color. He was a contrast to his wife. He dressed immaculately and was a hardworking man with immense energy, mostly nervous energy. The constant strain of hyperactivity made his smile inflexible, like a rectus. He talked incessantly, in an ocean of home spun wisdom. Harold looked exactly like his father with the same rugged handsomeness.

Mr. Harris tried his darndest to take the country, small town habits and characteristics out of me and delighted in doing so, too! I had a terrible time getting rid of old habits. For instance, I left doors unlocked, spoke to strangers, and in general forgot I wasn't in my small town. He would get furious when I did those things, and he threatened to send me home! Harold told me he was just kidding, but I wasn't sure. I got a little better toward the end of my stay, learning the potential dangers of living in a large metropolitan area, especially after hearing on the radio and seeing in the newspaper the daily human mayhem and carnage that took place there.

In accordance with our plan, we quickly went in search of summer jobs. Before long we met with success, if that is what one chooses to call it. We went first to the City Parks Department, hoping to supervise kids at one of the local parks. When we entered the employment office there must have been seventy-five people looking for jobs. I observed many of them to be black or of foreign nationality. When it came my time to be interviewed, I was told I would be hired as an instructor at one of the local parks. I said, with a surprised grin, "Great, when do I start?" The white, middle-aged male interviewer said, "You will have to pay me a percent of your first month's salary in order to get the job." I looked at him closely for the first time. He looked like the last rose of summer, almost professional, but not quite. He appeared tired of his job and disgusted with life and people in general. The suit he was wearing must have been the only one he had because it looked as if he had slept in it. His face was pock-marked, strained, sweaty and emotionless. He looked like butter wouldn't melt in his mouth . . . or anywhere else. It was then that I knew what medical schools did with bodies when students finished flunking out of medical schools. They were sent to work in the Chicago employment office!

But I calmed down. "What for?!" I said in an obviously naive way.

"That's the way it is fella – take it or leave it," he said.

"You can have it," I sneered. "Give it to one of them over there." And I pointed in the direction of the huddled masses of would-be contenders for the job. "They need it worse than I do," I lied, as I turned and walked away.

Harold said the same thing happened to him. "That's the way it goes in Chicago," he smiled. "So much for life in the big city," I murmured to myself.

Our next stop was Cicero, a small bedroom city on the westside of Chicago where the huge Western Electric plant was located. We had good luck there and were told to report the following day to the "degreasing" section of the plant. We were told to wear heavy shoes and protective work clothes. "What?" you may ask – the interviewer didn't want any money? That's right, no bribery this time.

We left Cicero that afternoon elated. We even put the top down on Harold's "pale blue" convertible Pontiac. I later learned that Cicero was one of the most racist cities in America. Several race riots had occurred there in the past and lots of trouble erupted there in the late 1960's, when Martin Luther King, Jr. demonstrated by marching thousands of his followers through the city streets.

We worked at Western Electric all summer long, not making very much money, but enough for me to send some home to Mom and Dad. I should say also that the job was easy, but dangerous. Our job was to degrease (dip) large metal containers that had paraffin clinging to the sides and its inner parts. Each container weighed about 30 pounds. We used pulleys with hooks to hold the containers and dip them in large open vats filled with some type of heated solvent. It boiled and churned constantly and gave off noxious fumes.

160

I would suspect they were dangerous gases. We wore safety glasses to protect our eyes. OSHA would have had a field day citing the company for this operational process if the same conditions existed today.

One final note about my Chicago visit. Harold had some female friends who lived near the 96th and Princeton Park area. One weekend early on we visited them in his pale blue Pontiac – with the top down, of course! My first impression when we arrived in the area was one of awe. I was shocked! The area looked like Ulen Country Club in Lebanon. The houses were mansions . . . and blacks lived there! I couldn't believe it. Manicured lawns, exotic flower beds, even swimming pools. The young ladies were gorgeous. One even liked me and we were friends for the remainder of the summer. My friends at home would have a hard time believing this. Little ole me, living in this different, wonderful world. Before the summer ended, I was beleaguered with pleadings from Harold and several ladies to stay in Chicago. The temptation was great, but I could not escape the prophecies of the "shimmering bush." I had a roundevous with destiny: the United States Air Force.

I'll never forget Mr. and Mrs. Harris. They were wonderful people. I bought them a lovely flower vase as a gift before I left. I have never forgotten Chicago either, and I still think it is one of the premier cities I have visited in the country. Marilyn and I still enjoy visiting the wonderful music and food fest called "Taste of Chicago." Our kids, when they were young, loved it too. And, of course, I'll never forget my friend Harold, and especially our rides through the magical streets of Chicago in his pale blue convertible. He came to visit Marilyn and me several times on his way to the 500 Mile Race. During one early visit, Harold, his wife and friends drove down in a huge Bentley automobile. We had a ball riding through the streets of my neighborhood. I made a conscious effort to wave at my startled neighbors. I'm sure they thought the "Goddess of Good Luck" had suddenly found favor with me.

Lebanon High as It appeared in the 1950's.

Happy students depart Lebanon High after another day of learning.

Lebanon High school coaching staff, from left to right, head basketball coach Earl Overman, asst. basketball coach "Doc" Heath, and head football coach Al Kincaid.

Standing left to right: Assistant Coach Doe Heath, Larry Riggins, Lynn Miller, Don Mambert, Bob Harshman, Aaron Stookey, Harley Sheets, Ross Pauly, and Coach Earl Overman.

Seated: Mgr. John Foster, Gerald Padgett, Jim Schulemire, Steve Scott, Sonny Walker, Dave Shirling, Marshall Sheets, and Mgr. Don Gillihan.

Standing left to right: Jim Parr, copy editor; Dave McGhee, sports editor; Judy Leerkam, art director; Steve Scott, business manager; Mr. Don Guilford, sponsor; and Suzie Lenox, senior and classes editor.
Seated: Shirley McGrigg and Jim Seering, co-editors.

High school friend Bill Lewellyn who died in a construction accident minutes after I was working at the same task.

Candelabrum Committee

The Candelabrum Committee is chosen by a vote of the Senior Class to carry on the ceremony initiated by Miss Lydia Bell in 1929. Traditionally, this ceremony takes place whenever the Senior Class has a class activity, such as the Dinner Party and Commencement.

Members of the committee are chosen for their speaking ability, poise, and dependability. The ceremony, with the seven-branched candlestick, represents the seven cardinal principles of secondary education.

Left to right: Dave Sherry, Sr. president; Suzie Lenox; Jim Seeright; Marilyn Jo Lee; Steve Scott; Charlotte Denger; Dave Shirling; and Shirley McGrigg.

Mom and some friends from Noblesville, a small town some 20 miles east of Lebanon.

Younger sisters: From left to right, Vera and Teya.

Neighbor Barbara Saltsman I later years with her daughter. Barbara, now famous for the bicycle she loaned me one summer evening long ago.

Home from basic training, Lackland Air Force Base. That's Dad and Mom, second and third from the left.

Brother Gary, home on leave

Dad dressed for his second job as
Chauffeur for the Standard family.

Older brother Dowane Jr. impressing my mother on the left and older sister Arthelma on the right.

Teya and Charles. Teya was May Queen.

A family group photo, Left to right, Charles, Gary, Mom, Don and myself. I was preparing to join the Air Force...hence my "spiffy" attire.

Dad, Dowane Jr. in front of our house. I don't remember who owned the car. It wasn't ours for sure.

Announcing news and sports at the local radio station. I began as a junior in high school.

TEPHEN LARUE SCOTT

Ath. Bd. of Control, Pres.; Span. Club; Glee Club; Concert Choir; CEDARS, Bus. Mgr.; Com'l Club; Hi-Y; Pennant; Essay Contests; Oratorical Contests; "L" Club, Basketball; Track; Candelabrum; Jr. Hist. Sor., Local Dir.; Golf; 3rd Pl.—State Oratoricals; 1st Pl.—Boys' Div.— Central Ind. Oratorical Contest.

I enjoyed being involved in LHS activities. Especially, the many friendships developed with fellow students.

Speech teacher Jane Ward, who guided me in speech and Drama.

CHAPTER 5

THE TRAIN

It was a Tuesday morning in mid-September when I walked the nine blocks from my house to the downtown United States Air Force Recruiting Office. I sure looked "spiffy" as I entered the office 10 minutes early for my 9:00 a.m. reporting time. Having just said goodbye to my mother, father and the rest of the family, I would soon be boarding a train for Lackland Air Force Base, near San Antonio, Texas. I had just bought a new pair of "white buck" shoes, white trousers and a dark red polo shirt to impress "Uncle Sam."

There had been no tearful goodbyes at home, just a lot of hugging and blessings of Godspeed. The family had already gone through similar ceremonies with my older brothers Sonny and Marlon both already in the USAF, having preceded me over the past year and a half.

Joining me at the recruiting office were seven other new enlisted men. They were from the surrounding farm counties, so I didn't know any of them. Some recognized me, however, as a basketball player from the "big city" of Lebanon. I didn't like the way they looked. Most were quietly huddled together on the folding chairs, looking like frightened deer, caught in the glare of car headlights on a dark night. Did they know some ominous secret of what may lie ahead that I didn't know?

Air Force recruiter, Major Howard Coghagen, gathered us together by barking out a command, the first of what would be hundreds of commands that I would hear and heed before I would leave the service four years later. He looked like General George Patton and acted like him too, as he snapped, "OK, you men, line up. We've got a train to catch. Your country and Uncle Sam await you." The Magnificent Seven perked up when they heard that, and away we went to the train station. We noticed, with some gratification, that three cars on the train were already full of recruits coming from other cities in northern Indiana. I was now ready for my first train ride, and I was excited!

As the train pulled out of the station, it passed right by my house! I could see all the old haunts that conjured up such wonderful, warm memories of my life at 911 West Pearl Street. As I looked out the window, I saw the train passing the area of the shimmering bush that revealed my life for decades ahead. It appeared to brighten and shimmer again, as if to bid me farewell. I gave it a small wave and a hearty salute! Then I settled back in my seat, folded my hands behind my head and thought about my next stop, San Antonio, Texas.

In my reverie I remembered how much Dad loved trains. He loved to watch the behemoth locomotives, whizz by, belching huge streamers of black smoke and steam. And he knew a lot about them. He knew the schedules for all the Big Four trains, the Pennsylvania and the Midland Railroads. He even knew that the engineer and brakemen had signals. He would sit for hours and watch them go by. When he bought his first car after decades of walking and riding bicycles, he and Mom would drive to different back roads in the county to watch the trains go by. One occasion, I recall he told us proudly of an incident in which he played a prominent role in preventing a train mishap. It seems while watching a freight train pass by, he noticed one of the cars had a "hotbox." I think that is when oil has escaped from a gear box on the wheels. It can cause a fire or even derailment because of the sparks from the friction of metal against metal. Dad signaled "hot box" to the brakeman, who in turn signaled the engineer, who stopped the train a short distance down the line. Dad was as proud as he could be that his knowledge of trains prevented a sure accident. It seems so ironic that Dad had never had the pleasure of being a passenger on a train, at least not to my knowledge.

I had promised the family I would try to write at least twice a month and they promised to do the same. I think we kept our word most of the time over the course of my military career. Dad did an excellent job of saving family memorabilia – newspaper clippings of baseball, basketball, track and football exploits of all of his sons. He saved all our track ribbons, trophies and letters. "You will never know what use you can make of them," he was fond of saying. "If nothing else, you can show them to your children and your children's children. It will help you to remember special events in your lives."

I'd forgotten about his commitment until one late summer day, about five years after he passed away, when my younger brother Jon brought me several shopping bags filled with my personal memorabilia. "Dad would want you to have these," he said. I put them on the shelf in my study, and swore I wouldn't look at the "booty" until the proper moment in time. After all, more than five decades of my life's history was in those bags and I wasn't anxious to look under those rocks just yet. But there it was, in yellow stained envelopes and newspaper clippings – my life. It truly brought a lump to my throat. As I began this writing, it was now time to look through the pile for relevant material.

I was totally ecstatic as I looked out the window of the train. I was being lulled into a deep state of unconsciousness, mainly by the metallic poetry of the train wheels' clickety-clack, clickety-clack, through state after state. Here I am, little ole Steve, who barely knew that life existed outside of 911 West Pearl Street, Lebanon, Indiana. Okay, I can throw in Crawfordsville, Frankfort, Lafayette and my brief stay in Chicago. But now I am watching the world pass by, right outside my window: strange cities flew past my view, cities like Terre Haute, Indiana; Effingham, Illinois; St. Louis, Missouri; Little Rock, Arkansas; Austin, Texas; and eventually, San Antonio, Texas. Daylight passed into night and on and on we rolled.

All through the night into morning, then mid-afternoon the train sped southward. Alas! We had traveled for nearly 12 hours, and we were still in Texas! I was thoroughly impressed with the vastness of the state, and all too soon impressed with something and someone else, as well.

We pulled into the train station in San Antonio amid a chorus of "Thank God that's over!" by the new recruits. The train ride had been wonderful and unique. I loved it but riding for 24 hours was getting on most of the fellows' nerves. We had not been permitted to leave the train during any of its several stops along the way. Peering out my window, I could see scores of blue USAF buses lined up, presumably waiting to transport us to Lackland Airbase. Although there was only a small contingent of us who boarded the train in Lebanon, many more recruits had apparently joined us at the many stops during the past 24 hours. The train was air-conditioned, rendering us impervious to the heat outside, but I could tell it was hot by looking out the window at people standing or moving about like zombies in the heat. It had to be considerably warmer than when we left Lebanon.

We quickly boarded the air-conditioned buses and away we went for the one- hour ride to Lackland. One had to be impressed with the vastness of the airbase. Barracks were everywhere, lined in perfect rows like dominoes. Tiny clutches of men marched to and fro. They were obviously in various stages of the sixteen-week basic training course, for some groups were marched smartly, singing songs in cadence with their marching step, while others bounded around in marching groups like bowls of Jell-O. Overhead, and over the near horizon, jet aircraft screamed through the air coming from Kelly Airbase. As one plane landed, another took off. Kelly was just one of the many pilot training bases in the huge state of Texas.

We were ordered to disembark and stay grouped by our bus, and we did as we were told. The caravan of buses soon left, abandoning us to the stifling Texas heat now starting to become omnipresent. We waited. We waited.

We waited some more. This was my indoctrination to the famous "hurry up and wait" doctrine of the military. After about an hour of standing in the miserable hot sun, most of us looking like melted paraffin, we saw a jeep pulled up. Out stepped what would be our worst nightmare for the next sixteen weeks – the drill instructor ("DI").

Our new DI was a mountain of a man named Alabovich! "Bo" was the nickname we gave him. Bo stood straight as a ramrod; indeed that's the only way Bo ever stood. He was about six foot five, with not an ounce of fat anywhere on his body. His close-fitting, well-starched khaki uniform revealed only muscle and more muscle. His barrel chest was emblazoned with rows upon rows of decorations he had earned in God knows how many campaigns and wars. The dry heat of the day's sun seemed to enfold him in an invisible cloud. He was a Master Sergeant. Clean shaven, lips curled down in a menacing snarl, he waved a swagger stick as he yelled, "Attention!" Most of us knew what that word meant – Stand-up straight, hands and arms rigid at one's sides. Right! For those uninitiated recruits, it only meant pay attention. We did, as we quaked with dread awaiting his next words. We didn't have long to wait. His next words exploded like a grenade. "I said attention, you miserable slime . . . that means stand up straight, with your arms stiff at your sides." That's what I thought, I said to myself. We again did as we were told! "You are the damndest sight I have ever seen in my three years as a DI at this airbase. Not only that, you are the ugliest too! I can see it now. None of you damn fools are going to be airmen in the United States Air Force. But I've got to try, because that's my job." I wondered how many young souls were frozen with such words. He bared his teeth again and began to walk among us, stopping here and there to "slam dunk" a recruit. He was getting closer to me! We were told to keep our eyes straight ahead, but I kept looking at him out of the corner of my eye. Oh, no! He's stopping in front of me, I thought. He looked me up and down, and in a voice too kind and with a poker-faced stare, he said, "Well, what have we here – the Sundance Kid! What in God's name have you got on?" He can't be talking about my spiffy new white buck shoes, my new white trousers and dark red polo shirt, I thought. My breathing was coming in thick gasps. Salty sweat slowly fell to my lips and chin. He seemed to enjoy my miserable plight with pleasure. "Don't you worry, Sundance, I am going to make you really sweat under this Texas sun before you leave here." He averted his gaze, pretending not to notice the resentment and disdain that flashed across my face. Nice start, Stephen, I thought. Too late now. You are too far from home. There's no turning back now!

Three other notable events occurred that day. First, the medical shots. I was totally shocked to see physically well-built young men faint while getting their shots. Some even had to be held tightly by male nurses as they cried unashamedly. I just tried to think of something pleasant as I received mine. Then our clothing allowance. It was hilarious! "What size trousers and shirt do you wear, recruit?" the store's sergeant asked. The recruits would proudly give their sizes. It made no difference, everybody got a size large. All of us ended up looking like "Pete the Tramp" in the old cartoons. After a couple of weeks, we got our proper gear. The military just wanted to make a statement about humility, and they did, but they weren't through yet! Next haircuts. This too was hilarious, especially with the recruits from the east coast. Many had "duck" haircuts, which were popular at the time. Some had long, greasy hair. The barber's razor did the same thing for all. After being asked politely, "How would you like it cut today, Sir?" We should have known right then and there that something was wrong. No one called recruits sir! We were told to call everyone else Sir! "Just a little off the sides," or "Can you give me such and such a hairstyle?" the recruits would say, with great aplomb. "Sure" the barber countered, smiling broadly, "anything you ask." And the razor would flick straight down the middle of the head, nearly to the scalp and the rest of the head would receive the same treatment. Howls and lamentations filled the room. Hair was everywhere! For obvious reasons, we black recruits had little to be concerned about. Our hair was short anyway! Now we were all the same, with egos left on the floor, along with the hair. What a sight! The whole affair still leaves me shaking with laughter.

For the next few weeks it was the same routine – up at 5:00 a.m., march, military classes, march, physical education and then march. Of course, there was the constant chewing-out by "Bo." After the first two weeks I managed to write my first letter to my parents. It is hard to imagine how excited I was to leave Lebanon and to begin seeing the world. Some of that excitement bled through in my first few letters home. I had also received some sad news about one of my high school friends.

Lackland Air Force Base
San Antonio, Texas
September 30, 1952
Dear Mom & Dad:

This paragraph is devoted mainly to you, Dad, and concerns the train trip down to Texas. First of all, Dad, realizing how much you like trains, you should know the trip was great! The route we traveled dissected the state of Illinois. It seemed to take forever to get out of the state. Take a look at your United States map and you will see why. It is a very elongated state. Then Kansas, the very "tip" of Oklahoma, a section of Arkansas, and of course, Texas. Some of us who are now "world travelers" can now toss around such names as St. Louis, Little Rock, Houston, Dallas, and San Antonio, Texas, as places we've been. The diesel train provided a smooth, quiet ride. You would have enjoyed the comfort.

Love,
Steve

Dad and Mom had bought a new Oldsmobile Delta 88 automobile just a few months before I left for Lackland. The family called it "The Green Hornet" because it was a gorgeous, pale green. It was their dream car. I don't recall their having any car at all prior to that except the old 1920s car that remained on blocks in the garage and was totally inoperable. I was very much pleased for them, because they derived such pleasure from it. They now could get away from the pressures of working and rearing their large family. Dad now had the mobility to explore all of the back roads of Boone, Clinton, Montgomery, and Tippecanoe counties – and he did so with great relish.

Lackland Air Force Base
San Antonio Texas
October 2, 1952
Dear Mom and Dad,

I've found a few minutes from the rigors of the day and evening tasks to say hello. I have just finished triple shinning my shoes and boots so I can relate what has transpired since my last "missive" to you. I suppose this time of year is affording you plenty of opportunities for sightseeing trips throughout the beautiful Boone County countryside, perhaps even to such places as "Hidden Valley." I recall that was some view when you showed it to me sometime ago. Be sure to take full advantage of the newfound mobility the "Green Hornet" provides you. Purely by accident, I heard of the disheartening and untimely death of Marilyn Kern, the oldest daughter of our family doctor. I was stunned by the news. We were such good friends in high school and I have many fond memories of her. Would you please include me in your expressions of sympathy to Dr. Kern? He has been such a good friend and physician to our family, performing so many free services and delivering all of your children. I know you must feel terrible, as well. I will send him a telegram as soon as I can. Dad, knowing of your love affair with airplanes, I am certain you would have a field day here at Lack land, observing all of the different types of aircraft as they come and go. Most fly directly overhead on their final approach to Kelly Air Force base. It is only a couple of miles from here. Kelly has hundreds of planes on site and is one of the biggest airbases in the country. I love to watch the 86s, F-80s and 84s. Even the huge B-36s fly overhead at a minimum altitude. What a great sight – you can almost see the pilots sitting in the cockpits.

You will be pleased to know that in a couple of weeks I will no longer be a "raw recruit." I will receive my first stripe and will be known as Airman First Class, or A/C.

I have to run now and get some sleep; 5:00 a.m. rolls around really quick . . .

Love,

Steve

P. S. Tell my sisters I am sorry to hear about their "broken arms," otherwise would have received a letter by now. Also tell Don and Gary to stop driving the "Green Hornet" so fast. I want it in one piece when I return from basic training. I'm jealous, you know (smile) . . .

Basic training continued to go well. Our marching "in step" had improved, and all of us advanced our individual and teamwork skills. We no longer felt like slime. Everyone had to pull solitary sentry duty, which means walking a post in a military manner, being alert for any unusual individuals or sounds in that immediate area. My shift duty called for me to "guard" a solitary garbage dump truck for four hours. Would you believe 1:00 a.m. to 5:00 a.m.? It was in a lonely and desolate part of the airbase. I did not look forward to that, believe me. First of all, I had never been awake at such unholy hours of the night in my life.

Second, I consider myself neither a coward nor a hero, but to be honest, my apprehension came in crowds.

The night skies over Texas are beautiful. The stars constantly showing off their brilliance. The line from the song "Deep in the Heart of Texas," The stars at night are big and bright . . . deep in the heart of Texas" - Those lyrics are right on target. I could pick out the constellations of Orion, the Pleiades, and Ursa Major and Ursa Minor with ease, as well as the constellations Virgo and the "Big Bear." However, I didn't spend much time looking at them. My flat feet were pulsating with pain and I started to get tired and sleepy. My shoulders were hunched and tight with fatigue, even though I was in excellent physical shape. My feet kept wanting to move my body, but they seemed to be fighting a losing battle. Then, mercifully, my eyes caught a magnificent, wonderful sight. To paraphrase Shakespeare's <u>Romeo and Juliet</u>, "What light on yonder horizon doth break . . . It is the east and dawn is breaking." I'm going to live, I thought. I've passed the sentry test. My sentry tour for the night was over. I was tired but proud of myself for conquering fear, fatigue, and flat feet. I suspect these were the lessons we were supposed to learn. Things were going well as I fired off another letter home. I hinted at some of the fun I had, including poison gas simulation and sentry duty.

> Lackland Air Force Base
> San Antonio, Texas
> October 10, 1952
> Dear Mom and Dad,

I'm getting as fat as an "ole butterball" turkey. Well, at any rate, I'm gaining a lot of needed weight. I believe I have gained about 15 pounds. They say the average recruit gains 22 pounds. With a few more weeks to go, I may reach that average.

Well, things are getting quite hectic this week. I got to see the stars at night. "Deep in the heart of Texas" the other evening. I had to do sentry duty for the first time. Walked my b... off. It also is quite dark and sinister when you are all by yourself on lonely stretches of the airbase. I'll not be anxious to do that again. We also went on an all-day march. I went to the gas chamber. I lived through it. I hope they don't try me again for the same crime. Ha! Ha! Ha! Actually, it was just a training exercise to acquaint us with the poisonous gases that could potentially be used by enemy forces.

There is quite a story behind this episode, but just let me say we were "attacked" with the following types of gases . . . if my memory and spelling serve me correctly, the gases were Mustard, Lewidite, clorepictorin, phosgene and tear gas. All of them are deadly and highly persistent. By persistent, I mean they will stay in an area for a long period of time. Man oh man! Phosgene was a real "gasser" – literally, a killer! Shew! Obviously they were all given to us in a mild form, but phosgene is a choking gas and kills by strangulation. Most of us got a little sick. They wouldn't let us wear our gas masks; however, they would let us use them for the tear gas. It was all part of the day's march, which was a simulation of real combat conditions. Frankly, it was a lot of fun! The worst enemy we encountered during the whole deal was the Texas cactus and sun. I've still got some of the tiny cactus stickers in my skin.

Give my best to the family and tell all I am thinking about them . . .

Love,
Steve
P.S. I'm Airman 3rd Class Stephen L. Scott now! I was promoted the other day.

Sooner or later the Air Force has to decide what they intend to do with each airman, career-wise. After all, they have now molded and shaped our minds and bodies into their own image. I had developed an interest in aircraft, inheriting that passion from my father. He could identify most World War II aircraft by sight. Dad had also taken my brothers and me to Indianapolis to watch the planes come and go at Weir Cook Airport (now known as Indianapolis International Airport). There was a vacant acre or two where one could park one's car and watch arrivals and departures from close proximity. Back home, if Dad was in the house and heard an airplane, he would rush outside to identify it, especially during the war years. We tagged along behind him. As a result of Dad's interest, my brothers and I could also identify most military aircraft plowing the skies over Lebanon.

One night, out of burning curiosity, I asked myself the biggest question: "You're in the Air Force; you love planes: Why don't you apply to go to flight school?" The short and painful answer was that I had looked into the prerequisites for pilots and had reservations as to whether or not I could qualify. The high performance USAF fighter jets were just coming on stream. The F-86F Saber jet, F-84 "Thunder Jet," the F-89 "Scorpion," and the F-94 "Panther Jets" were the backbone of US fighters during this period. No seat of the pants or blood and guts flyers here. Only briefcase types with calculators need apply. I would wait and make that decision at another time.

Lackland Air Force Base
San Antonio, Texas
October 28, 1952
Dear Mom and Dad,
I have gained another eight pounds and I'm really getting a dark suntan. [Yes, blacks do get burned.] The temperature continues to vacillate from the mid-nineties in the day down to nearly forty degrees at night. That's some variation!
I went to career counseling the other day. It looks like I'll be in either food service or medics. Just kidding, just kidding! It appears to be

communications. But, of course, the Air Force can do with you what they will . . . or, whatever their greatest needs are for the moment. If they need more men in food service, they will put more men in food services.

Several of my friends with some college education, some with graduate degrees are not getting the career path they want either. The career counselor asked me about cadets. They showed me part of the prerequisites and it looked more demanding than I am prepared for at the moment. Besides, the highest I ever care to go is to the top of our house, let alone flying a jet fighter at 50,000 knots. They also asked me to consider OCS (Officers Training School) at a later date, but I don't want that either. If their final decision is communications, I'll accept that. Tell my brothers Gary and Charles to keep shakin' and bakin' those hips on the gridiron for ole LHS. My sisters Vera and Teya are not going to get a gift if they don't stop fussing and fighting with one another [smiles] .
. .

Love,
Steve

It was now approaching the time to leave the "Lone Star State," and I did so with regret. I grew up a great deal at Lackland. I discovered many things about myself, including the importance of developing strong character, teamwork, diversity, new friendships, and conquering unknown fears and adversity too. Having loaded my military dufflebag on the shuttlebus that would take me to the train station, I said farewell and best wishes to my buddies. I had developed a close kinship with several guys from across the country. I even got to like "Bo" and shook his hand. "Get out of here, Sundance, and go make something of yourself!" he said affectionately. I thought I detected a sly grin on his face; the snarl seemed to have lost its menace.

As I gave one last look around the air base, I saw two clutches of new recruits huddled like frightened sheep in the Texas sun, waiting for another Bo to come fetch them and turn them into real young men. I simply smiled and entered the bus. More adventures awaited me in Cheyenne, Wyoming, home of the USAF Communications School. But I was going home first. I was definitely homesick!

Cheyenne

Gertrude Stein may or may not have been accurate in her oft quoted line about Oakland, California. [I've been there many times . . . and disagree!] However, if she were speaking of Cheyenne, Wyoming, in 1953 when I was there, she would have been right on target! Cheyenne looks like a land God might have banished Cain after he slew Able. Perhaps I am being a bit harsh on this famous western city. As the French say . . . "Even the most beautiful woman cannot give more than she has."

Cheyenne is one of the most historic towns of the "old West." It is the capital and largest city in the State of Wyoming. It lies in the southeastern corner of Wyoming, near the Colorado boarder, at an altitude of slightly more than 6,000 feet. Tourist enjoy the annual 6-day Frontier Days Celebration, which began in 1897. Cowboys show skill in roping, riding, and bulldogging steers. Sioux Indians perform tribal dances.

Of course this land ordinarily was claimed by the Cheyenne Indians, who were a warlike tribe of the Plains Indians. They were proud, and fanatically brave tribe and bitterly resented the coming of the white man. The Cheyenne probably lost more men fighting them than did any other Plains tribe.

Today, the Cheyenne area is one of the most important intercontinental ballistic- missile locations in the world. France E. Warren airbase is located near this facility. There were no missiles at France E. Warren when I boarded a train in Indianapolis and aimed my sights for two months of Communication Center Operations training at that location. I sent a brief note to my parents shortly after I arrived.

F. E. Warren airbase
Cheyenne, Wyoming
February 1, 1953

Dear Mom and Dad

As you can see I've arrived safely to my new "home" for the next 2 months. I completed my little jaunt west and arrived Thursday. I was really "pooped" after the trip, mainly because the Union Pacific train ran so slowly. One of the wheels was acting-up and we could only travel thirty -five miles per hour for a great stretch. Dad, knowing your interest in trains, I can tell you that the Union Pacific could use some modernization. One would think "Ole Abe Lincoln" must have traveled on same train. The scenery was really terrific, and I got to see my first mountains. They were something to behold. I think they were part of the Rocky Mountain chain. There were times I could see the engine and the lead cars snaking around bends in the mountains ahead. It was a little frightening as one looked from the window to see people and cars far, far below. We passed through the "mile high" city of Denver. It must be a gorgeous place and I hope to visit the city before I leave . . .

Love Steve

All I knew about the training I would receive at F.E. Warren was that I would be trained in the operations of a communications center. My next letter home provides a good summation of what was ahead for me.

F. E. Warren Air Base
Cheyenne, Wyoming

February 15, I953

Dear Mom and Dad

.....As you may recall, I came out here with the understanding I would be a Message Center Operator, but that is just the tip of the iceberg. I will be learning the following aspects of the standard Communications Center; teletype, weather and flight, facsimile, message structure, and code structure. Some deal huh!...

I have been assigned to the 9 week course, instead of the prescribed 13 weeks because of my typing skills learned in high school. Allah be praised for his mercies!...I am off to study hall now . . . talk to you later.

Love Steve

It is cold and windy in Cheyenne during the winter. Winds blowing, gusting with bone chilling cold, are an everyday occurrence. Giant "tumbleweed" can be seen blowing hither and yon. One thing is for sure, not even crows would dare come to Cheyenne. They would take one look and fly away in disgust. I couldn't fly away, nor could I escape another form on mans sworn enemies . . . the virus.

Strep throat was a common, but dreaded illness during the winter months at Cheyenne, and it was to be avoided at all costs. A few of days recovery time at the base infirmary might set a student back a couple of weeks. But, guess what? I caught the dreaded disease.

One Saturday, I woke up feeling feverish, sweating, eyes blurring to the point I could hardly see to read my lessons. But, I <u>had</u> to study for a test on Monday. I took one look at myself in the mirror, stuck my tongue out to get a good look at my throat. I swooned! I have never seen anything like the condition of my throat, and pray I never

191

do again in life. It looked like a "moss garden-green fungus was everywhere. Yuck! I screamed, but it was muffled by all of the growth in my mouth. I dressed quickly and warmly, and beat a hasty retreat to the infirmary. The doctor gave me a shot of penicillin and tried to keep me. I refused! I ran home, drank some hot tea, took aspirin, put on extra blankets, and stayed in bed for the remainder of the weekend.

My friends took care of me, bringing me any thing I needed. My fever spiked at 104 degrees that day. But dropped overnight to 101 degrees. Sunday I felt better and my throat cleared to near normal. I staggered to class for the next few days and slowly got stronger. I did not have to be phased back in my class work. I was nearing the end of my training, and the devil and all his minions would not keep me in Cheyenne. In my next letter home didn't let my folks know about my narrow escape from the jaws of hell.

F. E. Warren AFB
Cheyenne, Wyoming
March 20th, l953

Dear Mom and Dad.

....I've really been studying hard, but my time here is rapidly coming to a close. I have 14 more days of schooling, with two more test to go. They will be the hardest to date. It is "gut check" time. Mom, I'm sorry I didn't send you a Valentine card. Life has been a little hectic for me over the past week, and I was unable to get to the PX. You remain the best "sweetheart" a guy could have, and I will try to make it up to you later . . .

...I have just received orders today for my next assignment. It appears I'll be going to the Far East. We meet with the "big brass" tomorrow. For the moment, it appears I will leave Cheyenne on the 7th of April, and report to Camp Stoneman,

California on the l9th of April. All of us slated for an overseas assignment will await a shipping date from there. I get a 30-day furlough before I report to California. See ya soon!

Love Steve

I was now going home! I did not know my exact overseas assignment but I knew I where 911 West Pearl Street was and I would be happy to get there. I had already been to more cities and states I could ever imagine, and in 30 days I would be seeing other countries I had only read about in the history books.

I longed to see Mom and Dad and my brothers and sisters. I wanted to tell Dad, in more detail about my train trip, and trade stories about the old West.

Perhaps more importantly, I was rapidly becoming aware of the momentous job of parenting Mom and Dad had done in keeping our family together during times of supreme hardship and sacrifice. I wanted to let them know how much I appreciated and loved them.

I had a great 30-day furlough at home and returned to Camp Stoneman where I penned this letter.

Camp Stoneman, Calif.
April 22, 1953

Dear Mom and Dad

Well, here I am, safe and sound! A bit tired from the long train trip West, but . . .

First of all, I want to thank all concerned who had a part in making my furlough most enjoyable. Thanks also for being liberal in permitting me to monopolize the "Green Hornet". {The new family car] Tell my brothers and sisters I appreciated their forbearance. They can be assured I won't be using it again for quite a while.

193

I must confess this is beautiful country here. Camp Stoneman is surrounded by gorgeous hills that seem to roll on, and on, until they reach the Pacific Ocean . . . The train tripe again took a scenic route. The mountain passes are breathtaking. The train kept circling the mountains, climbing higher and higher. Then, all of a sudden, you find yourself situated precariously atop the mountain, thousands of feet in the air. I think the two mountain chains were the Rocky Mountains and the high Sierras, respectively . . . I don't know exactly what the deal is out here. I will advise you as soon as I know something . . .

Love Steve

Camp Stoneman, Calif.
April 23, 1953

Good Heavens! Me writing another letter so soon!...There is nothing to do here, but lay around and "shoot the bull" . . . We really have "thieves among us." Since no one knows anyone else. All airmen are easy pickings. We must have a clothing check, and those men who are missing items, steal what they need during the night. One ugly fight has already erupted. The men try to hide their money in their pillows only to wake-up, the next morning to find the pillow slit and the money gone. Ha! Ha! You won't believe the story a buddy of mine told me who lives in another barracks. It seems that this airman boasted that no one could steal his billfold because he slept with it in this short. But, that night, while he was asleep, someone took a razor, slit his shorts, reached in and stole his wallet. The culprit left a note on his victim's pillow which read: "Ha! Ha! The Phantom strikes again. Not only that, I didn't find anything else in your shorts . . . What kind of guy are <u>you</u>? It was hilarious!...I plan to go to "Frisco "and then down to "LA" to visit Hollywood . . .

Love Steve

Time was drawing nye to leave California and cross one of the Seven Seas. I was not apprehensive about the impending events that would lay ahead. I now knew one more thing that I was not happy about at all. "Lady Luck" was not going to smile upon me for the next few weeks. Or, as Don Marquis has stated, "Now and then there is a person born who is so unlucky that he runs into events which started out to happen to someone else." The reader may detect additional sarcasm in my next letter home.

Camp Stoneman, Calif.
May 5th, 1953

Received your letter the other day. Sorry I'm just getting around to answering it. It looks like we are about to go sailing. I have been preparing to leave and will do so tomorrow, which is Tuesday . . . My destination, heretofore unknown, seems now to have all the aspects of a tiny country called . . . Korea! The USAF never tells you anything precise, of course, but some of the other fellows orders stipulated Japan, others were going to Hawaii. Not mine! My orders were non specific which rumor says it is a war theater. I do know one specific. DI just received the "Purple Shaft" today. That isn't a medal or a compliment either. My name was " randomly drawn" [I don't believe that] for was is called, "Advanced Party " duty. We have to clean up the ship and carry out other lousy duties, like KP, for some 2,000 men who will be boarding the ship . . .

I went to "Frisco last night to see our ship, which was anchored in the Oakland Bay Harbor.

I'm impressed! It's huge! However, it needs to be twice as impressive to satisfy me, what with all that water I have seen, just over the horizon . . . You won't hear from me for a few weeks, but don't worry, I'll be ok . . .

Love Steve

CHAPTER 6

The winds are mad,
They know not whence they come,
Nor whither they go,
And those men are maddest of all
That go down to sea

Robert Burton

Place: <u>USS Mitchell</u>
Time: 1730 hours
May 20, 1953
Destination – Yokohama

<u>A SAILING WE WILL GO</u>

Dear Dad and Mom:

Hello everyone! I will dispense with most of the formal introductory talk and invite all of you to "climb aboard" the <u>USS Mitchell</u>. I plan to give you a day-by-day account of my ocean voyage. Shall we go? You may regret the first few days!

Wednesday: 1456 hours
It is a lovely day . . . not a cloud in the sky, a good omen for the trip . . . I hope! Dockside, the band is playing farewell music for us and the Red Cross is handing out coffee and doughnuts. It reminds me of a July Th celebration at Memorial Park in Lebanon. I don't want any coffee or doughnuts. I'm tired from my "advance party" duties

197

of the night before. The colorful band is playing its last number, "Till I Waltz Again With You." I could not care less! A lot of the married men, and I suppose others with bonding relationships are getting a lot of kisses and hugs. I turn my head from this scene (jealousy, I suppose). A loud, deep-throated, guttural sound comes from deep within the ship. It was time to go sailing. Men scramble aboard ship tearing themselves away from loves ones. The gang plank is raised . . . the ship glides slowly away from the dock and out into San Francisco Bay. Many of the men line the deck for a final, and in many cases, tearful view of the "Fresco" skyline . . .

....We are now passing under the famous "Golden Gate Bridge." MAN, OH MAN! What a sight! Not only is the vast open expanse of the bridge impressive, but I get a lump in my throat, and my stomach muscles tighten when I think of the men who "dangled" out over the bay during its construction. And can you imagine the dread of the men who paint the super structure on a regular basis? I'm not convinced I would like to drive over it . . . We have broken out of the bay and we are now at sea. The Pacific Ocean . . . no less!

.....The mood of the men is great! A lot of laughing and joking and pointing in awe at sights that lay before them . . . Its getting late. See you tomorrow . . .

Thursday 0800 hours
Everybody is sick! I mean everybody, including me!.....As they say in "The Mighty Casey at Bat," . . . There is no joy in Muddville, or on board the USS MITCHELL EITHER!....I have never seen so many sick men in all of my life. Everywhere you look, men are "heaving." It seems the ones that were laughing and joking the most yesterday, are the sickest ones

of all, today. They are heaving like crazy. I'm not! But, I feel like I could heave for days. Seasickness is like something an angry God would hurl upon his disobedient flock. No energy, just a heavy headiness . . . just a feeling of BLAH! All over!

.....There are about 1,500 men on this ship, two thirds must be sick and are up on deck trying to get some fresh air . . . or attending to the seamen' plague below deck . . . This floating tub is no sandbox. Normally I wouldn't bother you with such hideous details . . . but this situation is something else!....Oh well, I will have something to tell my children, and grandchildren at some future date, provided I live through this torturous ordeal. ....Yes, indeed! This story will be told around camp fires . . . anywhere strong men tell wild tales . . . I think I will go up on deck myself . . . I'll see you tomorrow . . . if there is one!

Friday 1800 hours
.....Feeling a bit better today folks . . . Pretty bad off this morning though . . . I'm beginning to eat . . . THINGS! Crackers, peanut butter, dry cereal, that kind of thing . . . Starting to enjoy the trip . . . We ran into a storm last night . . . no one allowed on deck . . . The ship, I'm told, was really rocking and rolling . . . Glad I was asleep . . . A lot of the men seem to feel a little better, but you can still see far too many of them heaving in place, or crawling into dark corners . . . I have not sought out a private corner for myself . . . Yet! I am pretty proud of that. Strangely enough, it appears the stronger men have fallen prey to seasickness, first . . . Just like the "shots" we received . . . The strongest men fainted.

Saw some whales today . . . Watched them for sometime . . . From the deck, all you see is "Water, Water everywhere . . . And not a drop to drink."...as

199

the poem goes . . . At 0800 hours today, we were 700 miles from "Fresco."...Only 4,013 miles to go! A long way to walk. Huh! I know the precise distance because the ship sends out a daily, one page, newsletter, which gives daily world news, t.i.d.-bits, including the nautical miles to our destination, Yokohama, Japan! This is the first time we have received word of our destination. I guess the Navy figures that "loose lips can't sink ships" if there is no one at sea to tell information to. I will remain for a week or so, for processing for Korea . . . I'll tell you more when I get the word . . . Going to a movie tonight . . .

See you tomorrow!

Saturday 1610 hours
.....I'm back again. I've just put in a hard day today . . . KP!. ...The smell of garbage, along with everything else is not an ideal way to spend a day at sea . . . I don't know whether or not I've told you, but we are going the northern route and the seas are getting rough again. We are going up by Alaska, then over to Japan . . . As of 0800 this morning we are 1136 miles from San Francisco. 3,633 miles from our destination . . . I was up on deck this morning and you would be absolutely astounded to find a flock of sea gulls, who have been following us all the way from "Fresco." Seagulls fly in the most unusual fashion. They never flap their wings . . . They seem to find just the right wind currents and glide gracefully on them. They generally fly alongside the ship or behind it, hoping to find the food we toss over the fantail . . . One naturally thinks back to the earliest seafarers who had these little friends as escorts during their frightening voyages into the unknown . . .

Another interesting sight is to see men scurrying around when the boatswains pipe the time to eat . . . I love that whistling, warbling sound. Then you hear orders being given. "All men berthing in section 401c. form a chow line on deck "c" on the starboard side."..Well, the first question for many of the men is "Where is starboard?" Some men run right some run left, some stumble "fore". some stumble "aft." It is a hilarious sight! Some men never got to eat the first couple of days because they never got to the chow hall on time. For many it was just as well because they were too sick to eat anyway . . . Pray that you never see such a sight as men trying to eat and then scampering away to find a hiding place for relief . . . One other phenomenon is that in certain places in the Pacific the water is so smooth that standing along the deck railing, one has a strong, compelling urge to just step overboard and go for a walk. It must have something to do with the water shelves in the sea bottom because at all other times you see waves . . . Even if they are calm ones . . . Don't worry though, I'll never try to walk on water. Man should leave that up to the man in the Good Book . . . I'm tired now and I'm going to hit the rack . . .

See you tomorrow . . .

Sunday 1830 hours

It's evening time now, but I experienced my first Sabbath day aboard ship . . . I'm feeling pretty good, despite heavy seas . . . That, as you know by now, translates into the ship bobbing up and down like a cork . . . More KP today . . .

The heavy seas brought about more sea sickness to some of my buddies. I can see them bending over cans now. I still haven't yet! I think knowing that I have to work has been helpful . . . I'm afraid that some men will be sick for the remainder of the trip. I have some friends who have never been out of the "rack" since the first day at sea. They just moan, eat crackers . . . and regurgitate . . .

.....Someone who was frightfully sick asked me the first day out, "Steve, you know a lot of things . . . the Captain is going to turn the ship around and go back home . . . Isn't he?" ...Poor guy was looking for any sign of hope for an end to his sickness . . . I told him only to "Hang on! We will be in Yokohama in a few more days." This didn't help. His spirits sank again. He's been in the "rack" ever since . . .

By the way, as of 0800 hours this morning, we were 3,106 nautical miles from Yokohama, and 1609 miles from "Fresco." How are you handling the trip so far? Don't worry, we'll get there yet!....

See you tomorrow

Monday 2030 hours
...It's nearly bed time and I'm a little tired and sleepy . . . but, I must remain true to my promise of painting a picture for you of the trip . . . The Pacific was simply beautiful today!..I haven't seen one person sick up on deck . . . You must remember that the only thing you can see is sky, water, and the seagulls, when they are within sight . . . I spent a lot of time on deck, fore, aft, and starboard, just sun bathing and day dreaming a thousand thoughts about what lies ahead . . . Can you believe it! The weather tomorrow is supposed to be . . . OH! NO! High seas!....

.....At 0800 hours this morning, we have almost reached the halfway mark. We are 2,036 miles from "Fresco" and 2605 nautical miles from Yokohama, Japan . . . Get ready for high seas tomorrow . . .

I'll see you then.

Tuesday 1730 hours

202

...Hi again everyone. Tonight we will reach a very significant milestone in our trip . . . Just before midnight the USS Mitchell and its human cargo of miserable protoplasm, will cross the International Date Line! What this means is that "Tuesday", when I go to bed, I will wake-up "Thursday." morning. Something like old Rip Van Winkle himself, Huh!...Today was another bad day weather wise . . . As predicted, the seas were very rough with high velocity winds. We can hardly go up on deck for fear of being swept over board . . . You guessed it! We are expecting worse weather tomorrow. So, we must display a little more forbearance. Let's all try to dream pretty dreams. They could be our last for a while. We shall see . . .

Thursday 1530 hours
....Back again folks! Feeling fine today, despite bad weather and rough seas. The ship is, at this very moment, really rocking and rolling. Everyone has been cautioned to stay below decks. Nothing much else of consequence happened today . . . Most of the men just played cards or slept.
.....As of 0800 this morning, we were 1742 miles from Yokohama, and 2972 miles from "Fresco" . . . Pretty warm today, temperature 58 degrees . . . That's it for today, folks. . . .
See you tomorrow.

Friday 1935 hours
...Hello!....Well, I intend to give you only a brief rundown today . . . Nothing much going on inside, or out . . . I'm feeling fine and hope you are handling this boring part of the trip with me. Rough weather prevailed again today. ...The waves breaking monstrously over the bow of the deck . . . The ship would heave high above the waves and then would come crashing down with such a

thunderous roar that I thought it would break in two . . . It is supposed to be calm seas and sunshine tomorrow. It's a funny thing. The weatherman never seems to be wrong with his forecast, unlike the ones on shore who never seem to get it right . . . As of 0800 today, we were 1389 nautical miles from Yokohama, and 3432 nautical miles from "Fresco.".....Friday didn't hold much action . . . Let's see what tomorrow will bring.

See you then.

Saturday 1633 hours
....Howdy! Hurrah! Several things of notable interest happened today. First, at about 0900 this morning we "spotted" a ship going toward "Fresco . . . The joke among the weary, disenchanted troops was . . . If they weren't past the halfway point, they would "jump ship," swim to the other ship, and go back to "Fresco." ...Saw another whale spouting and puffing water as it made its way through the water . . . Just think, we finally saw something material besides garbage over the fantail. It was really a welcome sight to see the other ship and the whale.

...Good troop show, comedy acts and singers aboard ship today. Good music was supplied and a very entertaining, happy time was had by all . . .

...As of 0800 today, we were 886 nautical miles from Yokohama, and 3956 miles from "Fresco."...Tomorrow is supposed to be a beautiful day. The seas smooth with warm temperatures. I will spend a lot of time up on deck . . . WHOOPEE!

See you tomorrow.

Sunday 1642 hours
...This is my last entry aboard the good ship Mitchell. Can you believe it?...We will be in Yokohama tonight sometime, and disembark in the

204

morning at 11:30 hours. Everyone is quite excited and preparing for the landing. We will be able to see land, lights, structures, ships . . . But we have to wait until tomorrow! ...All along I have forgotten to tell you that, just for the record, you can see only 9 miles in any direction. On a clear day, at that. This gives you a feeling that you are staying in one place at all times . . . You can clearly see why the "old sailors" thought the earth was not round. ...As of 0800 today the ship was 4713 nautical miles from "Fresco", and 472 nautical miles from Yokohama. ...getting close Huh!...It has been quite an experience overall. But, I wouldn't be anxious to do it again right away. I say right away, because I hope I will return in about a year. ...Tomorrow is the big day! I'll include my first impressions of the new land, and then send this chronicle home to you.

See you tomorrow.

Monday Evening

....Here I am, a land lubber again. We arrived today amid cheers and a brass band. I was immediately struck with awe at the quaint little, brown-skinned people and their small huts and buildings. ...I feel like Gulliver among the Lilliputians. It is truly another world! ...You should have seen the train taking us to our barracks. The gauge of the tracks was so small compared to ours back home . . . I love to view the countryside. It is so green and calm. The train trip took three and a half hours to go 27 miles. ....I shall endeavor to tell you more the next time. ....Right now, I must bring this chronicle to an end. I hope you enjoyed the trip as much, or more than I did. ....There is much, much more to tell, but time is against me. .....

....I'm flying to Pusan, Korea Saturday. Pusan will be my permanent base . . . or for the foreseeable future. ...Until next time, here is wishing you all . . . God Speed and take care of yourself. ...I'll attempt to do the same . . . Love and kisses to all!...

Love, Steve

...P. S. Tell Don, . . . Don't join the Navy! Ha! Ha! This place smells like an indoor outhouse!

"YOU May not be interested
In War, but War is interested
In you"
Leon Trosky

KOREA - "LAND OF CALM"

Pusan, Korea
17th Communications Squadron
May 30, 1953
Dear Mom and Dad,
I have just a few spare moments and wanted to see how everyone is doing "stateside." I'm doing fine, no need to worry. When it rains here, it rains in "torrents" and continues for days. However, the sun is very hot and all water soon vanishes.

I'm working on a deal that could lead to a change in my career. I was listening to the "Far East Network in Tokyo" and they indicated in an announcement that the "American Forces Korean Network" was accepting applications for radio announcers in the Korean theater. I called the Pusan radio station and asked them about an audition. I was quickly okayed for an audition the same week, but I had to work. I'll try again.

Love,
Steve

Pusan is now beginning to yield some of its pleasures, despite the fact that South Korea is fighting for its life. There are a very curious and disturbing, yet intellectually compelling aspect about war zones. If one is not physically or actively taking part in war, life elsewhere just goes on, seemingly oblivious to the fact that soldiers and civilians are suffering and dying. I had been guilty of this contemptible malaise myself. I would go to the flight line and watch war planes taking off, heavily laden with bombs,

207

heading for the North. Most of them would come back. Some wouldn't. For example, I would be playing basketball for our communications squadron while the planes headed north. For the most part, they would go about their deadly business, unnoticed.

Once the planes would leave, or even while they were being armed with their deadly arsenals, men would absolutely insist on drinking their coffee at <u>exactly</u> 9:00 a.m. I often thought if the enemy ever attacked the airbase, they should do it at <u>exactly</u> 9:00 a.m. and hit the chow hall, where most of the men would be. I don't drink coffee to this day because when I recall those days, something seemed terribly wrong about indulging oneself in such pleasures while others suffered. However, according to my next few letters home, I seemed to be doing the same thing. Shame on me!

Pusan, Korea
17 Communications Squadron
June 6, 1953
Dear Mom and Dad,

I have just finished playing basketball for our squadron team and I'm pretty tired. We had a tough team to play. We won 40 to 38. Your son managed to get 19 points of the 40. My commanding officer, who was quite an athlete, has taken a liking to me. Maybe I will make corporal soon. Ha! Ha!

Do you remember the broadcasting position I auditioned for a few weeks ago? Well, would you believe the radio station called me yesterday to tell me I had been accepted? It's true! They want to know when I can come to work. A funny thing though, the city of Pusan is nearly 8 miles outside the airbase and I have no way of getting back and forth. Nevertheless, a tape recording of the audition tape I made has been sent to 5th Air Force Headquarters in Teague, Korea. The generals and other "big wheels" have to give their "OK" before I can be formally accepted.

As you know, I rarely brag about anything I do, but if all goes well this move has the potential of being a major break for me in the future. Most of the announcers have considerable commercial broadcasting experience, including staff announcing for the major networks, NBC, CBS, and ABC. I don't think any blacks have ever been accepted, so . . .

Mom, I hope you are still enjoying driving and showing off your gorgeous "Green Hornet" Delta 88. Try not to "fly" too low, will you? Also Dad, you will not be pleased to know that your son remains all "fingers" with his camera. I picked up my pictures the other day – two rolls – and nothing. I'll try to get some instruction . . .

Love,
Steve

17th Communications Squadron
Pusan, Korea
July 3, 1953
Dear Mom and Dad,

Lately, things have been rather calm, just a few demonstrations on the part of the South Koreans. I'm pretty isolated from the political realities here. You probably know more at home than I do. Nevertheless, we are still restricted to the base. "Old Sigmond Rhee" is supposed to land here sometime today. The base is being "spruced-up" for him. I think I'll mosey on over to the flight line to see what I can see. Sometime in the distant future I can say I witnessed a small fragment of history by seeing, up close, the President of South Korea!

I went down to the beach yesterday (Pusan Harbor) – nothing like it. Life is really not too bad here, especially if one keeps busy in one's spare time. Here are some snapshots of "the kid" shooting the basketball during a game. Notice the number 4 on the back of my jersey. You may recall that it was the number I wore at LHS. The guys really go for sports activities here, and if you play basketball for the squadron you are a pretty "big cheese." Oh yes, I'm taking college courses in English and history. If I pass, the grades are transferable to any college in the USA. The courses are given through an alliance with the University of California.

Love,
Steve

Pusan, Korea
17 Communications Squadron
July 19, 1953
Dear Mom and Dad,

We have had two floods in and around the area lately. Two days ago, I had to fill sandbags to protect the airbase perimeter. The rains were washing away the bomb dumps and that is a definite no-no. It doesn't rain long here but when it does, the heavens really open up. I had to look twice when a small boat went by. A boat at an airbase, no less! I wanted to make sure it wasn't heading for the river Styx.

Recently, I took a little jaunt into Pusan, just to make sure I could recall one day, when I'm in my "rocking chair," what this war was all about. The city is just teeming with people . . . most of whom I feel really sorry for. The Koreans are constantly busy, just trying to exist. The small streets are filthy and impossibly full of people going hither and yon. It reminds me of a beehive. There is no drainage or water system, and the women wash clothes right in the street. Sanitation just doesn't exist. One should not have to live like that.

The black market is an underworld that permits some semblance of an economy. I was offered $85.00 for my watch. I paid $25.00 for it. A person of devious character could make thousands. The penalties are severe if caught, though. I'd rather not make money on these terms. What is most irreconcilable to an observer is that just beyond the squalor, there are beautiful green rice paddies, with Pusan Bay and 3,000 foot mountains as a backdrop to them. One questions how it can appear to be so peaceful, and yet be so deadly. In history class, we are writing an essay on "What America Means To Me." It was easy to write after witnessing the sordid sights in Pusan . . .

Love,
Steve

It had been nearly two weeks since I had written home. Rumors were flying that the war was nearing an end . . . again! I was anxious for the killing to stop . . . on both sides. No more B-26s with their bomb loads heading north to bury men, women and children under piles of rubble. No more refugees carrying their worldly belongings on their backs . . . and above all, no more vacant stares in the eyes of the children. I was thinking about these things when I wrote to the family.

Pusan, Korea
17 Communications Squadron
August 1, 1953
Dear Mom and Dad,
It looks like the "big show" is over, at least for the present. The day all of us, friend and foe, have been hoping for, has finally arrived. The Armistice has been signed. It has been a hellish and costly war. Let's hope there will be a lasting peace this time. It's strange, but there was no rejoicing here on the base. It's hard to believe, but everyone went

about their daily jobs as if nothing had happened . . . nothing at all. Can war really be that routine? They have already told us that the Armistice will not have any bearing on my coming home any sooner. In fact, there are rumors that our tours may be extended a couple of months, because the marines, pilots, army guys, the ones risking their lives daily will have priority for shipping out. They deserve it. I wouldn't mind deferring to them. Well, promotion time rolled around and I was excluded from the elite few who made corporal. When I say few, I mean few – only 3 out of some 60 men. Air Force policy states it must be six months since your last promotion before you are eligible for your next promotion. Those that made it had up to 20 months eligibility time, so . . . !

Love,
Steve

Pusan Korea
17 Communications Squadron
August 23, 1953
Dear Mom and Dad,

It has been some time since I have written. I apologize. The weather here is still hot, but I go to the beach every chance I get. Fortunately for me and others of us here at the base, we are doing so much better than those soldiers, marines, and others near the front line. You should see me now, I'm really dark from the sun . . . I mean really dark! When I take a shower at night it looks like I have a pair of "white" shorts on. One of my white buddies even asked me what nationality I was . . . come on! My kinky hair should be enough for them to go by . . .

Well, I went down to the radio station in Pusan again. They wanted to talk to me about getting a transfer out of my unit. A couple of officers are

212

working on it now. I don't know how they are doing, but there are no footprints for Negroes in this field so they must be doing a lot of "head scratching" . . . I'll keep you up to date.

Love,
Steve

Pusan, Korea
17 Communications Squadron
August 28, 1953
Dear Mom and Dad,

I'm feeling fine. Most of us are just trying to find ways to keep cool during the hot weather. We are about to enter the monsoon/typhoon season. Believe me, we have already experienced a few big blows that have winged their way down the peninsula. Possibly you have heard of one of them. It was tagged with the name Nina. Nina was not a nice lady! Thankfully she narrowly missed us, so there was "no sweat."

I got a B grade on my history final exam so that's one college course I won't have to take when I go to college stateside. I won't be able to take the next course in sequence because I won't be here in Pusan much longer . . . I hope!

The radio station called again and I went to Pusan for an audition. One of the fellas was assigned to drive me there in a jeep. He was white and didn't like that very much, knowing the purpose of my visit was to be a contender for such a prestigious slot. That's his problem!

I spent the full day at the radio station and had no way to get back to the base. What an experience that was! I'll tell you about it in a minute, but first, more about the audition. I had to ad-lib for 5 minutes about my background and radio experience. Next I had to pretend to be a disc-jockey and do a 5-minute show. I had to make up

213

my own title, introduce 5 records and then close the show . . . all without notes. I had no problem and called my show, "Platter Party" . . . now, just how original can a guy be, right?

The rest was really easy – just announcing news, sports – that kind of thing. The audition ended by me "selling myself" to the network. I must have done well because they said, on the spot, "You've been accepted, Airman Scott! All that remains is a higher security clearance. If all is okay, and I see no reason why not, you will be sent to anyplace in Korea where we have radio stations. There are nine of them."

Now only one more hurdle remained, and it was a big one. I had to get back to the airbase at Pusan! It was late afternoon and no one at the station had transportation. OH NO! Can you believe that! My base was nearly 8 miles away. There was no place for me to stay at the station. I was told by my commanding officer, who didn't want me with the AFKN outfit anyway, that he would not assign me a driver to go to Pusan, but he had to! He then told me I would have to find my own ride back . . . and don't be AWOL. So . . . I did . . . I walked.

I really didn't mind the idea of walking. I had been playing basketball back at the base and swimming daily in Pusan Harbor. Physically, I felt in great shape. I knew the road well enough because I had been to Pusan several times, as you know. As I began my solo trek, I became so engrossed in watching the bright green rice paddy fields and watching the "mama-sans" and papa-sans" walking by wearing their traditional long, white, loose fitting outfits, that it suddenly dawned on me it was getting dark and I had only gone about halfway to the base. Darkness was sure to catch me soon . . . and it did. I began to suck in my breath with some sense of urgency! My walking stride became more brisk. I had no weapon because they wouldn't issue me one, unless you would consider a "mess kit knife" I borrowed at the radio station for a weapon. Anyway, black night was falling fast and the road was becoming obscured. You must remember, there were no street lights in Pusan, and of course none in the countryside.

Suddenly, a huge water buffalo and a farmer were right upon me . . . I didn't even see or hear them. This was getting to be more than I bargained for. It was now "blacker than a thousand midnights . . . down by the cypress swamp."... as the poet says. About another mile down the inky black road I heard a voice coming from a person I couldn't see. "Hey GI . . . you go K-9." You must be kidding me. How can someone see me? I can't see them, I thought to myself. My head turned in all directions at the same time. Suddenly, my straining eyes could make out the outline of what turned out to be a South Korean soldier. I gripped my knife as I said, "Yes" in Korean. "I go with you" he said in a voice much too eager. We walked the remaining few miles together, chatting away like two old friends. I even got to practice some of the Korean words and phrases I had learned. As it turned out, he had made his way from the front lines near the 38th Parallel after the Armistice and was going to see some of his friends who worked at the airbase. Finally, I could see the "lights" of the airbase. My Korean friend and I parted company and wished each other farewell. To this day I have no idea what my "friend" looked like or wore. It was too dark. The lights of K-9 airbase were a welcome sight to end an exciting day.

Love,
Steve

Pusan, Korea

215

17 Communications Squadron
September 14, 1953
Dear Mom and Dad,

Hi Folks! I have an extra moment on this end and the best way to spend it is to chat with all of you. I have been busy flitting here and there, trying to work through all of the details of my career transfer.

I flew up to Teague a couple of days ago for an interview at 5th Air Force Headquarters. The weather was rather bad and it was nighttime, so I didn't experience quite the same visual and physical sensations I did on my flight from Yokohama, Japan to Pusan, Korea. But I still kept my nose pressed against the aircraft window like a starving street kid looking into a bakery.

Just a few particulars for you. We flew 6000 feet in the old C-47 aircraft. It took about 45 minutes from take-off to landing. Would you believe I wore a parachute and a "Mae-West" life preserver? During our pre-flight check, they quickly went through the uses of the devices and other safety matters. I doubt I would be able to manipulate everything properly in case of an emergency anyway. You know me . . . all thumbs!

Nonetheless, I sat next to several envoys from communist countries. They were in South Korea to ensure there are no violations of the Armistice agreements. They were all bedecked in splendid uniforms. Very impressive! Several South Korean officers were on the plane as well. I'm glad another war didn't erupt on the plane (smile). Koreans include a staple food in their diet called Kimchee. It consists, as far as I know, of fermented cabbage and other assorted vegetables. It smells to high heaven, believe me! I literally wanted to bail out of the plane . . . emergency or not. Then reason

216

returned. They probably think some of the things Americans eat have a terrible odor as well.

Here is the latest information I have on my being transferred. Enclosed is a letter of my acceptance! I will be doing news, sports and a disc-jockey program. The location will be Teague for a while. There are nine radio stations throughout South Korea. To be chosen is quite something, because many apply, but few are chosen (didn't someone important say that?) This move will be permanent until my return to the states, which will be about seven more months. YIPPIE!

I haven't left yet, but this will be my last letter to you from Pusan. I'll write again when I get to my next base. So don't write until I give you more information about my exact location. It may be two or three weeks before you hear from me, so don't worry about not hearing from me.

Love,
Steve

17th Communications Squadron
September 18, 1953
Dear Mom and Dad,

Well, things have really been "hopping" around here lately. About a week ago a fighter jet, an F-84 thunderjet, was coming in on its "final approach" over the end of Pusan beach and the runway and it crashed! As usual, I was "shooting baskets" and as always, keeping my eyes glued to the aircraft taking off and landing. Dad, you shouldn't have gotten us all fascinated by aircraft. The basketball court affords a panoramic view of the beach and of the airstrip. The fighter jet looked okay for its approach, a little low and hot, but okay, he thought . . . wrong! He suddenly realized he was going to crash. He jettisoned his wing tanks for fear of fire and explosion. The plane smacked the beach, lost its nose gear and began spinning and careening across the runway. It lost its right wing, part of its tail and skidded a hundred or more yards and came to a halt. All of this happened in the space of a few seconds. You'll never believe it, but the pilot "walked away!" Remember the old saying "Any landing you can walk away from is a good landing." He'll be grounded and chewed-out, but he's alive.

Another incident happened the other night that will demonstrate that this is not the Hilton Hotel. There I was, fast asleep, the time being about 1:30 a.m. I guess I was dreaming the usual dreams when suddenly I was awakened by terrible, frightening screams. I first thought the base was under attack, or some of the guys were horsing around. The screaming continued. One of the airmen, brandishing a gun was screaming, "I can't stand it any longer. Nobodies come near me. I'll kill you all. Get away! Get away!" Well, you know me, no hero here. I got out of my bed and got away from the poor, demented soul. We summoned the APs, who had a hard time hauling him away!

He came back to join us after a couple of days at the psychic ward, apologizing for his unseemly behavior. It appears excessive drinking brought about by a "Dear John" letter he received from home caused him to "flip his lid." All of us nearly flipped ours as well that night – Ha! Ha!

I'm glad to hear brothers Gary, Charlie, and Larry are doing well in athletics at "LHS." . . . give them my congrats! I hope Don goes into jets or OCS – I would be proud to salute him. On second thought tell him I'm not about to "salute" any younger brother (smile).

Love,
Steve

It may come as a surprise, but I thoroughly enjoyed walking in the beautiful Korean countryside. Life seemed to slow to a pace only suited to a small-town person like me. At least once a week, I walk for a couple of hours through the fields or on the small country roads and footpaths. The oh-so-green rice paddies always seem to have high hills and mountains as backdrops. The view of the landscape is gorgeous!

I even met a couple of families and stop to chat with them. It didn't hurt that one of them had a beautiful, unmarried daughter about my age. Her name was Kim. Both the family and Kim taught me Korean words and phrases that would help me "get by" in the marketplace and with our Korean houseboy.

I recently climbed one of the low relief hills and was happy and proud of myself for that achievement. I again wrote my parents. I was also now working for AFKN radio and was at my new air base in Teague, Korea. It had been some time (a couple of weeks) since I had heard from them.

Teague, Korea
8241th Army Unit
October 3, 1953
Dear Mom and Dad,

It has been quite some time since I have heard from you folks, but no sweat, I tell myself. I will be going to Tokyo, Japan, on "R & R" sometime next month and you will be expecting a nice little gift, but there will be no hope for you. Ha! Ha! Ha! That should get some action. I started work at the station as I told you in my last letter. Everything is going quite well in my new position. There I was, doing the "Rice Paddy Ranger" disc-jockey show, 12:00 to 2:00 a.m., when one of those usual blunders of the radio business took place. I had just finished playing a record. I introduced the next number (I think it was one by Sarah Vaughan). Anyway, I introduced it and relaxed for a minute while it was playing. Suddenly, I heard a terrible buzzing sound in my earphones. I quickly diagnosed the problem. I had forgotten to turn the mike off. Thinking it was off, I began shooting the breeze with a friend of mine sitting next to me in the studio. Would you believe all of our conversation was going out over the air? Half of South Korea heard the goof, no less. "Woe is me." Fortunately, we were not talking about anything unsavory. Nothing came of it, so there is no cause for alarm.

Oh yes, I climbed to the top of a large hill/mountain today. It must have been 1,000 feet at its highest point. It was very rocky and climbing was rather difficult, but my buddies and I made it. You know me, I'm afraid of heights and trust me, I was nervous all the way up. It was all worth it, though. We had a splendid view – no, it was spectacular! I saw a wondrous green valley, far down below, dotted with little villages all seen to their greatest advantage from my lofty perch atop the hill/mountain.

Love,
Steve

I didn't remain in Teague very long. My stay in Teague was really just a holding point until I could receive my permanent broadcasting assignment, and the time was at hand. Despite the fact that my new assignment was to be war-ravaged Chunchon, near the 38th Parallel, I was happy to be there.

Chunchon, Korea
AFKN
October 11, 1953
Dear Mom and Dad,
Well, I have done it again. Yes, I have moved! Now here I am, way up north, in South Korea. Can

you believe that? Just keep in mind that there are two Koreas, Communist North and the Republic of South Korea. I will now be stationed in a city called Chunchon, which is about 25 miles south of Seoul. Chunchon is a village of about 20,000 people. The radio station is about 5 miles away. I hate to say it, but it is a dirty, stinking place. I suppose most war-ravaged cities cannot be expected to be anything but total devastation and squalor.

There is a small airbase about a mile and a half from the radio station. AT6 aircraft fly in and out of the airfield. During the war, the small propeller aircraft, called "mosquitoes," were used as enemy spotter planes. They would drop flares on or near enemy troop concentrations, providing targets for the much faster U. S. jets. The mosquitoes could linger over target areas for long periods of time, until the jets would arrive to hammer the enemy positions. They also played a major role in protecting downed US pilots from enemy ground troops, again suppressing enemy ground fire until the rescue choppers arrived.

The radio station itself is really paradise compared to my last location. It is located in a Quonset hut, as opposed to the other stations which were in huge vans. It is the most sought-after station by AFKN personnel in Korea, so I can't complain. I'm told I will remain here until my rotation back stateside.

I am working the morning shift now. I will be on the air from 0500 hours until 0800 hours. As you can see, I will be the lucky one to sign the station on the air. I have a variety of shows to do during those hours, but I think they will present no problem. I'm happy. Oh yes, the station is called "Rambler." Who knows why? We are required to wear patches on our sleeves that are inscribed with "AFKN-The American Forces Korean Network," with a picture of a microphone. No rank, it literally means we can go pretty much where and when we want and receive all rights and privileges benefiting high positions. How about that for prestige?

Mom, when I go to Japan I will try to get some of the famous Japanese china for you. I've seen pictures of various name brands and you will love the china. Tell Dad I'm at a loss as to what to get him, so please advise . . .

Love,
Steve

Prior to my R&R, I had received word from home that the Air Force officially considered my brother Marlon killed in a plane crash in the remote Alaskan mountains. Among my dad's memorabilia, years later, I found this release capturing the end of the dreadful affair.

November 20, 1953

PRESS RELEASE FROM ANCHORAGE, ALASKA, BY ASSOCIATED PRESS

A faint radio signal was the only tenuous clue today to the fate of 52 men aboard a giant C-124 Globe master which vanished Saturday night over the Gulf of Alaska. They cautioned, however, against any undue optimism, pointing out that the signal was not picked up again, and past experiences in Alaskan air tragedies has shown that mysterious radio transmissions are not uncommon and have proved valueless in searches. Names of the crew, including Marlon L. Scott, Airman 3C, Lebanon, Indiana, were released yesterday. The passengers have not been identified.

Twenty-four search planes are poised here, ready to fan out when weather permits, over the 150 miles to tiny Middleton Island, the four-engine transport's last checkpoint. The weather outlook was poor. The 41 army and air force passengers and 11 crewmen yesterday were listed officially as missing in the continuing plague of United States military air disasters throughout the world.

Since November 7, six planes have crashed or disappeared. They carried 162 men, of whom 82 are now confirmed dead, 72 missing and 8 survived. Three of the troop carriers were lost in Alaska, two in Korea and one in Montana.

A graduate of Lebanon High School, where he played both basketball and baseball, Airman Scott had been stationed at McCord Air Base, near Tacoma, Washington. The weak radio signal, which could have come from emergency equipment carried by the Globe-master, was picked up yesterday by the CAA station at Yukatoga, on the Alaskan Coastline about 150 miles east of Middleton

223

Island. The S.O.S. was so dim no bearing could be taken, but authorities at Elmendorf Air Base here said the signal on the navigational distress frequency might have been "Gibson Girl" radio transmitters attached to the C-124's rubber rafts.

My memories of these events were later captured in letters to home and reflected my hidden sorrows.

> November 28, 1953
> Dear Mom and Dad,
> Yes, it's me again! I know I had just written to you the other day. I've got some things to send you and I want to convey to you my sympathies over the finality of Marlon's death. Dad, I will look into the matters you asked me to when I go on "R&R" in Japan. But for now, I would like to take this time to respond to the questions you sent me.
> I want you to know that it leaves a terrible empty feeling inside me when I think about the grief both of you are experiencing now. I feel the same way and really have no one to talk to about it. It just seems so unfair that a shroud of mystery and doubt will always remain about the events connected with Marlon's death. I suppose we must live with the fact the Lord still moves in mysterious ways.
> For you, Mom and Dad, please accept my deepest sympathies and know that I am sorry it had to end this way. Perhaps it will draw our family even closer together. We must remember always how much happiness he brought to all of us. Take care and God bless!
> Love,
> Steve
>
> Chunchon, Korea
> AFKN Rambler
> November 30, 1953
> Dear Mom and Dad,

The cold weather is really beginning to show its hand here. The mercury dropped to 7 degrees overnight, however, it has climbed back up to the forties by mid-day. We have all received our winter clothing, so I'm not worried. You should see me in my winter gear. Man! I look like Nanook of the North. I have this wonderful fur-lined parka coat. It has a huge rabbit inner liner. The coat itself is heavily lined at the knees. Then there are Mickey Mouse boots that are huge, just like Mickey's. They are fur-lined and insulated against rain, snow and ice. Bring on winter! I'm now doing a morning disc-jockey show called "Coffee Shop." I'll send an audio tape of the show home when I get some other items to go with it.

I don't think I will be going on "R & R" in December because I'm going to be operated on in a day or so. Don't worry, I'm just going to get a minor clipping of my vital parts. Very vital! I hope I don't sound like tweety bird or sing soprano when it's finished. Try to read between the lines! One last hint, all Jewish boys endure this indignity when they are born. Give my best to the rest of the family.

I would like to know if there have been any new developments about Marlon's missing plane? Please advise me as soon as possible. Is there anything I can do on this end?

Love,
Steve

One gets a sense of what was in store for me from this letter. Male children born when I was were rarely circumcised and this inconvenience was being remedied by a lot of military men during their stint in the service, I had made the decision to avail myself of the same hygienic benefits afforded the Jews thousands of years ago. Waiting until you are nearly 21 years old to have the procedure done

225

was a true adventure and above all, not recommended!

The doctor told me, "Airman Scott, you seem to be getting on the beautification bandwagon that's traveling through this place." I suddenly took a look at the surgeon for the first time. He was a Major about forty years old. He had sagging skin that only a body shop could fix. His eyes looked as if something he feared was catching up with him. It might have been alcohol at the Officer's Club. "No," I said, "I'm not trying to get on any bandwagon, it's just that while I have a lot of free time, I might as well get it done. When can you do it?"

"Tomorrow," he said, his words coming out like the croak of a frog.

I was beginning to have second thoughts about this guy, especially about entrusting my future potential for children to this man whose hands now began to become a fixation for me – hands that would soon be waving a scalpel over me and my secret places. They seemed to be withering like spider legs before my eyes. "Be at the dispensary at 8:00 a.m. tomorrow. You'll be a little sore down there for a few days, but there will be no problem."

8:00 a.m. came and the procedure was done following a spinal tap. No sweat! I hobbled back to the barracks with his admonition to see him in five days, no lifting/no strenuous exercise, and there will be some edema. Take two aspirin every four hours until the pain goes away.

The five days were up, I went back to see the Major, whistling because the edema made me more than an ordinary man. I looked as if I could conquer the earth. But the edema went away and I was a mere mortal again. Unwrapping the bandage, he stepped back as if in mortal shock. "I've been too aggressive with my scalpel, but then you colored men have more than your proper endowment." I started to hurl myself at him, when he broke out laughing. "Go forth and multiply, Scott – you're fine." I laughed all the way back to my Quonset hut. How many airmen, black and white, had he scared half to death?

Love,
Steve

The Christmas holidays were fast approaching. This would mark the first Christmas I had ever spent away from home. I had also planned to delay going on "R & R" because of the "shearing" operation, but things had gone so well that I was able to speed up my vacation.

I had flown to Japan for 10 days and was really looking forward to the trip. I had not tasted a glass of milk, real eggs, or a steak in what seemed like ages. Quite frankly, I was getting a little despondent looking at war-ravaged cities and refugees. I was also dismayed by the arrogance of some of my friends' treating the Koreans as if they were their slaves – calling them "gooks" and pretending they were socially, physically and intellectually inferior. Back home many of my white friends would be considered lower class. Who knows, maybe that is why they felt superior. I always thought it curious when they command the Koreans to "Speak English!" when none of them could or tried to speak Korean. Anyway, I was tired of it and was excited when I boarded the C-54 for the flight to Japan.

I had heard many stories of guys who had gone to Japan with about seven hundred dollars or more. After three or four days living a sultan's life in Japan, they were belittled at the airbase because they were broke. For me, I had a grand plan. As previously mentioned, we network boys wore no rank, just the AFKN radio patches. I intended to use that to my advantage too, but first I intended to eat some real food (we had powdered eggs and processed meats as standard fare) at the hotel, buy my mother a set of Japanese china and find a present for dad. I took only three hundred dollars, so I had to be extremely frugal, calling upon all my Pearl Street knowledge to escape the fate of many others. As events unfolded, I would have to call upon those skills much sooner than expected.

I had heard my friends talk about the Pearl Hotel, and that was my destination. The cab driver spoke reasonably good English. He said his cab was a Hubba! Hubba! cab. Great, I thought. Hubba! Hubba! must mean fate had smiled on me and I was getting privileged treatment. Wrong! I should have known I was wrong about my receiving special treatment as a member of the advance party when I boarded the <u>USS</u> <u>Mitchell</u> many months ago. What Hubba! Hubba! meant was we were going to go real fast, and we did! Laying on the horn, driving as if the devil himself was after him, we streaked toward the Pearl Hotel. When we arrived, I thought I was more dead than alive – frightened to death would be the proper description. The cab driver just grinned. The bill was $19.00 plus tip.

I immediately went to the dining room, ordered a quart of milk, a filet mignon steak, eggs and a chocolate sundae. I felt like a king until the bill came – $61.00 plus tip. This R & R business was going to be no joke. I had taken a cab, eaten one meal and spent nearly $80.00 including tips. I didn't even have a place to sleep yet. The room fare was $35.00 per night. I was in trouble. I groaned miserably.

However, not to worry nor despair - I still had a Plan "A", didn't I? I stood up from the table, having just devoured my scrumptious meal, made an unapologetic belch and dashed straight to the manager's desk. I introduced myself to this wonderful gentleman, who bowed and smiled at me warmly. I bowed in return. "Good morning, Sir," I said, grinning from ear to ear. "I am Mr. Tannase," he said, smiling and bowing graciously. "I have just enjoyed the most wonderful meal here at your Pearl Hotel. I'm on R & R from Korea, having just arrived this very day. I have ten days of leave and would be honored to spend them here with you. If your excellent service and divine food are any indicators, you and your hotel will receive my highest endorsement when I return to Korea." I pointed with pride to my AFKN radio patch on my sleeve and with similar pride detected that he recognized it. "Sir," I said, "I would like to make you a proposition. Permit me to stay at your hotel, give me one meal a day and provide me with a female companion to show me the sights of Tokyo. In return, I can guarantee you that hundreds of GIs within the sound of my voice over the Korean airwaves will spend their R & R leaves here at the Pearl Hotel." I handed Mr. Tannase my greeting card with a great flourish. The world began to rock beneath my feet as I awaited his response.

I was astonished when he smiled, bowing gently from the waist and said, "Di jobbie, Airman Scott, it will be my pleasure to assure you that the Pearl Hotel will be at your service for the remainder of your stay. One of our finest female escorts will call on you this evening. I will take care of the other arrangements. Be sure to see me before you return to Korea." We both bowed deeply! To this day I am not sure how to accept the fortune I had that day. I do have my faults, but I honestly did mention the Pearl Hotel during one of my disc jockey shows upon my return and Mr. Tannase, too.

My escort and I spent a wonderful afternoon shopping the great stores of downtown Tokyo. I bought my mother a 20-piece place setting of Noritake china dinnerware, which she absolutely adored. When my father and mother passed away, I commandeered the set, which rarely, if ever, was used at home. It sits in a prominent place in my home to this day. I smile every time I think of the Hubba! Hubba! cab ride to the Pearl Hotel, Mr. Tannase, and of course, my escort.

Following my R & R visit to Tokyo, I wrote a brief letter home to my parents. Naturally, I deleted any reference to my good fortune. As Mae West was fond of saying, "Too much of a good thing can be wonderful." I wasn't about to break my silence on such matters.

Chunchon, Korea
AFKN Rambler

December 18, 1953
Dear Mom and Dad

I regret the delay in writing to you. I offer only the normal excuses, but you can try this one. I've been very busy, writing Christmas plays, radio drama, announcing and traveling. Remember I informed you I wasn't going on "R & R" this month? Well, I did, and have now returned. I was very disappointed with myself for not taking much money with me. There were so many things I wanted to do and there were many things I wanted to buy for you and bring back to the States. I hope what I did purchase are items you will enjoy and cherish.

I went to Tokyo for seven days. After riding in nothing but jeeps and trucks over bumpy roads and mountain passes, it was like being in another world. I rode in Oldsmobiles, Chevrolets, and other new car makes. The people were wonderful to me – so polite and willing to do anything to ensure my needs were met. I hated it when they called me "master." I had steak once a day, real milk, eggs and bacon. Oh, by the way, if you look closely at the envelope, you will see that I have received a promotion. What about that!

With the coming of Christmas and a brand new year on the horizon, I would like to take this time to wish all of you a Merry Christmas and the most joyous of New Years. Your presents have been mailed and I hope you enjoy them. I hate to say it, but they took some effort to get. Someday maybe I can tell you how much effort!

Love,
Steve

> "The worst sin toward our fellow
> creatures is not to hate them
> — but to be indifferent to them;
> that is the essence of inhumanity"
> Bernard Shaw

In the bleakness of winter, life in Korea was grinding slowly along at a snail's pace. This fact became abundantly clear to me when I reviewed the old, yellow, stained letters I sent home to my folks.

I had sent a tape of one of my disc-jockey shows home to my dad. He thought it might be of interest to the radio station in my hometown, WINL-FM radio. Alas! Dad informed me that they rescheduled their regular programming to play the two-hour show. I was kind of embarrassed, but pleased he was able to pull it off. Mom and Dad were excited that many listeners called the radio station applauding them for playing it.

During that same period our station was terribly busy wrapping up a marathon for the "March of Dimes." We played nothing but music, twenty-one hours a day for three days. Pledges were taken by phone and we played whatever record the GIs wanted to hear. Most were romantic love songs dedicated to their loved ones back home. We were literally swamped with calls for the three days. Pledges amounted to $33,000 dollars, believe it or not! That is an awful lot of money for that time - four decades ago. Some pledged one dollar; one verified pledge was $4,000 dollars! We had fun doing it for such a good cause. There was a big write-up in "Stars and Stripes" along with my picture and those of a couple of my broadcast associates.

A few days after the grueling March of Dimes marathon, my buddies and I decided to go into Chunchon to do a bit of sightseeing and shopping. It was a bright sunny afternoon but very cold, perhaps 20 degrees. We were wearing our "Mickey Mouse" boots and fur parkas, so we were pretty much oblivious to the weather. The marketplace was busy as usual with Koreans hawking their wares. Women in their native dress sat huddled behind their heating pots, wares, hand-woven blankets, jewelry, clothing, rice, and dried squid, along with other unrecognizable foods.

We were not interested in buying indigenous fruits, vegetables or fish products. I was constantly reading public service announcements to the GIs warning of the dangers of hemorrhagic fever, a very debilitating and potentially fatal disease caused by bacteria found in Korean fruits and vegetables. The bacteria is particularly virulent because Koreans use human fecal material as fertilizer for their fields. No question about it though, their fruits and vegetables really grow extra large and looked great. However, digestive systems of Americans are just not accustomed to the sneaky little bacteria.

One of the great experiences of life is to be out of doors when the Korean farmers are spreading the fertilizer contents from "honey pots" on their fields. The ominous odor hangs heavy. It is so strong it would make a billy goat puke. For miles around there is no escaping the odiferous odor. Trust me, you don't get used to it. In any event, as the sun muscled its way high in the sky, we muscled our way through the teeming crowds. Suddenly, I heard a young voice cry out "GIs, help me!" We turned as one to see the most forlorn sight I have ever seen, and pray I never see again in life. Approaching us was a young Korean child, perhaps eleven or twelve years old. He was as dirty and unkempt as any wretch could be. He was several somethings all wrapped into one: something precious, something shattered, and something battered and bereft of hope. A feeling of the utmost dread overcame us as we noticed he wore very little clothing and regrettably no coat either. But most of all, what caused our souls to shiver, was the way he walked as he approached us. "That can't be," we said, collectively. "He's hobbling on one leg and the other leg (what was left of it) was exposed to the hip. It couldn't be, no way – or could it? He had leprosy!"

My two friends hurled curses at him, and told him to get away from them. They began to run! I stood transfixed. The child and I stared at each other. The anonymous looking at the anonymous. "Help me please, GI," he said again. "Give me food!" My mind instantly flashed back to the time I was nearly his age, and probably just as hungry. I forced myself to tell him to come closer. I instantly realized that my words came out of my throat like the sound of the croaking of a cricket - thick and staccato. I dared not look too closely into his eyes. My first thought was to give him my fur parka for warmth. I could always get another. But then I thought someone older or stronger would just take it from him, or worse, kill him for it.

I did the only thing I could do. I gave him some chocolate which I always took with me when I went into the village, and five one dollar bills, all the money I had, thinking at least the dollars could purchase a generous supply of food for several days. I finally looked him directly in the eyes. They were sad and vacant, resembling those of a dying animal. He thanked me in Korean. I knew his life would soon be over – such a small, frail, lonely human being with no one caring whether he lived or died. I had seen such pathetic sights before as I passed by several orphanages. In the past I, too, simply turned away. I'm glad I didn't this time. I began to feel moisture welling in the corners of my eyes. Could it have been caused by the chilling breeze? A dirt speck in my eye? A sadder and wiser young man I was that day. I remembered that so many of God's children die young.

As the month of March wore on it was fast approaching the time for me to begin thinking about my rotation back home. Several of the fellows were volunteering to extend their tour of duty from six months to a year, but not me! Although I thoroughly enjoyed my tour, I wanted to go home! I had seen enough of Korea, but one more pleasant surprise awaited. I was about to meet movie stars – FEMALE movie stars. In reviewing my letters home, I pleasantly remembered that fact. And the meetings were a little more than casual.

Several military decorations were bestowed upon me and the other fellows in my unit. During a brief parade assembly, I, along with others in my old outfit from Pusan, received another campaign ribbon. This made a total of three, with two battle stars. They represented spring, fall, and winter campaigns of support while the war was raging. Actually, I'm not so sure, even to this day, how much pride to feel. The GIs, living and dead, who did all the fighting should receive the medals, as I'm sure they did. The civilians I saw fleeing for their lives from Seoul, carrying their miserable belongings, should have received special decoration and certainly special place in heaven because their lives were hell in Chunchon, Pusan, Teague and countless other villages that were ransacked, leaving human wretches strewn across the land. One needs only realize that it was the Chinese who stopped the Americans, not Russia! Stalin lost! Mao was the big winner. He got half of Korea, the longtime enemy of China. Stalin and Russia did not want all out war with the West; American air and sea power, plus the atomic bomb caused Russia's timidity. There was no such timidity with China.

The Americans lost more than 50,000 men and suffered countless wounded in order to stop the Communists. Who knows how many losses occurred on the other side? President Truman may one day be recognized as a great President for his foreign policy that stopped the ever-expanding Communist land grabs. I leave it to the historians and time for such judgments to be made!

On a much, much lighter subject, our broadcasting studios were moved from a huge van to a comfortable Quonset hut. The van studios were practical for what they were originally designed, mobile broadcast communication with the troops. Some very bright person deduced that if the enemy forces were advancing, their first objective is to silence enemy communications. This is a fact of modern warfare on a global basis. But if the broadcast facilities can be moved quickly, then communication was still possible.

In our case something extraordinary happened. Coincidentally to our move to a permanent studio, the USO was performing at a one-day stopover at K-47, the Chunchon airbase I spoke of earlier. Marilyn Monroe – yes, THE Marilyn Monroe, along with actresses Terry Moore and Susan Zanuck, were part of the entertainment troop. While I was on duty in the new studios, Marilyn Monroe, by pre-arrangement, stopped by to help dedicate the new facilities. I interviewed her for about ten minutes during a DJ show I was doing. I asked her if she would sing a few bars of any song of her choosing. She obliged by singing, in a voice that was sweet, bubbly and sensuous, "Diamonds are a Girl's Best Friend." We both giggled a lot when she finished. She was delightful. Marilyn even extended a personal invitation to all of the staff announcers to a party being given by the base commander that evening, although the commander didn't know of the invitation. She released her driver after asking me if I would like to take her back to the airbase. With a sly grin and a gentlemanly bow, I said, "I will be honored." Night was gently falling as we climbed into the jeep. We were chatting merrily away when I asked if she would like to see the lights of the airbase and Chunchon from a bluff I climbed frequently. She said, "We don't have much time; the base commander is waiting." But we went to the bluff anyway and arrived at the party much later than planned. Later she introduced me to Susan Zanuck and Terry Moore. My buddies and I received a lot of attention that night. The base commander didn't like it much as he looked at me all evening with a stare that only a man condemned would fling at his executioners. My smile inside was as warm as morning sunshine.

Several weeks later, I received orders for my next assignment and was to go home soon! I would receive a 30-day leave before reporting to Newburgh, New York, home of Stewart Air Force Base! I didn't write home about that, but I did about another strange occurrence.

Dear Mom and Dad,

Guess what? You'll never believe it! About a week ago I was doing an early morning DJ show from 4:30 p.m. to 8:00 a.m. I closed the program with, "This is A/3C Steve Scott, wishing you the very best of everything." After the show was over, the phone rang and a voice said, "Is this the Steve Scott I know from Lebanon, Indiana?" It was <u>Bob Kincaid</u>, Bob Kincaid who lived just a few houses down the street from us on Pearl Street. Bob was in a special unit that builds small to medium-sized airfields throughout South Korea. I nearly fainted! We are going to get together soon to reminisce. He says he lives in a tent complex about 15 miles from here. I'll tell you more after we get together.

I'm sorry Brother Don does not intend to go to flight school or OCS. He would have been a great leader.

Love,
Steve

I shared as much as I could about the impending cold weather and other adventures in my letter. Winter was starting to roll in fast. It was not bitterly cold, but it certainly got our attention. I continued to go into Cancan. I loved the market places where the merchants sell everything, and I mean everything – huge pears, plums and freshly caught fish. I had heard of the bitter cold winters in this area. We will probably soon be "battening down the hatches."

CHAPTER 7

GOING TO GOTHAM

A young person today may never understand the lure of New York City that we felt in the mid-1950s. I did not escape that lure, the intoxication of the "City That Never Sleeps," "The Big Apple." I like the name "Gotham" better.

Nearly everybody now knows not only the past of New York City but also the sordid present as well. Four decades ago, a trip to New York City, would be like a trip to Mecca for a young man from Lebanon, Indiana. I had briefly visited the major city of Tokyo, Japan, but until I had seen New York, well, I had not really seen anything. The sun was just making its way above the southeastern horizon when I set out alone for Gotham, sixty miles away from Stewart A F B. The air was soft with a hint of spring, winter and fall, all mixed together. It was to be a day both of welcome and unwelcome surprises. It seemed as if the whole state of New York was dressed up for my intrepid adventure. The vile blows and buffets of the world ceased to exist as I silently reviewed plans for my day in the city. I had a whole day to taste its favors. The George Washington and the Brooklyn Bridges, the Empire State Building, Central Park and Cinerama to explore by daylight, and then Greenwich Village and the jazz hot spots, like "Birdland" and "The Village Gate." I would see as much as I could and drive back to Stewart by 10:00 p.m. Yeah, right!

The threads of my plan began to "unspool" as soon as I reached the George Washington Bridge. I needed to cross the bridge to enter the city, but I was in the wrong lane. Being in the wrong lane for crossing the bridge, I learned one thing quickly. New York drivers are not courteous.

They wouldn't let me over the necessary two lanes, despite my hand gesticulations. They thought I was giving them the "finger." They returned the "finger." I gave a final gesture to a driver who wouldn't let me over, but I was swept by the heavy traffic on past my designated crossing point – way past! After several miles of going in the wrong direction, I was able to make a turn and tried it again. This time I made it. To paraphrase the poet Dante, "The arrow seen before it cometh is less rudely received." No, Gotham was not going to meekly submit to my bidding!

Undaunted, I headed for 42nd Street. I wanted to see Cinerama. I had heard that this new cinema technological miracle utilized a huge screen and the unbelievable photography put you right in the picture. I parked my car along a side street. I don't remember the name or street number, but cars were everywhere. I walked a few blocks to the theater and saw "Holiday in Cinerama." I was dazzled by the movie. I was dazzled by the Gothic splendor of the buildings surrounding the theater. There was a lot to make me uneasy too! People were elbow to elbow and walked with a different purpose. I did neither as I made a quick hop to Wall Street but didn't go inside the exchange. I merely wanted to see the temple where the money changers gather. I had a wry thought: Here they don't mix religion with business – business is their religion!

I walked several more blocks to the Empire State Building, trying all the time not to look like a tourist from Kansas, or Indiana for that matter, and observing as I went the snaking lines of people passing aimlessly by. I didn't do a good job of seeking anonymity because I kept looking up, and up, and up, when I got closer to the enormous skyscraper. What a sight for the little guy from Lebanon to see. I was very much impressed. I went to the top of the building and witnessed the wondrous panoramic view of New York City. I was spellbound; New York was everything I had heard about. But I had this chilling feeling that a person could disappear anywhere in the city and never be heard of again. Blacks were very good at disappearing,

238

you know. However, I brushed that chilling thought out of my mind and continued my adventure.

For some reason, a feeling of uneasiness began creeping over me. As I walked back toward the spot where my car was parked among all the other countless autos, I was shocked. My car was the only one on the street, but the hour was only nearing 3:00 p.m. Still baffled at why my car was all alone, I got in, started the engine and began to move. Out of nowhere appeared a horse – a horse with a man on it. Since horse and rider were right outside my driver's side, they both looked twenty feet tall. The giant on the horse bared his teeth, grimaced, and said, "You're parked in a 'No Parking Zone,' Mister." My heart did an eclipse! "No parking after 2:30 p.m.," he continued. His forehead crinkled into furrows like an alien specialist on "Star Trek" as he gave me a look of exasperation.

"I am sorry officer. Look at my driver's license and my plate. I'm from Indiana and this is my first trip to New York." I wondered if it would be my last. "I'm on my way back to Stewart AFB in Newburgh, " I lamented and looked to him for pity. "Okay," the giant said, "this is your lucky day. I suggest you do just as you indicated. Leave New York and return to your airbase, and the next time get more acquainted with the city before you return." You got that right, I said to myself. I took his advice and headed straight back to Stewart. All in all I had a pretty good day. I did see lots of people and sights, had plenty of things to write home to the family about, but one thought still remains deep in the crevices of my brain, no matter how many times I've returned to New York City, and there have been many over the years, I always have the feeling that I am being hunted – hunted by unseen people with criminal intent!

BRUSH WITH THE LAW

The City of Newburgh is located in the southeastern part of New York State. It lies on the west bank of the Hudson River opposite the small city of Beacon. It is 58 miles north of New York City. Newburgh is an old city which was settled by Germans in 1709. It served as General Washington's final headquarters and was a key American command post in the strategic Hudson Valley during the Revolutionary War. The estimated population of Newburgh at the time I was there was 25,000 people. About 15 miles west of Newburgh was Stewart Air Force Base, home of the USAF Eastern Air Defense Command. The basic mission of the Command was to provide protection of the air space over the northeastern seaboard. The aircraft used to perform this function were F86-D Saber jets and F89 Scorpion fighter bombers. Stewart Air Force Base was to be my home for the next 2-1/2 years. In my letters home I constantly referred to the beautiful settings of the cities of Newburgh, Beacon, West Point, Poughkepsie and, of course, the grandest city of them all, New York City.

There is no question about the uniqueness of Stewart Air Force Base. The buildings were in a campus-like setting, the only exception being the wide expanses between buildings. Living quarters were not the typical barracks made of wood; red brick was used instead, and the esthetic landscaping was immaculately tended with lots of flowering trees and beautiful flowers. The airbase runways and flight center ran vertical to the base headquarters, living quarters, chow hall and the communications center where I worked. I never sought the numbers but I would guess that perhaps 5,000 military personnel worked at this base. It's difficult to be precise because many of the airmen were married and lived off base with their families. After several months of spending my time becoming acclimated to the communications center, work assignments and the surrounding environment, I applied for a staff announcer's job in Newburgh the first summer that I was stationed at Stewart. I was offered a job, but unfortunately it was a full-time position and I couldn't accommodate the station's work schedule with my military requirements. The Air Force needs did come first. The station manager was impressed enough to offer to call a friend of his who managed a radio station about 35 miles away who needed part-time help. However, I did not have a car at the time and commuting that far was impossible.

I also made one feeble, low-key effort to be transferred to the European theater and the Armed Forces Radio Service there; however, personnel informed me that my classification as a communications center specialist was vital to the Air Force interests at the time. So for the moment, I could forget that idea. I did and never made the attempt again.

Meantime, I was beginning to enjoy my tour of duty at Stewart. I was playing basketball for the squadron team and was playing very well. So well, in fact, that I was selected along with two other Stewart athletes to represent the base in the annual "all-star" basketball tournament held at Loring AFB in Limestone, Maine. Every person alive should pray that he never visits Limestone, Maine, particularly during the winter. The year was March 1955 and the weather was horrible. As our plane bearing the team circled the airbase, I looked out the window and noticed the wreckage of a B36 bomber that had crashed in a terrible snow storm the night before. The crash left only the tail section intact. Several men were badly injured, but luckily there had been no fatalities. The pilot of our plane, a C54 transport aircraft, informed us over the intercom that there were 46 inches – yes, 46 inches - of snow on the ground. In fact, after landing, we made our way to the chow hall for lunch by walking through a tunnel made of snow.

The tournament was delayed for two days because of bad weather. When it finally got under way, our Stewart AFB, all stars played their first game with An Otis AFB, rolling over them 80-64. I was fortunate to show the way for our team by racking up 22 points and got my picture in the local paper – sailing through the air; not, however, like a modern day Michael Jordan. We ended the tournament in second place out of 16 airbase teams and were duly proud of ourselves. I was selected to the first team, all tournament squad. However, I considered my major accomplishment to be just getting out of Limestone and Loring AFB, alive!

One night I had been in the city of Newburgh for entertainment provided by some friends of mine. Somehow the evening hours began to pass by fleetingly without my really being aware of their passing. The old axiom that time flies when one is having fun was just as true forty years ago as it is now.

The hour struck midnight! The hour struck one! I needed to leave and I did. My rank was now Airman First Class, having received another stripe on my return from Korea. I was now a supervisor of my work shift at the communications center. Driving with care, I thought, through the streets of Newburgh, I headed toward the airbase. Most airmen wore civilian clothes when they were off duty, and I was no different. Suddenly, the dark night lit up like daytime and the interior of my car was ablaze with amber, flashing lights. It was a patrol car.

Like any good driver who never received traffic tickets, I slowed, pulled right to let the patrol car pass to catch the speeder up ahead. The patrol car didn't pass. I rolled down my window and motioned the police officer to pass. Deep in my psyche I knew this was developing into a no-joke situation. The officer now gave me a sign of his own. The international sign for "Pull over." A long, grizzly arm with an even bigger finger pointed directly at me in a sweeping motion toward the side of the road. I who had never received a traffic citation before, brought my car to a complete stop and got in two or three practice charm smiles before the officer reached my car.

His shoulders were hunched and tight. His eyes, as red as hot coals, immobilized me. His face resembled a crocodile when he opened his mouth. "You just ran a red light, Mister, and we don't take kindly to that in this city," he said in a voice much too eager.

"I'm sorry, Officer," I countered, while attempting to stifle my anxiety. "I won't do it again," I groaned.

"Where are you from, where is your driver's license and where are you going?" the crocodile asked.

"I'm an airman at Stewart AFB and I'm returning to base."

"Not till in the morning you're not," he said, "because you're going to jail. Your fine is $10.00 plus court costs and you'll have to pay that in court, which won't convene again until 7:00 a.m. I can't accept any payments. " His smile curled and broadened as if invisible fingers were pulling across his face. Hey, a decent cop at least, I thought to myself. "Follow me," the crocodile said, and I did.

The time was now nearing 3:00 a.m. Having been fingerprinted, I made my one phone call to the airbase and was able to reach a friend of mine. I was assured someone would be on his way to get me . . . no . . . to <u>save me!</u> Because now, I was headed for the lock-up. I was a disconsolate man; going to jail, being fingerprinted and now facing the lock-up for running a red light. I felt fear as never before. It began as a vague feeling that something was out of place. Then I felt it creep up in my spine, slowly tightening as it clawed its way upward through my body.

In the lock-up, the men were drunks or homeless or desperate. Just before I was released, the jailers tossed in another of life's misanthropes, a Chicano who had just knifed a man to death. I crawled into a corner and waited for my Savior. After another hour passed, I was released into the custody of Stewart AFB and I was out of there. I knew then and there that I was really more Hoosier than East Coast.

This woeful tale ends with one of my friends sending home to my parents a small write-up of the event appearing on page 4 of the <u>Newburgh News</u>, dated Monday, September 9, 1956.

Airman Stephen Scott, age 23, forfeited $10.00 dollars for passing a
red light. Also, Ms. Gwendolyn Burns forfeited $2.00 for speeding.

Well, Newburgh was a small town, but one could still have assumed there should have been something better to write about than me and Ms. Burns paying a combination of $12.00 in minor traffic violations, and including my age, no less.

All in all, my tour of duty in New York was a pleasant one. I attended Army football games at West Point, attended the World Series in New York, went to the theater, even saw <u>Oklahoma</u> on stage. I went to Greenwich Village and the Village Gate to hear all the jazz quartets, Dizzy Gillespie, Charles Byrd, Bobby Hackett, Maynard Ferguson, Oscar Peterson and others. I listened to other great singers and legendary musicians at the legendary "Birdland," such singers as Cris Connors, June Christy and Sarah Vaughan.

In 1954, during my first year at Stewart AFB, I played a lot of basketball and even played my first game of golf in several years. I had dearly missed playing this game. I had so many fond memories of playing golf the game with Dad and my brothers. All care seemed to disappear when I was on the golf course. Obviously, I wasn't able to play in Korea. But, strangely enough, I had played the game so many times in my formative years that I felt my skills would easily return if and when I had a chance to play. That chance came on a beautiful fall day at the West Point Academy.

By happenstance, and for reasons unknown to me, the base commander, a General, found out I could play golf.

He loved the game, but he had trouble finding golf partners. One day I received a phone call from the General. "Airman Scott, this is General Smith. I would like for you to go to West Point with me this afternoon. I'll send my driver by to pick you up and we'll drive down for a leisurely round of golf. I've made all the arrangements."

Well, the man had made me an offer that I could not refuse. First I was just dying to play golf again anyway, but secondly, and more important, an airman doesn't refuse a request from a General. I didn't know then and I don't know now the military code of conduct that regulates officers fraternizing with enlisted men. I do know that one of the base fighter pilots, a Captain, scrimmaged and played on the base basketball team with me.

The most highly acclaimed painter could not replicate the rare beauty of the New York countryside as we made the trip to West Point. The landscape of rolling hills and trees, dressed in a gorgeous kaleidoscope of wondrous colors, looked primordial and untouched. My breath seemed to leave me as I wondered at the spectacle that lay before me. But, even this sight grew pale compared to the grandeur of West Point itself. The campus complex sits on a high bluff, the mighty Hudson River cutting a breathtaking ribbon below.

As a military man and accustomed to seeing military marching men, I was awed by the West Point cadets who were in a class by themselves, marching in a synchronized lock step. I witnessed dazzling displays of precision drills, heard rousing martial music from the Corps band and most of all, I was impressed by the heart stopping pride these young men displayed in themselves.

The golf course appeared manicured. It probably was maintained by the terrified hands of some band of freshman plebes. I did not play particularly well. I think I might have shot in the low nineties. Nevertheless, whatever my score, it was good enough to beat the General. I never received another invite to play with him again.

I never played "customer golf" when I played with men above my status, even in later years when I played with my business associates. I was of the opinion that they might be able to give me orders and make demands of me during the normal intercourse of business, but all rank and privileges were "stripped bare" on the golf course.

What an afternoon! What an experience it was for me to say forever more, that I played golf at West Point more than forty years ago. I kept the scorecard and sent it home to the family. Dad loved it.

"Look up skyward . . . "
Yahweh said, speaking
To Abraham as he made
The Covenant with him

LO...AND BEHOLD

The following event is one of those things I have to prepare people for. I have to say, "Now this is going to sound pretty weird, and it is, but maybe not as weird as it sounds, and you'll see this once you have a bit of understanding." So in the meantime, don't prejudge it, or casually dismiss it.

"Look up skyward," Yahweh told Abraham as he made the covenant with him. That we have done. Since the earliest of times, earthmen have lifted their eyes unto the heavens, awed as well as fascinated at the starry nights. Astronomers now know the positions of the stars, the cycles of the moon and sun. We now know of galaxies and how they are formed, and of the wondrous quasars, black holes and super novas in the depths of the deep. As we stand at the threshold of a new age, when sunrise on the day of the spring equinox will occur in the zodiac house of Aquarius rather than as in the past 2000 years in the house of Pisces, many may wonder what the change might usher in - good or evil, a new beginning or an end, no change at all, or if we will see wondrous sights.

We now boldly go on a side trip into the realm of the bizarre, as I witness a wondrous sight. Historical sightings of Unidentified Flying Objects (UFOs) over the last century have provided human kind with one of the greatest mysteries of our time. Gallop polls indicate nearly 20 million Americans believe they have seen flying saucers. Not aircraft, not meteors, not migrating birds, not high altitude balloons, not Venus, not swamp gas, not temperature inversions, not plastic garbage bags lit by

247

candles, <u>not</u> visions of half-crazed psychotics, but real sightings of unknown, unidentified flying objects. UFOs have been seen by President Carter, commercial and military pilots, radar experts, police officers, astronauts, trained observers and by an entire airbase!

At the risk of my credibility, and with your incredulity accepted, you deserve an explanation, or explanations. So, try these!

First, my wife Marilyn, and my two children have watched me read incessantly for pleasure, and to relieve the tensions of the day, the subject matter ranging from history, autobiographies, philosophy, science, economics, business journals to physics, particularly quantum mechanics. I didn't understand the math or equations of quantum mechanics, but I could read. I recall reading about a reporter asking Mrs. Albert Einstein if she understood her husband's Theory of Relativity. She remarked demurely, "I understand the words, but I don't understand the sentences." Mainly, I couldn't understand how the chair that I am currently sitting upon during the writing of this chapter could be made up of empty space and tiny, very tiny atoms, interacting randomly to create matter . . . my chair.

As for UFOs, I saw one along with more than a thousand others at the same time over Stewart Air Force Base. Ever since that event I've probably read hundreds of books on the subject of UFO'S. My conclusions must remain my own. I will say only that there is more to heaven and earth than we know and probably ever will know.

The American public first became generally aware in a dramatic way of the UFO phenomenon in June 1947. The incident surrounded a Boise, Idaho, businessman named Kenneth Arnold. While flying his private plane near Mount Rainier, Washington, Arnold observed a formation of nine disk-like objects moving at high speed and in an unconventional manner. Later reports would indicate that he actually said, "They were moving like a saucer would if you skipped it across water."

According to Ralph and Judy Blum, co-authors of the bestseller, <u>Beyond Earth</u>, such a description had been used before. On January 24, 1878, near Denizen, Texas, a farmer named John Marlin looked up and saw a circular object in the sky. Marlin said the object was very high and moving at a wonderful speed and that the only way he could describe it was like a large saucer floating though the air. According to the Blums, the story appeared in the <u>Denizen Daily News</u>, but that was as far as it went.

Surprisingly not many know that the sky in our near atmosphere is not a simple place and it can play tricks on people. For example, St. Elmo's Fire can turn a perfectly ordinary airplane into a bright, multicolored halo of twisting light. The planet Venus, when viewed under certain conditions will appear as a long, glowing orb that moves in the most extraordinary patterns. Comets, meteors, balloons, satellites, flares, fireworks, certain cloud formations, can all look like bright solid objects. For instance, a high altitude balloon, if struck at a low angle by the rays of the setting sun, will resemble an enormous disc flying at tremendous speed. What will appear to the observer to be the flaming exhaust of the disc will actually be the swirl of dust and ice particles left in the wake of a high altitude balloon and also reflection of the sunlight. The same is true of temperature inversions. These are various layers of air all at different temperatures, which bend and twist and generally distort the rays of light to create a mirage. It is possible for a temperature layer to pick out a boat at sea, and project it as an image in the sky, and that mirage will be viewed by a competent pilot or other observer as a long, dark shape filled with bright windows. As for plasmoids and ball lightning, both are basically formed by electrified gas that, when burning brightly, oscillates, vibrates, wobbles, flies horizontally, climbs vertically, and glows in the blue and red color ranges. But what we saw was none of these things.

THE SIGHTING

It had been a long busy day at the communications center during the late summer of 1955, much busier than usual. Messages of a routine nature, secret and top secret, had been flying across the nation and around the world all day. I had just finished my shift and several of my fellow airmen friends and I headed for the chow hall. I was famished. The time now was approaching 5:15 p.m. Amidst our rehashing of the day's activities and our light conversations about sports, baseball mainly, things changed in a hurry. Suddenly, our remembrances and small talk were interrupted by a commotion within a small group of airmen who had just entered the dining area. One of them yelled in a strident voice, "You gotta come outside, you got to come outside and see!" he exclaimed. The terror of the voices got higher and higher. "I'm not going outside to see anything," I said to myself and to no one in particular. " It's just another fight or something and I don't want to see it," I demurred. I was hungry. However, airmen began to rapidly shuffle outside to attempt to find out what the devil was going on. Reluctantly, I followed.

It seemed the whole airbase had emptied from offices and barracks, and the entire personnel was standing in large groups and small clutches, in the yards and streets, staring and pointing toward the northern sky. Some crossed or clutched at themselves. There was still plenty of daylight. The sky was cloudless. Following the gaze of the spectators I saw, hanging majestically, and motionless, without apparent noise, a huge luminous object. Making an educated guess, I would say it was at an altitude of 7,000 feet, right over the northern end of the airbase. I repeat. It was huge! It must have been 200 feet long and as wide as a football field. I noticed its cylindrical shape and metallic gray color. Its rotation, in a counter-clockwise fashion, a most fascinating mixture of colors which emanated from the bottom quadrant. The lights were shimmering and oscillating from reds, blues, oranges and dull whites, like he colors given off by a blow torch. I stood transfixed and not without some angst, I might add.

Again, noiselessly, it tilted nearly vertically, wobbled and moved slowly off at the same altitude away from the base. After gliding off about a quarter of a mile it stopped instantly! I could hear airmen around me exhale and groan, pitifully. Some wrapped their arms around one another. Others fell to their knees in fear, other scurried like in random directions like mice when a light is turned on in a darkened room. I could only sigh and say, to anyone listening, "Good Lord." Off in the distance I could hear the familiar growl of F86-D fighters taking off in tandems of twos, six fighters in all. Within minutes we could see them streaking toward the object, but they were not nearly at altitude yet. Still, they began to close in short order. The next series of events was incredible! As the fighters closed, the UFO alternately increased and decreased its speed as if in a taunting dance with the fighters who were pursuing it. The cat and mouse game did not last long, perhaps three to five minutes at the most. Then, as if in total disdain, the UFO suddenly shot up to a great height! The curious thing about this maneuver was that it was at a great height, perhaps 50,000 feet, within a blink of an eye. It remained there for perhaps five to ten minutes, glowing with incredible brightness and swaying back and forth, covering small degrees of the sky, and then vanished, literally, just blinking out of sight in a nanosecond – perhaps out of existence, for all we observers and the F86 pilots knew. The maximum ceiling height the F86-Ds could achieve at that time was approximately 40,000 feet.

I turned to my friend; his face was a frozen mask. Other men near me mumbled oaths. More groans emanated from the other spectators, perhaps 1,500 of them. All were stunned by the visiting UFO, and right over an airbase. Did we see the past and the future right before our eyes? What it was, what it meant or might mean for the future of mankind was concealed from us. I did not go back to finish my dinner meal. It would have been fruitless – too many people talking, too many unanswered questions. The next day at the communications center, I heard that a top secret message was sent to the Air Technical Intelligence Center, based at Wright Patterson Air Force Base in Dayton, Ohio.

I had never read a book about UFOs prior to this event. I had only heard the phrase in Korea, but never paid any attention to the tales of these wondrous craft, if craft they be, tales that circulate around the communications center.

So, what did I make of this? I think there was and is a cover-up of the first magnitude! Either our government and other governments around the world know what they are and persist in keeping the truth from us, or they don't know what they are and are keeping that secret as well. I do know a little bit about secrecy as taught to me by the military. The first lesson of secrecy is to spare the total workforce of complete knowledge of any project or mission. No one knows about the individual parts they are making, or the information they have is not enough to form a whole. The second, and perhaps the most important, is that men will not believe their eyes, or that men, if they do believe their eyes, will be ridiculed for it if they speak openly. Finally, some secrets can't be kept; however, they can be protected. To protect a secret you must give away part of it, and turn it into a rumor – mix half-truths with lies; speculation does the rest. As for me, I'll settle for the principle of Achams Razor, i.e., the simplest solution is the best one. UFOS exist and have for millenniums.

For anyone interested or half-crazed enough to dare read more about the UFO enigma, let me say there are literally hundreds of so-called factual books on the bookshelves, most of which are well worth avoiding. I have several I feel are worth reading. The Hynek UFO Report (Sphere); The UFO Experience, A Scientific Inquiry, The Report on Unidentified Flying Objects (also by Dr. J. Allen Hynek, Doubleday and Company, New York, 1956), and Project Blue Book, copyright 1976 by Brad Stieger, Ballantine Books, a division of Random House, and Project Saucer, Book Two, and Genesis, by W.A. Harbinson, Dell Publishing, copyright 1980, 1982.

THERE'S NO CHEER IN LOSING

The messages for processing just kept coming the night I nearly ended my career in the Air Force. The messages were for processing, i.e., typing them on the teletype machine for transmission to airbases in the Eastern Air Defense Command and other air bases across the country. Usually they were classified as Top Secret, Confidential, Secret, Priority and Routine. The first three classifications were to leave the Communication Center first. The Communication Center was operated in three shifts around the clock, seven days a week. During the daylight hours, a duty officer, usually a Lieutenant, was in charge. A non-commissioned officer, a sergeant, was in charge during the night time hours. Nearly 20 communication center specialists comprised a shift. When a working shift was nearly over it was common practice to police the area and sanitize it for the next shift.

On the evening in question, I was the supervisor on the night shift. I had the airmen and airwomen working their tails off during the night to process and send all of the strangely over-abundant backlog of messages. I had never seen so many of them. Most of them were classified in the secret, priority, "must get out" category. Meticulous records had to be maintained of all incoming and outgoing messages. We had just finished sending the last of the messages when my shift ended. It was time for the early morning shift to report for duty. No time for clean up. I went around to everyone and thanked them for their extraordinary effort. They were bushed – dead tired. I told them they were relieved of duty and I would take the heat, if any, from the oncoming duty officer. My assumption was the next shift should be happy all the messages were gone and they would gladly do the tidying up of the area. I was wrong!

In walked Lieutenant Barnes, a white officer from Macon, Georgia, smoking a cigar and drinking a cup of coffee. The next scene was straight out of an old war movie. "What in the hell hit this place," Barnes said, pointing his cigar directly at me. Then he bellowed, "Scott, I want your people to stay overtime and clean this mess up, and you and your people are not relieved until you do, is that clear?" I pulled on adrenaline like an old pair of socks. The staff started moving around like bats caught in bright lights.

"Lieutenant, check the incoming and outgoing message log. We have just set an all-time record for processing and sending messages. I'm proud of these people, and they are going home," I said in a voice quivering with emotion.

The head of Lieutenant Barnes appeared to swell. The coffee he had been drinking dripped from the downward curve of his mouth. He tried to grin but failed. As for me, I wasn't faring much better. I was all ice and fire at the same time! "I'll go to the dingy gates of hell before I ask this staff to do another thing," I croaked.

Every man and woman tried to calm me down. "It's okay, Scott! It's okay. We'll do it!" they clamored.

"Like hell you will . . . I want all of you out of here . . . now!" I said, waving my hands wildly. I stood there trembling in a state of grandeur and lunacy. Barnes and I faced each other like maniacs, like two horned rhinos protecting their territory.

"You're now on report, Scott, for disobeying a direct order. I'll have your hide for this," Barnes said. "You can have more than that . . . and in case you don't know what to do with it . . . I'll be happy to draw you a map!" I screamed. I was insufferable.

Poor Lt. Barnes was not faring any better. He was staring at me with eyes that looked like they had just seen the hereafter. What piteous scenes had he just witnessed? Perhaps my own horrible death. He could only whimper, "Get out — all of you!"

The base commander reviewed all men on report. That afternoon I received a call from the general. "Scott, what in the name of Caesar have you done now? You're really in trouble, judging from this report I have in my hand." Aldous Huxley reminds us that many excuses are always less convincing than one. I simply restated my case. No fait accompli here — I was through. "Apologize to Lieutenant Barnes, Scott, when he reports on shift tonight and with all persons present last night, witnessing the apology." Remember, I had just played golf with him at West Point a few weeks earlier. I knew when I was beaten. I had him in a tight spot, too. I agreed, and told him so, completing the ceremony in front of Lt. Barnes the next morning. My staff was furious at Lt. Barnes and would have backed me all the way. Unfortunately, none of us knew where "all the way" meant. The stockade?

I retained, through the years, my contempt for irrational people in authority forcing their irrational decisions upon others who feel compelled people to follow in lock-step. But I had other more pressing things to worry about. In one week I would be discharged from the United States Air Force and enrolled at Indiana University.

CHAPTER 8

ROOMMATES

Most adults who have attended college look back upon those years as highly important in the development of enduring friendships. Chances are strong that the college roommate is from another region of the state or country, and that his association adds to personal growth. Roommates bring a certain amount of personal baggage that may influence each other in a positive or a negative way. I had a certain advantage over many of my peers in college because of my Air Force experiences with other airmen from across the country. But, I must admit I was not very approachable. I had built up many defense mechanisms to isolate me from people or to avoid events that would get in the way of my accomplishing certain goals. It was a definite advantage for me at Indiana University to have the comfort and companionship of my brother Don. I was a sophomore when he arrived on campus, after his tour of duty in the USAF. My brother Larry would eventual join us when we were upperclassmen. Fate did not permit any of us to be roommates. In fact, I had only two roommates in college, both of whom I remember with fondness. For different reasons, both played a major role in my understanding of what a friend in need can really be.

Howard Griffin had a soft, androgynous voice that came from a face, sprinkled with freckles, that possessed a constant grin; and his large head was adorned with curly red hair. His cherubic grin gave one the impression that he knew some secret that bode well for all mankind. He was black, of course, but very light-skinned. We became roommates in my junior year. Howard wanted to be and became a psychologist. At that time, he was a zoology major, and a bright one at that. I was now living in the men's dormitory, Trees Center, on campus, having saved enough money during the previous summer to move from the Cottage Grove barracks housing, off campus, where most of the poorer Korean GI's and married students stayed.

Howard and I never socialized much together but we liked each other's company and spent a great deal of time talking in our room about the challenges of our different career paths. There was no doubt he was going to be successful in a field that required hard and long periods of preparation, including an M.D. degree.

I was fighting my usual losing battle with Spanish, but it was required and I had to persevere. We were nearing midterms and were both studying late one evening. He was prepared to study all night. I wasn't, but I agreed. About one o'clock, I said to Howard, "I've had it. I'm going to bed. I'll get up early in the morning and continue the effort." My eyes were already veiled by half-closed lids. Worrying about doing well on the Spanish exam sat like a small stone in my belly, but I needed the sleep.

Howard knew that I needed to continue studying, and he offered the most curious solution. "Steve," he said, "I have some pills that will make you stay awake." He laughed a cracked note that echoed too loudly for my "powered down" mental status. I had never ingested anything into my system that was foreign except for a few beers at the hole.

"No thanks, Howard, I'm going to sleep. Wake me early," I said. My eyes were now nearly closed.

Howard was ice and fire. He had all the cunning of a rat. "I'm telling you they won't hurt you. I take them all the time when I have to stay up all night. You'll see, they just make you stay awake. Even truck drivers use them. They're called 'pep pills'," he said.

I licked my dry lips and took the two tiny white pills he offered. Time passed. "Howard, this isn't working, I'm going to bed," and did. Howard grinned again. Why does he always grin, I thought. The grin wasn't normal. It left me with the feeling that something was about to happen that was definitely worth escaping. Suddenly my eyes shot open, not just open, but wide open like a person who has just been surprised with a birthday party. A burst of energy walked the ladder of my spine, climbing up into my brain, bringing lightheadedness. Howard threw me another grin like a fishing line. "I thought you said it wasn't working," Howard smirked. I continued to lie in bed. I started to see and hear things way too clearly. All extraneous audio clutter seemed stripped away, leaving just the essence of things. The normal late night sounds, even dogs barking, came through huge megaphones in my head. Colors were brighter and even the light on Howard's study desk became pure, dancing photoelectron packets. Howard continued to grin.

I stayed awake the remainder of the night, studying and the next day took my two morning mid-terms. I think I passed them, but without knowing it. My biggest challenge lay just ahead. I had to sign the radio station on the air at 1:00 p.m. that afternoon. I felt fine when I arrived and signed on the station and opened the first program. Then it happened! Instantly, and without warning, I became terribly sleepy. The show I was doing was a disc jockey show that called for introductions of each selection, a five-minute newscast and weather sandwiched in on the half hour. The newscast came and I began to read. Things went spiraling out of control. I seemed to be searching for words just in front of my eyes. My adam's apple would not function properly. It acted like a turtle that cautiously sticks its head out and sucks it back quickly into its shell when it senses danger.

All programs were monitored by professors as well as by the chief announcer, who was usually a senior. The senior announcer, John Brand, came running into the studio to see what was wrong with his premier announcer. I had previously received two awards from the station as its outstanding radio announcer. "Scott, what in the world is wrong? Are you okay?" he asked. I must have looked like someone who just escaped some days ago from prison. I couldn't keep my eyes open. I could hardly tell John I needed a replacement as I wasn't feeling well. John took over my shift and had someone drive me back to the dormitory. Everyone was concerned and called me several times during the evening. Mercifully, I slept like a baby and felt nearly reborn the next day. Howard, with that grin, asked me how I felt and I told him, "Just fine." I never asked him what it was I had taken, and he never volunteered to tell me. I think it was some type of strong amphetamine. But I never took any more drugs without prescription. I highly recommend that practice.

My other college friend and roommate was Curt Jones. Curt Jones was an young ordinary man. Just plain ordinary, except for one thing: Everybody loved him. Curt was my freshman roommate in college. He was very dark-skinned with a strong, finely chiseled face, large full lips and a deep baritone voice that commanded attention. When he smiled, his teeth flashed like a neon sign. His body was perfectly proportioned on a six-foot frame that I know was fashioned by the Marine Corps. He had just finished active duty in Korea.

Although he never talked about it, he must have seen a lot of terrible combat because he had fitful dreams and nightmares, He would stay awake until late at night, not studying, just brooding as if staying awake protected him from his own private demons. This was not good for my study habits because when he slept or brooded he had to have the lights on. But I tolerated his behavior because we had became good friends. He would lend me the shirt off his back, which he literally did, many times. Curt loved pizza. Often when we studied late, I would use my best radio voice to describe a pizza and what it would taste like if we were eating one at that very moment. Since I never had money and he did, it was often a lifesaver when he would weaken after about ten minutes of my whetting his appetite. He would laugh like crazy when he would finally say "Okay, okay, Steve, I give up. Go ahead and order a large Mother Bear's pizza."

Curt always seemed to have money; he had a car, too. As it turned out, neither of these was necessarily a good thing. Everyone borrowed his money and his car. Many never repaid the money or replenished the gas they used. Several times Curt was left stranded – out of gas. That was the case one October afternoon. I had just finished my afternoon classes and was walking across the football practice field. Adjacent to Cottage Grove apartments was a side street leading up a slight hill to my dorm. As I reached the bottom of the hill, I stared at an unbelievable sight. To paraphrase "Alice in Wonderland," the more I stared, the more "curiouser and curiouser" the sight became. A man was blocking traffic and was breaking out windows in a car. It was Curt, Curt Jones, my roommate. I bit my lip gently to start my brain to working on the problem of how to calm Curt down, all the while thinking that the Christians stood a better chance against the lions that I did with my maniacal friend who was possessed and tormented with rage and a baseball bat!

Curt was howling like a dying animal and hurling curses at the wind. "Curt! Curt! Come on, that's enough," I said in a pacifying voice. "Quiet down and tell me what is wrong." At the same time I told the small crowd of students, "It's over, go on about your business!" Curt looked terrible. He had turned into a real Frankenstein. He had a crooked smile on his face, saliva foamed in the corner of his mouth, and his eyes glazed.

"That's the last time they'll ever borrow my car again! Out of gas! Out of gas!" he bellowed. I held him in my arms for a few minutes. It was over. Curt wept! He also sold his car the next day, poor fella!

In retrospect, Curt should never have gone to college, at least not when he did. I don't think he had gotten the war out of his system and he missed his Marine buddies. He often talked about them. I guess today they would call his condition post-traumatic stress syndrome.

Curt left school after one year, returning to his high paying job at the steel mills in East Chicago. I liked Curt and have since tried to locate him, without success, to see how he was getting along. Word has it that he is doing fine.

TEMPTING THE GODDESS OF GOOD LUCK

It would be fair to say that most people believe the real attraction of gambling lies in the thrills and tension of uncertainty, the daring involved in taking chances, and the challenge of testing one's skill or luck. It is both the satisfaction of beating an opponent, and the dreams of good fortune. Despite my long narrative on the goddess of good luck, it was the latter that gripped me one evening in a poker game at "the hole."

The day broke with much anticipation for me. It was the first of June, payday for veterans. One hundred and ten dollars would be safely tucked away in my wallet by one o'clock that afternoon, after the mailman made his welcomed delivery. That delicious moment meant treating myself to a better than average meal, gas in my car and perhaps even a movie. I whistled through the morning. Normally, I worked at the radio station during summers and even though it was Saturday, I had to do a two-hour radio show, starting at three in the afternoon. I cashed my check and went to work. When my duty shift ended, after a scrumptious late supper, I studied until around ten p.m. then my brother Don and I decided to go to the "hole" and have a beer or two and "jaw" a bit with friends.

The "hole" was the black Elks Club located on the west side of Bloomington, in the middle of a cluster of black residential homes and next to a graveyard, no less. The "hole" got its name because it was the basement level of the site where the Elks members were to build their future, permanent structure. The future appeared to be a very elusive target, because it remained as it was for countless years. It contained a large bar, an area for dancing, a juke box for music entertainment, a kitchen area for food preparation, and a small back room used for gaming purposes.

When we arrived, we drank a couple of beers and chatted with friends for about an hour or so. Then we saw a few of the guys heading for the back room where a poker game appeared to be taking shape. I said to Don, "Let's gamble." He looked at me with a Cheshire cat grin as if he, too, knew this might be our lucky night.

So just like out of an old western movie scene at the local saloon, we hitched up our belts and swaggered toward the back room, which was hidden from view of the patrons. We had to negotiate a storage room where sundry items were stored in a dark, dingy hallway to get there. All that was missing over the entry door to the poker room was a sign Dante spoke of at the gates of hell – "Abandon hope, all ye who enter here." I was soon to find out what Dante really meant.

As we entered, we were greeted by three men, two of whom I recognized and a third I did not. The two I recognized were local residents, and Don and I had played poker with them before. The third appeared to be a graduate student. Henry Duerson, the local resident, was the first to speak. "Well, look who we have here – Steve and Don! Come on in, fellas." Henry's voice sounded strained, which made his grin inflexible, like some martyred maniac in an old wax museum. Henry was an excellent poker player, but from that look on his face and the small stack of dollar bills and coins in front of him, it appeared things were not going too well for him. The other two groaned a hollow, "Hello, how are you?" Don and I did the same. Well, what else could we do? Things were about to get serious, very serious.

Henry Duerson looked like a man who knew some deep, dark and sinister secret. He was of medium build, dark complexioned with thick eyebrows that masked sleepy eyes. He was very quiet by nature. Henry was a member of the Elks Club "hole" and was pretty much in charge of any poker game that was played there. The other two men at the table were fairly non-descript, other than to say they took poker very seriously. The older of the two was called "Bugs," I think because his eyes were unusually large and protruded beyond his forehead. The younger college kid was named Buck.

Our entry into the game was gradual as we began observing the play and feeling out our opponents' strategy for the evening. The game was dealer's choice, which meant five-card stud, six-card straight or with a wild card, or seven-card straight poker, with or without a wild card. To enter the game one had to start with a minimum of $20. If you thought you had a winning hand there was no limit to how much you could bet. Those who know the game of poker, realize that this is a form of very high stakes and volatile risks. Don and I were accustomed to such games from our early exposure at home and in the armed forces.

The game wore on toward twelve midnight with the normal ebb and flow of winning and losing hands. Buck had long since succumbed to fate, ill fate, if you will, and departed the game leaving Don, Bugs, Henry Duerson and myself. The games usually ended at midnight and with me safely and comfortably ahead, I watched the clock and idly counted my winnings to this point. They were considerable. Most good players at this point in the game normally fold their hands unless the cards they are dealt have more than a casual chance of being winners. After all, why risk the winnings you have so skillfully amassed on long shots and tempt the Goddess of Good Luck at such a late hour. So I watched the clock. It was now five minutes to midnight. I fantasized about how I would spend the extra money the Goddess of Good Fortune had given me.

"Six cards, deuces wild," Henry Duerson proclaimed, and he glanced at me and the stack of money I had in front of me. He dealt the opening cards around the table with a sense of urgency. I casually looked at the two hole cards as I had a jack up. "What!" I said to myself as I gazed fondly at the little beauties . . . two jacks in the hole! Henry continued dealing the cards to the players and slowly, too slowly for my tastes, gave himself a card. Henry had a king up. "Five dollars on the king," Henry said. All called the five-dollar bet. Henry Duerson dealt the cards again. My eyes glazed over as I saw a wild card deuce appear through the mist of my glazed eyes and lightly touched down on my jack. Oh no, Henry's card was a king. Henry Duerson now had a pair of kings up. "Twenty dollars," he said, nonchalantly. Now this is getting interesting, I thought to myself, as I double-checked to make sure I had four jacks. All players called the bet, including my brother Don. "I call your $20 and raise you back $30," I hissed. I became painfully aware of the grating noise of chairs being pushed back from the table. All players folded their cards with sighs and oaths to heaven but Henry Duerson. He called the bet in silence and dealt the cards again. It was now mano a mano!

I began to have a creepy feeling that the events were now beginning to swirl faster than I had planned at this stage of the game, and my stack of money was rapidly dwindling. If things continued on much longer at this pace, I would have to go into my pocket for more money, which would not be a wise thing to do. It was, after all, only the first of the month. "Mom Mayes" needed to be paid her room and board and other necessities and commitments needed to be met. But with my four jacks I calculated I still had a superior hand. Nevertheless, my breath was coming in heavy, sucking motions, barely moving through my nostrils. The game must go on.

"Next cards," Henry Duerson said, with a smile too broad for my comfort as he dealt me a five of hearts and himself a ten of spades. All right, I said to myself, I didn't improve my hand, but neither did he. I confidently bet $25. "I call your $25 and raise you $25," he said. "Now wait a minute," I thought to myself. I know I have four jacks, an almost unbeatable hand to this point, and this guy is raising the bet. The most I could reasonably figure his hand would be is a full house. I win, he loses. I called the bet.

"Last card coming," Henry Duerson cackled. He flipped the card in the air. It seemed to float in slow motion toward me. My eyes strained to see it. Another Jack! It was another jack! Now I had five jacks. Allah be praised. He then gave himself another card. Oh Blood! It was another King, a King of Spades! He now had three kings face up and I had three jacks face up. "I bet $30," Henry Duerson said. I reached into my pocket and discovered I had only $35 left to my name. I tossed the $30 dollar bet toward the swollen pot of money lying in the center of the table. Looking at the other players around the table, who were now spectators, I saw only thick tension and suspense in their eyes. I glanced at brother Don for some sign, any sign of hopefulness. All I got was a face the color of cold ashes. He looked like he was about to have a small, cardiac incident. "Five Jacks," I exclaimed and, instinctively, I began reaching for all that money in the center of the table.

"Hold on just a minute – five Kings, Steve," said Duerson as he reached with both hands to scoop up the money. I looked at the clock. It was midnight! The game was over and I was doomed. I made a sound that came deep, deep inside me. It was a sound I hope I never hear twice in my life. It was born of despair, gloom, misery and anguish. Don and I walked out of the club, into a starlit night . . . but I couldn't see any stars. For me, black night had fallen.

That night I played and replayed that hand in fitful dreams. I always won. Ha! Ha! Ha! I always won! I am glad I laughed in my dreams because I would not laugh again for another 30 days.

I faced a full month with no money. I hadn't even paid my landlord, "Mom Mayes." However, she did let me stay, but no food. For the rest of the month, I lived by my wits – eating with friends, calling in all the chits I was owed when I had helped others in similar straits. Somehow I got through the month, but barely. For the last two days of the month, I didn't eat at all. The night before the next GI bill check was to come, I was so hungry I could barely climb into my upper bunk at Mayes' house. I dreamed I was in ancient Egypt and was a much-loved king. I had declared a feast in my honor. I was surrounded by dancers and court jesters. I clapped my hands and was brought honey, butter, wine, milk, grain, olive oil, dates and grapes and mutton. All piled in a delicious heap before me. There were other treasure troves of foods untouched by fire or oven stored in all corners of the room. Freud would have had a field day doing an analysis of my dream. I woke up hungry.

The next morning I began to laugh through my misery as I planned my strategy when I got my check. I had no gas for my car, perhaps less than a gallon, so I would have to walk ten blocks to the bank. There was a small food store across the street from the bank. I would get a candy bar for quick energy, then walk back to my car and hope there was enough gas or gas fumes to get me to a gas station a block from Mom Mayes'.

What's the use of prolonging this hideous episode, for even attempting it has been like deep dental drilling. Suffice it to say lessons were learned from it, primarily that the Goddess of Good Luck sits only fleetingly on your shoulders and she cannot be tempted by folly or personal greed. I'm happy to leave this part of my time travel.

WHEN YOU STRIKE GOLD

. . . . YOU SHOULD STOP DIGGING

Love! Socrates tried to explain it to the Greeks, Ovid to the Romans, Shakespeare to the English, Cervantes to the Spanish, and Goethe to the Germans. Love and lost loves have inspired great thinkers and countless art forms throughout human history. Now, it was my turn to be inspired by love as I soon met and found my heart's desire.

The fall semester of 1958 at Indiana University began with all of the sameness of the previous two years. I was doing reasonably well in school, and I had been working full time as an announcer during the year and summers at the University radio and television station, still collecting a dollar an hour. I wonder why we never got a raise. Anyway, as usual, brother Don and I would study until about 10:00 p.m. and then go to the "hole" for a couple of beers.

One particular fall Friday evening, Don and I were enjoying our beers when a friend of mine who was working toward a master's degree, Bill Russell, walked up to us. He told me there was a young lady and her friend there both working on their master's degrees, and one would like to meet me. Her name was Marilyn.

Although I had several female friends whose friendship I enjoyed and whom I dated occasionally, I was really not looking for, or interested in, any permanent relationship. I knew that upon graduation I was going to travel a rocky road trying to find a job in my chosen profession. Any thought of marrying, or establishing a lasting relationship, was not on my immediate agenda. I had things to do and places to go. Nevertheless, I was never opposed to meeting young ladies, so I told Bill, "Why sure, I would like to meet her. Where is she?"

"Follow me, and you're going to owe me one, Steve." Since it was a Friday, which often means a packed house, I had not noticed the general comings and goings of fellow students nor of this young woman. So we elbowed our way over to a section of booths in a corner. That's when my heart did another of its profound eclipse fluctuations.

As I stood before the two gorgeous young ladies seated at the booth, Bill said, "Steve, I would like for you to meet Marilyn Gayle from New Orleans, Louisiana." My lips moved as if to speak, but nothing came out. Sitting before me was the most beautiful young lady I had ever seen. She looked simply radiant with her black hair hanging loose and spilling down to her shoulders. Her face was olive color, with large brown eyes that seemed to dance above full contoured lips that begged of red, ripe plums. The smile, crowned by two rows of perfectly shaped teeth that literally flashed with brilliance, had a tenderness that begged intimacy. I sucked in my breath for strength enough to say, in a barely audible voice, "It is my pleasure to meet you," as I extended a sweaty hand in her direction. I was rewarded with a delicately warm hand with long arching fingers, adorned by bright red finger nails. "May I join you?" I asked, trying to hide my joy.

"Please do," she said. As I slid ungraciously next to her in the booth, I caught a hint of her perfume, which smelled of jasmine, or fresh-cut spring roses. During our eventual courtship and even years later that frozen moment of time led me to call her my "Southern Flower."

My friend Bill excused himself and left me alone with the two ladies. I introduced myself to the other young lady, whose name was Rae Francis Chapman from Atlanta, Georgia. Through our conversation, I learned that she came to Indiana University to work toward a master's degree in music and Marilyn had ventured North to earn a master's degree in speech and drama. Our conversations were easy and delightful. I then excused myself and told them I would like them to meet my brother, Don, who eventually joined us and sat next to Rae. We had a delightful time. I asked Marilyn if she would be join me the next day for the IU football game. She agreed, we exchanged telephone numbers and she gave me directions to the graduate center, where she lived. One more pleasure awaited me. When we all stood to leave, I couldn't help but notice that she was also tall, stately, and her physical proportions were such that any model of that day or this would be envious. She was five feet ten inches tall, and weighed 135 pounds. Each pound was arranged in exquisite design and proportion. As Don and I left the "hole," I happened to glance skyward and noticed the moon high in a cloudless and star-studded sky. The moon appeared to look straight at me and smile as if it knew something special had just happened.

I had a two-toned Mercury hard-top convertible that I had purchased in Newburgh, New York, mostly with poker winnings. However, one problem remained for tomorrow's date. Unknown to Marilyn, I had only a dollar or so and my car was running on gasoline fumes. Don had even less, so I could not borrow money from him. As the next day dawned, I decided to make an extraordinary decision and gamble that I would not run out of gas. I would pick Marilyn up in my gorgeous two-toned, yellow bottom, green top Mercury convertible, go to the game and take her directly to her residence without stopping for cokes or coffee, and without running out of gas, I hoped. I then would be home free. Few men had cars on campus in those days so I would have accomplished a major goal by letting her know I had my Mercury hard top convertible (two-toned). All went well. We attended the game and she was the fairest maiden among the meager fans on hand. That was usually the case at IU football games in those days. I even sneaked a kiss as IU made one of its improbably first downs. Not touchdowns, but first downs, for the entire game! IU never, ever won football games in those days.

Don and Rae eventually married. As for me, I could only think of the sudden chill as my mind glimpsed once more the "shimmering" of the golden bush by the railroad track in my youth, when I eventually went on to married my "Southern Flower," Marilyn. But she would not be an easy capture.

THE WORST OF TIMES

The Goddess of Good Luck also favored me with my roommate, Howard Griffin, who became a good role model for me. I was actually a few years older than he was, but he was a college senior when I met him and we became roommates. I was a junior. Remember I had spent four years in the Air Force before going to Indiana University. I admired Howard's study habits. Seniors just seemed to understand how to stay focused and confident in their approach to academia. His undergraduate major was zoology and it required that he remain focused, effectively managing his time and establishing priorities. Through Howard's constant prodding I began, for the first time, to understand what it really meant to be a student. In simple terms it is the quest for knowledge. The more knowledge you acquired the less you really knew. But that was all right, in as much as the search for truth is a life-long process and pursuit. That discovery was sobering for me because, known to everyone but me, I discovery I knew everything!

In the previous semester I had studied Plato's <u>Republic</u>. Among other brilliant insights, Plato talked about the pursuit of truth. He illustrated his point through the use of the now famous "Allegory of the Cave," in which he stated, "Learning is absolute truth and the meaning of life, or reality itself, is beyond human comprehension. The best one can do is simply interpret, or glimpse the shadows of the truth." The overall effect of discovering the truth is like being in a dark cave and moving toward the light; one is blinded by the light or truth and cannot see. The best one can do is move toward enlightenment by interpreting "shadows" on the cave walls. Thus, absolute truth and understanding would remain forever just outside of our view, reality, and comprehension. A staggering precept and certainly a humbling one. I would have to remember this many times over the years as the vagaries of life closed in on me. My initial encounter with this mystery did not take long!

Howard and I had been studying for final exams. It was a Tuesday in May, 1957. We had decided to study late that night, and it was now about 2pm. Suddenly, without warning, I fell asleep, dreaming dreams . . . fitful dreams. Shortly, the phone rang waking me from my dreams. On the other end of the line was my brother Sonny calling from Lebanon. In his usual soft-spoken sincere voice, he said simply, " Our mother is dead! She had a stroke. I'll come down to Bloomington to get you as soon as I can." He hung up and my world ended!

Somewhere in the distance I heard low, piercing screams and moans of an unearthly nature. Where was that dreadful sound coming from? I suddenly became aware of a giant's hand, shaking me violently. It was Howard and the screams were coming from me! I cried for days on end. Where was the truth now? Where were the answers now? Mom was only 52 years old. I had promised her many times that I would eventually make something of myself. I would make a lot of money and she would never have to work again. She could have so much fun doting over her grandchildren, as she had done over the twelve of us. There would be fine dresses and fine foods. New furniture. New cars and travel. Now, all of those dreams were gone forever. The only tie to the here and now was the telephone receiver, dangling from the phone on the wall.

Socrates was right after all. We can never understand the truth, the real truth, or the real whys of this world or perhaps even God. I didn't want to go home. I didn't want to see friends. The house. The kitchen. The bedrooms. I wanted only to grieve alone. I wanted to think of the days, long ago, when Mom had been alive and young. And how she and Dad, even during the worst of times, sat in the living room, gazing fondly at one another, proud of the children they were rearing. How they felt and looked so young, beyond the reach of time and death. Now, all of her dreams would have to reach across the outer limits, beyond time and space where they touch us still.

When I try to think if there is anything left for me to say that authors, poets, philosophers, fools and kings have not said before, it all comes down essentially to the same thing. The mothers of all races, religions, and stations in life have traditionally been superwomen. They hold the family together in good times and in bad. They are strong. They do their best to make a house a home. They are icons. They put everyone's needs ahead of their own. And, in the end, they usually miss out on much. So very much!

FINDING A WAY

Things did not get better for me, as my soul continued to sink lower into the depths of despair. I made a terrible decision, more out of haste than anything else. Only marginally recovered from grief, I decided to take the final exams. They were only a couple of weeks away. I was taking sixteen hours of subject matter and didn't want to take any incomplete in the courses. It was a mistake of the highest magnitude! At the time of my mother's death, I was doing well enough in school, but not great – a C+ average. I made mostly Ds on the finals so, therefore, were my semester grades. It was a disaster! Why under those circumstances, did I decide to take the final exams rather than take incompletes? The short and correct answer is – I shouldn't have! My grade average spiraled down to the point where I was placed on probation and asked – no, *requested*, to withdraw from school for a semester. Quite frankly, though, I wasn't traumatized by this state of affairs, having already been traumatized by my mother's death. But I learned something that I have tried to pass on to others: "When life is pressing you down, rest a bit, but don't quit. Use the time to improve some aspect of your life that you have found lacking."

I took a job as a night watchman at a manufacturing firm in Lebanon. It was a great time for reflecting and reading. I concentrated on reading history, science, religion and philosophy. I devoured books! Reading late at night, when all is deathly still, is a religious experience in itself. I would make my rounds, punching in times on a special recording station, and rush back to my books. Reading also served another purpose: it kept my mind off my current condition and off the bumps, creaks and groans I would hear in the night. However, I was making very good money, and I was being reborn. I made a commitment that summer to finish college and forge ahead with whatever life presented me in the future, and to be a winner for my mother.

HEADQUARTERS
AMERICAN FORCES KOREA NETWORK
8214th Army Unit
APO 234

31 August 1953

SUBJECT: Letter of Acceptance

TO: Commander
        17th Communications Squadron
        APO 970

1. A/3c Stephen Scott, AF16428031, of your organization has
expressed a desire to serve with the American Forces Korea Network.

2. Provided no military objections exist Amn Scott will be accepted for duty with this unit as soon as he can be released.

3. Subject Airman has the professional experience, training, and
the basic qualifications desired in radio broadcast personnel

                    ROBERT N BERRY
                    Capt   TC
                    Commanding

Pusan Korea intra squadron basketball game. That's me, #4, firing one up from the left corner. It went in, of course.

277

F. E. WARREN A. F. B. WYOMING

My class of Communication Center Specialists, Cheyenne Wyoming.

Colonel William B. Reed and S/Sgt William W. Briner look on as M/Sgt Raliegh W. Smith presents a $1,000.00 check to Captain Warren S. Bollemier the local chairman of the March of Dimes Campaign.

other contributions were, Air Base Squadron $739.00, Officer's Club $371.20, Maint and Supply $330.47, 942nd $295.52, 48th $182.35, AACS $160.00, 49th 148.00, Group Hq and Postal Detachment $113.27, Dispensary $84.00, AC & W $52.00, Air Terminal $13.50 and Miscellaneous 13.34, for a grand total of $4,029.35.

All personnel who donated money can be thankful to Radio Rambler for the fine job they all did in the collecting of $40,000.00 in pledges. At 0500 hours 30

A/2C Steve Scott holding record, Pfc Ralph Harris flipping switch and Sherry at the mike keep on the job spinning records for your pledges in the March of Dimes Drive.

January, T/Sgt E. W. Bohl came on the air to start the three days of continuous broadcasting to collect pledges for the March of Dimes. For the next 72 hours the weary disk jockeys at Rambler played, talked, begged and pleaded for all personnel to dig for that extra dollar. All personnel at Rambler take great pride in the fact that the competitive spirit originated by them at Rambler

(Continued on Page 2)

279

Local Airman Serves On Radio Staff In Korea

A/3c Steve Scott, son of Mr. and Mrs. Dewaine Scott of this city, is a key member of the staff of Radio Rambler in Korea, where he has been stationed for the past 11 months.

Rambler is one of the northernmost stations in Korea, located near Seoul, and its staff is composed both of Air Force and Army personnel. Airman Scott is serving as an assistant in the record library.

A member of the Armed Forces Radio Service, the station recently observed its first anniversary. Its initial broadcast was made on November 5, 1952. Since that time the station has been on the air constantly during normal operating hours with the exception of short periods when there was radio or power failure. A mobile-type unit, Rambler is currently operating 21 hours a day, seven days a week and generates its own power.

Rambler not only broadcasts programs supplied by the Armed Forces Radio Service in Los Angeles, major producer, but also presents locally produced shows of which Mail From Home, announced by a nurse from a local mobile hospital unit, is considered the favorite. Rating second, is news presented throughout the day. This proved most beneficial before the cease fire was called as alert warnings were given over the air before the siren was sounded enabling the men to find cover more quickly. When any outstanding entertainment is brought to the airbase or surrounding Army units, Radio Rambler records the performance and sends it out later on the air. The broadcasts drama, music, mystery, comedy and news has brought many hours of entertainment to the service men.

Personnel manning the station are well qualified for their jobs as previous experience in the radio field is a prerequisite for receiving a position on the staff. Airman Scott, while attending high school here, was a popular announcer with the original staff of WINL.

Recently Airman Scott through his work with the Rambler, was heard by another local airman, Gail Barton, and they enjoyed a reunion later. Scott is expected to return to the states next spring, but will continue radio work - broadcasting to Korea - until his four-year enlistment period is completed.

Personnel of Radio Rambler crowd around the 'mike' awaiting the sign from the engineer that one of the many locally produced programs is going on the air. With radio programs, the timing is split second, so the programs do not over-lap.

CHAPTER 9

**He is a bold man who first swallowed
an oyster...But even a bolder man
who first ate gumbo!!
Steve Scott**

NEW-AH-LEENS

I now gladly roll back the years to make a profound bow to my wife Marilyn and her family, the Gayles from New Orleans. I was now back in school, had my old broadcasting position back and my grades were improving dramatically. I had achieved the two promises I made to myself following my mother's death. I had not broken any promises since I was young, but I hadn't made any either, so I was feeling pretty good about myself.

I have already told you about my brother Don and me being smitten by Cupid's arrow on the same night at "The Hole" or Elks Club? I must commend the Gods and Cupid for hitting two young men with one arrow! I now pick up that story. Don and Rae were getting their respective degrees – Rae a Master's in music and Don a B.S. degree in psychology, and they were getting married, too. It was the Christmas holiday, 1959. They were off to Atlanta to take their vows. I was to be Don's best man, and Marilyn was invited to the wedding as well, following which Marilyn and I had made plans to go by train to New Orleans to meet her folks. Now, it came as a surprise to me that when a gentleman comes to meet the parents of a southern belle, this lone, innocent act has profound meaning for his future.

Nevertheless, Don's wedding was world class. Everything proceeded without fault. The bride and bridegroom beamed a thousand flashing smiles and headed off into what would be a wonderful life together. Anyone who knows me well enough and is aware of my many misadventures will be delighted to know that I didn't lose the ring, step on any gowns or otherwise screw up that gorgeous wedding. This fortunate state did not last long for me, however, as Marilyn and I proceeded to board the train for the crescent city of New Orleans.

It had been nearly seven years since I was on a train bound for Lackland Air Force Base in San Antonio, Texas. The familiar clickity-clack, clickity-clack sound of the iron wheels whizzing along the track brought back the same physical sensations of welcome adventure that I had felt then. Thirty-five years ago the city of New Orleans was not exactly on the travel route for a lot of blacks from the North. Perhaps, even today, some readers may not know very much about New Orleans, a city of immense charms. It is often called America's most interesting city. But its most popular nickname is "The Crescent City." It got that name because the Mississippi River sweeps past New Orleans, forming a giant curve. Part of the city is below the normal levels of Lake Pontchatrain and the Mississippi River, and I am told that when the Mississippi River is high, a person standing at the base of a levee sees an awesome sight - ships steaming on the river above his head! Even the cemetery tombs rest above ground because the water lies just a few feet below the surface. For the same reason, most homes do not have basements.

Blacks make up about 45 percent of the New Orleans population. The city is remembered as the birthplace of jazz. It is famous for traditional black musical classics as, "Basin Street Blues," and "Way Down Yonder in New Orleans." And Black jazz bands still play for funeral processions to and from cemeteries. And of course Mardi Gras, that gay holiday, reaches its climax on "Fat" Tuesday, the day before Lent begins.

284

The French Quarter is the oldest and most famous section of New Orleans. One quickly notices that the area looks much as it did in the 1700s and 1800s. The streets are narrow and buildings crowd them. From these narrow streets, visitors can look through small, intimate passageways into colorful courtyards and patios. One cannot help but be impressed by the homes and gardens on St. Charles Avenue. Many of these large mansions have lovely, well-manicured gardens with magnolia and oak trees. The graceful trees provide cool relief from the muggy, hot and humid days of summer. Trust me, New Orleans in July and August will make one hurl curses at the sun. Events that lay just ahead for me were about to make things even hotter.

But, for the moment, I was feeling important and as if all things were now in a steady state, I pondered the upcoming scrutiny that I would be under from Marilyn's family, the Gayles of New Orleans. My steady state soon evaporated, giving way to fear and misgivings now punctuated by the wheels' clickity clack. I walked back to the club car to rehearse in my mind the tests I would have to pass within the next 24 hours to win the hand of "My Fair Lady." Now let's see, Steve . . . there's the bourbon test, the gumbo test, the gentility test from Uncle Eddy and cousin Fanny, her grandparents, and other of the senior Gayle's aunts, cousins, friends of the family, and Dr. Adams. Just thinking about it made me thirsty. I decided, while in the club car, I could rehearse for the bourbon test. I sauntered up to the bar and sat next to a medium-height, moderately dark-skinned gentleman who appeared to be about fifty years old. He looked at me with sleepy eyes that dropped below large, thick eyebrows. His engaging boyish smile prompted me to introduce myself. "Steve Scott, from Lebanon, Indiana," I said. "Robert Gayle from Washington, D.C.," he said, with that boyish grin. A lightbulb should have beamed in my head with his answer, but it didn't. After more chatting away like old friends and downing a couple more practice bourbon tries, we eventually realized that I was talking to Marilyn's uncle! He was on his way to New Orleans with his wife Lucille . . . to meet me! What a marvelous coincidence! We sipped more bourbon!

Upon arrival in New Orleans, I went immediately to Marilyn's house to meet her parents. The next evening a dinner was to be given in my honor. Meeting Marilyn's parents was a real thrill. Her father, James Gayle, was a short, dark brown-skinned man who spoke with great confidence and bearing. He was the principal of a large elementary school in the heart of a large, severely economically depressed area. He ran the school in a highly professional manner, insisting that all his staff treat the children with the utmost dignity and teach them the basic skills they would need if they were ever going to escape poverty. The teaching professionals today could sorely use a James Gayle as a model for all that is good with an educator. I respected him greatly.

Marilyn's mother, Ruby Gayle, was a beautiful woman. Her stately manner, high intelligence and absolute devotion to her husband and daughter were manifest in everything she did. She was an excellent and impassioned housekeeper and cook. She possessed the strongest of principles and the of highest moral values. Over the years, some thirty odd, I would eagerly anticipate our trips to Marilyn's home to luxuriate in the warm and sincere hospitality that was afforded me by the Gayles. One incident at this initial and formal meeting at the Gayle family dinner truly epitomizes this quality.

I really didn't know that at the dinner I would be on such a dramatic stage. There was Marilyn's grandfather, a tall stately, dark-skinned man of keen observation and intelligence. He was the proprietor of the Gayle Religious Bookstore. Starting with virtually no capital, he had guided the business into becoming one of the largest black religious book stores in the South. He was a proud and taciturn man who richly deserved the success he had engineered. His wife, Estelle, appeared to walk in his shadow but was duly proud of her role as housewife and mother to three sons and a daughter. She gazed curiously at me all night, as if to say, "Who is this stranger from the North who has come to try to lay claim to my granddaughter?"

Marilyn's Aunt Mildred was a delight! I immediately called her "Auntie Mame" because of the way she dressed and flitted hither and yon like an excited bird in a cage. She knew all of the social graces. We got along famously. I was to be her house guest during my stay in New Orleans. I met Marilyn's cousins, Fanny and Eddie Rose, a wonderful couple who grilled me in a kindly humorous way. Finally I met the longtime family friend and surgeon, Dr. William Adams. Dr. Adams, like so many black professionals in the South, was a highly respected man. He was an outstanding surgeon, but he was also a civil rights advocate. Schooled in the liberal arts, he was a sterling raconteur.

So there I was, trying to be dazzling, and probably failing, but I loved it, especially after I had another glass of famous Southern bourbon. Remember, I had drunk hard liquor only once, in Korea, with my friend and neighbor from Pearl Street, Bob Kincaid. I say I drank only one drink, but, it was probably more like three! Anyway, I was passing the bourbon test with flying colors! So I pressed on, trying to ignore a faint hint of tipsiness. I continued to talk faster and louder, hoping that the hint would fade. Control was the word, and I demurred to myself, "Steve, you can't lose it, not even once. You have to keep in control."

Next up was the gumbo test, and I just knew I would hit this one out of the ball park. Later, I would regret the arrogance of that thought. Anyone not familiar with Louisiana gumbo should hope that someone will pray for his soul if at some unguarded moment he tries it; he needs a description of the dish. Keep in mind, I came from this little town in the North where the staple meals were chicken, ham, pork or roast beef and the usual potatoes and gravy.

The Gayle's recipe for seafood gumbo:

Heat bacon drippings over medium heat, add flour slowly and stir constantly until it is a chocolate brown. This takes a long time. Add to a large pot of water, adding celery, onions, green pepper, garlic, and parsley; and cook 45 minutes to one hour, stirring occasionally. Fry okra in shortening until slightly browned. Add to the first mixture and stir well for a few minutes. Pour into a large pot and add chicken stock, Worcestershire sauce, Tabasco sauce, catsup, tomatoes with juice, salt, ham, bay leaves, thyme, rosemary. Simmer 2-1/2 hours. Add chicken, crabmeat, shrimp, and sausage and simmer 30 minutes more. Add brown sugar and lemon juice. Serve in bowls over hot rice.

There you have it – that's gumbo. NO . . . THAT'S POISON! There are several variations to the recipe but essentially that's the grueling, time-consuming and prodigious number of ingredients used in the making of this famous New Orleans dish. Gumbo proved to be my undoing.

LOSING IT, LITERALLY- YET WINNING

When I arrived back at Aunt Mildred's, I didn't feel like taking a shower. I needed to go to bed. Gumbo mania had me in its dizzying grip. Deja vu of my Pacific ship crossing when I was seasick haunted me. Sleep came but I dreamed dreams within dreams. Light boughs of magnolia trees swooped low over my bed, telling me secrets, but they were lost in waves of nausea. I woke up and ran to the bathroom. I retched. Fighting back with mind control didn't help. I retched several times more over the next hour. <u>I flunked the gumbo test!</u> To the credit of Aunt Mildred, she said nothing to me the next day nor to the Gayles nor Marilyn. She didn't have to — everyone could see that I was in bad shape. My eyes were immobile ashen coals, peering from a puffy face that looked like two loaves of bread stuck together. My face ached when I tried to smile.

In spite of this miserable misadventure, I fell in love with New Orleans then, and I still love it now. Marilyn's parents were as warm and gracious as two people could ever be. I attempted to eat seafood gumbo twice more over the next few years. The results were the same. I found out later that the real culprit was the shrimp. I'm allergic to shrimp! Today when my wife serves gumbo to our friends for dinner, I eat steak and potatoes. Just what a good native Hoosier should eat anyway!

As I reflect on my attempts to be gracious and macho, perhaps I could have escaped with my pride and nearly my life if I had eaten only one bowl of gumbo. But, no, not me. "May I have another bowl, please?" I had said, hiding subtle rumblings in my lower regions, three generations of Gayles watching my every move. Despite the disastrous results of the gumbo test, I was batting 2 for 2 on my mythical test. The bourbon test and gumbo test were now behind me.

Now I had to draw Dr. Adams into my corner and impress him with spirited conversation. We talked science, medicine, music, art and civil rights. We talked philosophy, religion and the origins of the homo sapien species. I could tell I was doing well when he followed me to add to or subtract from some minor point I "scored" earlier in some particular debate. We were both loving it.

I hate to admit it but, at this time in my life I was a young man of very decided opinions some of which frequently misled me into shark-infested waters. Once I had formed my opinion, I never changed it except if I discovered that by some strange accident I was incorrect in the first place. On the chance of seeming a bit pedantic, I knew a little bit about a lot of things – often a most dangerous state. A strange thought occurs to me now. I was really no different from most men, including intellectuals with whom I had been associated. As someone once said, we frequently find that what is well-known is poorly understood and what is taken for granted is taken without thought. Humility was not a character trait that I possessed much of at the time; only aging brings that about. Actually, I will admit now that under the brittle pretense of amusement, I spoke very fluently but too loudly on every subject under the sun. My cynical smirks due to alcohol and gumbo gave me a feeling of superiority. Undoubtedly, I was an ungrateful swine.

Marilyn continued to look lovingly in my direction to see how I was faring in my debate with Dr. Adams. She would smile her most engaging smile and give me the 1950's equivalent of a thumbs up. But then her hand signals became more furious and agitated. I was also getting early warning signals that the gumbo and my constitution were in serious disagreement with one another. The gumbo was getting the upper hand. Marilyn kept pointing to me and her dad and the kitchen area. It dawned on me that the time was at hand when I needed to talk with JG about my plans to marry his daughter.

Suddenly I became visibly nervous, my throat became dry and my lips puckered like prunes. My stomach churned even more. It was now crunch time for discovering our future. I had to venture now into the most formidable realm of all – a heart-to-heart talk with Marilyn's dad to seek his permission to marry his daughter. Pulling on courage like a new pair of socks, I guided JG away from other conversations, saying something profound like, "JG, let's go into the kitchen and discuss the future of your daughter." He smiled, put his hand on my shoulder and we glided toward the kitchen. "JG, I'm in love with your daughter – I have been since the moment I first saw her. I respectfully ask your permission and blessings for us to marry." Simple and straight forward, right? Wrong! The warm, gracious and congenial Southern charm that JG had displayed all evening vanished in a nanosecond. "Young man, we Southerners are not accustomed to such directness. For example, what would you say to a question I would propose to you – Steve, how do you intend to take care of my daughter?" I blanched, as if I had just faced pursuers in a darkened forest. "Ahem!" I said , sucking in my breath (remember, broadcasters are never lost for words). I began to remember things. "J. G., you have heard that I come from a large, humble, yet proud family. I am still in college, but I do remember Socrates, that old master of discourse, said something like, 'Human nature will not easily find a helper better than love. And I do have potential." He laughed as if I was preparing to tell him another folktale. I couldn't help laughing myself as we returned to mingle with the guests. And I finally heard the magical words, "You and Marilyn have my blessings for a wonderful life together."

"Why have I not a rich wife?"
asks the Roman Poet, Martial.
"Because I do not wish to be my
wife's maid."
Roman Poet-Martial

MARRIAGE

Even as early as 131 B.C., the Roman censor Maccabaeus had to publicly exhort Roman men to marry. But his appeal clearly reflects the cynical attitude that generally prevailed with regard to the marriage relationship. He said something to this effect. "If we could do without wives, we should be rid of that nuisance, but since nature has declared that we can neither live comfortably with them nor live without them, we must then look more to our permanent interests than to passing pleasure." This attitude stood in sharp contrast to the reverence for the institution during my day.

When my life was laid out for me at the railroad track, when the Spirit Guide at the "shimmering bush" spoke to me, I knew that I was going to marry. I was told that I would marry by the age of 28. I would be 28 years old on August 25, 1960. The wedding date was set for August 19, 1960 and the plans were in full swing. I was now speeding down destiny's track.

My younger brother, Charles, had agreed to be my best man. I loved all my brothers, but circumstances dictated it would be Charles. I couldn't have picked a better candidate. Charles had taught me so much, particularly about the beauty to be found in art and classical music. Charles in many ways was a family favorite, and why not? If you couldn't like him, you couldn't like anyone. He was about five feet nine inches tall. His face seemed to be sculptured out of the finest olive colored mango melon one could find in all South America. All of his features, his nose, lips, chin, were perfect. But as finely chiseled as these features were, it was his eyes that drew you to him. They were green, a soft green like the wheat one would find bobbing and waving in the spring breezes of Indiana. His voice was soft as gentle rain. He talked of all things with great passion and flamboyant gestures. He loved life and was a good athlete, too, winning letters in track and football. He attended Fisk University and majored in Art.

While I was in high school, I would make up schedules for "chores" for all the family – running the vacuum, taking out the trash, mopping floors, washing, wiping the dishes, and bringing in coal from the coal bin. When it was my turn to wash or wipe the dishes, I always paired myself with Charles. We would close the kitchen door, bring in the portable record player and he would introduce me to classical music – Beethoven's Fifth and Ninth Symphonies, the Rossini Overtures, particularly the "William Tell Overture." He thrilled me with the Capriccios "Italiano" and "Espanol," "The 1812 Overture, Ravel's "Bolero" and Aaron Copeland's "The Rodeo." Charles introduced me to Broadway musicals: "Finian's Rainbow," "My Fair Lady," "Porgy and Bess," and "Oklahoma." It seems so incongruous that a poor struggling black family would have as one of its members one with such knowledge and passion for classical music and art as Charles.

Before I proceed with the wedding, I would like to make one final confession. Since I was just completing my college education, I had very little money. I was forced to ask my brothers, Charles, Gary, Jon and Larry to lend me money to help with the wedding. My sisters, Vera and Teya, helped me as well. Not only did they help me with my expenses, but they all came to New Orleans to be in the wedding.

Charles and I drove to New Orleans a week before the wedding. We stayed at the home of Marilyn's Aunt Mildred. She and Charles got along famously. They would sit up late at night chatting away. Yes, he passed all the tests I had a year earlier, but he went one step further – he passed the gumbo test as well!

The day of the wedding had come. My general feelings of angst were lessened by the sound of harps and the scent of jasmine in the air. The day was sunny, hot, and humid, typical New Orleans in August. The ceremony was to be held at the St. James AME Church with the reception on the lawn at Marilyn's house. Mrs. Gayle told me of the history of St. James Church having been built in the early 1800's by its black parishioners, many of them were former slaves. It is one of the oldest churches in New Orleans, also it is one of the oldest black churches in the nation. From the account given by my mother-in-law, the following details emerged. In the latter part of the year 1844, a group of men known as "Free Men of Color" organized them into a religious society under the name of the African Methodist Episcopal Church. Free Men of Color were permitted to worship with the white members of Wesley Chapel M.E. church; however, the black men were required to worship in the balcony, a place reserved for them. The black men resented this treatment and other ill practices against them and determined to have their own church. A white minister, Charles Daugherty, broke away from the main branch of the AM Church and rented a site next to a blacksmith shop on the corner of Valerie and Bienville Streets. There he and the Free Men erected a temporary place for holding services. The congregation grew in membership, although services were frequently disrupted by the local authorities. It seemed that slaves would occasionally come into their meetings for the purpose of worship. Nevertheless, the first Louisiana Annual Conference was held in St. James AME Church in the year 1865. The Civil War was in progress and it was during this time that the church became the center of activity in aiding the cause of freedom for slaves. Daugherty's church survived all adversities and vicissitudes. There have been only 18 ministers at St. James over the period of 1844 -1994. The minister that married Marilyn and me was Rev. C. E. Hayden, 1958 - 1964. I believe that the success of my marriage began with the legacy of St. James AME Church.

On the day of the wedding, I awoke with butterflies fluttering around in my head, luring . . . promising. Magnolias and other perfumed flowers put on their finest display for Marilyn and me. But, knowing my propensity to screw things up, things no one else could possibly do, I waited, sweat sticking to my skin, for something unfortunate to happen. Would I faint from the heat? Drop the ring? I had the feeling I was embarking on one of those British Colonial explorations in the jungles of tropical islands: they were pretty sure there was a tiger in the jungle, but they weren't sure where. So the explorer warily cracks sticks until he hears a roar. Likewise, I was waiting for the roar – but, miracles of miracles and Allah be praised and his children multiply – the roar never came. The wedding went off without a hitch. Marilyn and I now faced the future together as we rode out of town headed for St. Louis. I kept thinking of the railroad tracks and that day by the "shimmering bush." I was still on target – "married by the time you're twenty-eight," I heard whispered again as we headed north on Highway 10, the lovely oak and magnolia trees majestically bowing to us as we passed. Life was now good! New life, new energy, new hope suddenly had come my way.

We arrived in St. Louis late in the afternoon. We were to spend the following day with a family friend of her grandfather. We needed a place to spend the night, however, so we went looking for a hotel downtown. The one we selected was really nice. Since neither of us was familiar with the customs of St. Louis, we decided to change clothes – in the car! We took our cue from hotel guests we watched coming and going. They were fully dressed. We were an unholy sight. We laughed at ourselves as we changed in the parking lot. Legs, arms and naked skin flashed in the setting sun. We both agreed, if the police happened to be passing by, they would never have believed our miserable tale. Surely we would have gone to jail for indecent exposure. We were very lucky indeed.

The next day we found Marilyn's friends without much trouble. They were a delightful couple and extended their hospitality far beyond that for which friendship would call. They served us a wonderful lunch and dinner. In between, they drove us on a sightseeing tour around the famous old sections of St. Louis and East St. Louis. I was thoroughly impressed as we visited famous jazz spots and honky tonks. The black people looked carefree and gay. I seemed to hear the "St. Louie Blues" everywhere. We wished our wonderful hosts well and promised ourselves we would send them a gift once we returned to Indianapolis. Unfortunately, as so many well- intended promises go, we failed to do so. One additional thought, it is a pity the city of East St. Louis has fallen on hard times. I read recently that the city was broke, that the jobless rate was sky high, that garbage had gone uncollected for months on end. What an unfortunate postscript for a grand old city.

Our next stop was Chicago, Illinois. We wanted to visit Chicago because of my fond memories of the time I spent there with my friend, Harold Harris, nearly ten years earlier. We arrived there much later than we had intended, around 8 p.m. I called Harold anyway. He was married at this juncture. I talked briefly with his wife, whom I didn't know. Anyway, she disappointed me when she said, "Harold is sleeping and must get up in an hour. He plays piano at the Playboy Club and needs his rest." I was a little miffed because if Harold had called me, day or night, I would have set everything aside for him. Most importantly, I wanted so badly for Harold to meet Marilyn, but I could tell his wife was in no mood for company, no matter how good friends Harold and I might be. Marilyn and I both agreed neither of us would be so inhospitable to friends of ours. We had a great time anyway, sightseeing and listening to great music at several jazz spots. The following day we set our sights for Indianapolis and not a moment too soon. Would anyone would be surprised to hear that we had less than a dollar between us when we arrived at our apartment?

The next day, Marilyn caught a train for Grambling University in Louisiana. She had secured a professorship in Speech and Drama at the school. I was very proud of her when she told me that she would soon be directing "Raisin in the Sun." I was even more proud when several weeks later she called to tell me she was pregnant with our first child. Opalescent light shimmered through my apartment, my spiritual guide was busy again fulfilling his prophecy and right on schedule.

A CHILD IS BORN

Humanity shows itself in all its splendor when a child is born, like the sun showing itself at dawn, or a flower first unfolding its petals. Children have been chronicled in letters, stories, essays, poems, drawings, pictures, musical compositions, autobiographical documents, musings, and case histories. All of these rich sources capture the wonders of children coming into a family. Interestingly enough, Charles Darwin in the mid 1800's, recorded the growth and development of one of his own children, collecting data pretty much as if he were studying some strange new species.

Marilyn, beautiful, radiant, looked supremely happy and very pregnant as she stepped off the train in Indianapolis that cold December day in 1962. She had been riding for a full day coming from Grambling University in Louisiana. It was the Christmas holidays at Grambling; she could take a break from her teaching and join me for a week. She burst into her million-dollar smile when she saw me standing at track side. I flashed my cool "father to be " smile in her direction as well. My walk had a purpose as I moved to embrace her.

I had recently rented a two-bedroom apartment at the "Campus Apartments," near Indiana Avenue, in Indianapolis. These apartments were considered as up scale living for up and coming, or professional blacks at the time. Many of our friends who were doctors, lawyers, teachers and others with reasonably good jobs lived there. My brother Don and Rae, lived there as well. So, we were not without great company. My two bedroom apartment, sparsely decorated, and certainly had the look of a bachelor apartment. Two days before her arrival I became a veritable whirlwind cleaning, and polishing and hiding things in secret places. Despite my heroic actions, she spent the next few days making that humble abode our

298

home. It took some doing too, as she has always been a thoroughly fastidious person.

We also spent considerable time and a great deal of our meager funds buying furniture. A good description of our purchases would be eclectic: Some of the furniture was early American. Some was contemporary. Some was early Salvation Army. We made a bookcase out of bricks and boards, as did many struggling newly married couples in those days. This device had the distinct advantage of taking up a lot of room and giving the impression that one had a lot of furniture.

Marilyn bought the usual things for our newly expected baby: a bassinet, baby bed and a wonderful, movable mobile to hang over the bed. She continued cleaning and scrubbing everything-windows, stove, bathroom, walls and floors. Then we purchased the piece de resistance: a grass rug for the living room floor, for heavens sake!

After several days of creating a new world for us, Marilyn rubbed her hands together. "Ah . . . That is good," she said. And it was so.

Now, the big job lay ahead for me. "Keep it clean!" she admonished, as she waved goodbye for her return trip to Grambling.

Several months later she returned. Her school commitment to Grambling College was completed and we could now be together . . . forever!

During the time Marilyn was gone, I read every book I could get my hands on that dealt with child birth and the rearing of children. I could have been a pediatrician. I knew all about trimesters, first, second, and third. More important, I knew what bodily changes should be taking place during each phase. I read Dr. Spock's baby book three or four times. I deemed it necessary to be a strong bulwark of a fellow to my wife. I had to know all the answers to any questions she might have. I made dry runs from the apartment to the hospital. I secretly dreamed of running red lights at full bore hoping to be stopped by the police. I fantasized and fanaticized my spiel to the arresting officer. "Officer, out of my way, or turn on your siren . . . I'm having a baby!" What a great story to tell around campfires and other places where men tell tales.

The fateful day of birth came. The pains, the panic. I held my ground though. "Not yet dear." I would calmly say as I plotted each time of the pain on a graph. Then I would average three pains for frequency. I had read somewhere that when the pains averaged 15 to 30 minutes apart there was sufficient time to grab the overnight bag. During the morning they had not broken the one hour barrier. Into the afternoon the pains were now into the 45 minute bracket. I dutifully alerted the doctor to standby for my next call, which would be when I was leaving for the hospital. He didn't like the idea, but my bravado was beyond all measure. I didn't know it yet but it was nearly beyond all reason, as well. I was dutifully waiting for the fifteen minute average ranges. All the while I kept Marilyn busy, washing clothes, dishes, hammering, nailing, anything to occupy her mind and divert it from the ordeal that lay ahead.

Suddenly, my eyes did a double take. The last three pains averaged just less than ten minutes! I couldn't believe it! How did I let the averages sneak up on me? My eyes began to blur as I stared again at the graph. I tried to remain calm, but dread was coming on fast. I called the doctor. I began to stutter as I told my wife, "It's . . . It's . . . time . . . It's time to go, darling, as I reached for the small overnight case. I really did speed to the hospital and I did run several red lights. This was serious business now!

When we arrived at the hospital, the nurse gave me hell for waiting so long. They scarcely had time to prep her, it seemed, when the doctor, Dr. Frank Lloyd Sr., came into the waiting room and said, "Congratulation's Steve, you have a fine son. They both are doing fine. Give the nurses about a half hour to make your son ready for your greeting." My soul floated six feet outside my body. My wife's best friend, Gloria Adams, was with me during the delivery room phase. We waited, chatting quietly in the waiting room Some of the poor expectant fathers had been there for hours. Some for days. Yet, I had pulled off my delivery in less than an hour.

Gloria and I made our way to the nursery after stopping by Marilyn's bedside. I gave her a big kiss and a "thumbs-up" for a job well done. I gave the head nurse my name and passed along the word to bring forth my new son. There was a huge viewing window where parents could peer at their little darlings. The attendant held up my son amidst all of the other screaming babies in the nursery. I opened just one eye. I wanted to see shadows first before seeing the entire portrait. Slowly he came into focus as I discerned minute features. The face was sublime. Those deep fathomed eyes, chiseled nose, and sculptured lips all showed a certain regalness. Steve Jr. was marvelous! I stared. I stared, and I stared some more. He suddenly started to turn red from screaming. Was it because he saw me and thought better of the whole thing or because he was completely naked? He finally quieted down. I continued my gaze from his head to his toes to see if he was ok, physically. Ah, plenty of coal black hair . . . all right! A gorgeous smile like his father. All right! My soul did an eclipse. Through a haze my mind now ran the whole gamut of emotions, as I noticed something for the first time. "Why" I asked, if he is naked, is he wearing blue shoes?" Something was terribly wrong here. I became giddy and dizzy at the sight of my boy, the first born and his "blue feet." The question, badly put, was, " Is he deformed?"

Gloria must have heard me. She began to steady me as she comfortingly said. "Steve, the blue shoes is only a matter of circulation to his feet. The lower extremities are the last to reach normalcy after birth."

The fog lifted! Not only was he alive . . . but he was physically fine. "All right!" I said loudly enough to be boorish! I motioned for the nurse to bring him to me, which she did, straight away! I noticed another thing as I hoisted him high, he had no odor, just the smell of new!

Seven years later, over early morning breakfast, Marilyn complained of a headache and flu-like symptoms. Newspaper headlines had been screaming over front page stories and television contained several news items about a growing contagion called the "Hong Kong flu." There was an extremely virulent new flu virus sweeping the country. "You're catching the 'Hong Kong' flu," I said. " Drink plenty of juices and water today. Also, take two Tylenol every four hours. You'll feel much better by this evening" I opined, using my best pseudo-medical doctor voice. I was wrong! The "Hong Kong" flu lasted a week, a month . . . No. Nine months. She was pregnant. So much for my pseudo-medical knowledge, which would rarely be trusted again.

June 1, 1969 was an especially bright and cheery morning as Marilyn indicated to me that this would be the day when our second child would be born. I had gone through all of the same rituals that I practiced when Steve Jr. was born. After all, seven years is a long time between children. But things seemed to go much faster this time. Same graphs, same rehearsals for getting to the hospital, the same "calm" approach to timing for the trip to the hospital, Only this time, the interval for our arrival at the hospital, was even shorter, and the nurses' sharp tongue lashing was even more biting. I was still a swine.

We had already decided that if we had a baby girl her name would be Wendy Gayle Scott. The play on the words windy gale had such a marvelous ring to it. Can there really be an intellectual approach to naming a child?

Wendy stole my heart immediately. It would be no exaggeration to say that I was truly born in that moment. A baby girl. Wow! Some say that Wendy arrived on this earth talking and smiling. She was an absolutely magnificent looking baby with her mother's large expressive eyes, full lips, perfect skin. She was just perfect! Even the nurses scurried to Marilyn's bedside, just to catch a glimpse of the person who perfected this child. Fathers never get any credit.

I drove home from the hospital that day taking the scenic route along White River Parkway. The trees bowed in a salutation toward me. Was that a "shimmering, dancing, glow" coming from a clump of low lying bushes? I had my second child, just as foretold when I sat next to the railroad track a long, long time ago.

FALCONS DROP O_A E, TAKE 331st AIRMEN

A new court combination, the 329th Falcons, made up of basketball talent from the 329th Headquarters and Air Base Squadrons got off to a good start in the Second Round of Intramural play by both winning and losing a game. The Falcons having plenty of height, speed, and bench strength are out to prove tough opponents for everyone on their schedule.

Last Monday night the 329th Falcons were nipped by 42nd Comm Sq 46 to 44 in a thriller all the way. If it were not for the steady foul shooting of Steve Scott (17 points,) of Comm, the score could have been quite different. The Falcons guard combination of James McNutt (10 points) and Ira Bennett (14 points) led the team in scoring with Gardenbrock (4), Jackson (4), Smith (4), Widdig (6) and Enderline (2) rounding out the scoring.

Base Basketball Team Chosen For Entry in NEAF Tournament

Through a vote of the Base Intramural Basketball League managers, the 15 most outstanding players on the base have been chosen as the base team for the North East Area Air Force Basketball Tournament.

This group will begin practice at the base gym on Monday, 23 Jan., from 1:00 to 2:30 P.M. and continue daily until tournament time.

M/Sgt. Harold Tipson of Hq EAADF will act as coach, cutting the squad down to 12 players before 27 February, when the Stewart JETS will journey to Sampson AFB for the tournament. The Base Athletic Section would appreciate the cooperation of the selected players section heads in allowing these men time off to attend the practice sessions. This is the year, if ever, that Stewart has a good chance of winning the conference crown and to do it we need the best possible court squad representing us in the tournament.

Players chosen for the base team are Steve Scott and Robert Barnitz of the 42nd Communications Sq.; Charlie O'Dell and Charlie Butler of the 329th Infirmary; Joe Hollins, Tom Buford, and Walter Wilkins of the 329th Materiel Sq.; Hank Gillis, Herb Blackwell, and William Bowes of the 330th FIS; Dick Waterson, Angelo Cincotta, and Arnie Staub of MATS; Ira Bennett and James McNutt of the 329th Falcons.

Steve Scott of 42nd Comm takes to the air for two points against the 329th Air Base Sq. in the opening Intramural Basketball game of the season. Emmons and Tolleson of 42nd Comm. are pictured on the extreme left and right. Members of the 329th Air Base team on defense are (L-R) Jackson, Watts, Erwin, and Bowes. (Photo by Katz)

304

331st Teams Win In 'Hoop-Loop'

Last Monday night the 331st Officers jumped into an early lead in the first quarter and played steady ball for the remaining three periods to defeat MATS (12th Weather and AACS) 54 to 45. Leading the 331st attack was Williams at center with 18 points. Thompson with 15 and Boxhorn with 10 points rounded out the double figure men for the officers team. In defeat the MATS team was led by Waterson, 14 points, and Cincotta, 12 points.

In one of the higher scoring battles to date, the much improved Hq 329th team was edged 58 to 50 by the 331st Airmen. Each quarter of the game was close, but the 331st Airmen picked up the added two or three points in each period to make the difference. The 331st Airmen had four men in double figures: McCally, 14; Wilkins, 12; Waddle, 10; and Ozen, 10. The Headquarters 329th team was led by Bennett, the high scorer in the game, with 19 points from his guard position. Clooback was also in twin figures for 329th with 13 points. The 329th team with a bigger squad are showing steady improvement and should make some trouble in the second round.

On Tuesday night, the first game of the evening was a wild affair with Hq EADF using their height to slap down 42nd Comm Squadron 51 to 43. Greenwald led EADF with 21 points from his center position; while 42nd Communications had Scott as their high point man with 20.

Some sort of scoring record (the least amount) for the Intramural League was set in the second game of the evening when the 329th Air

(Pix) The opening jump of the 1954-55 Base Intramural Basketball play-offs at the base gym Monday night; between 42nd Comm and EADF.

42nd COMM NOSES OUT EADF 58-55
OPENING INTRAMURAL PLAYOFFS

The 1954-55 Base Intramural Basketball playoffs got underway this week with 42nd Comm., EADF, and Prep School the participating teams.

Opening the double elimination tournament were EADF and 42nd Comm. who squared off at each other in what proved to be a close contest all the way. COMM lead 13-11 at the end of the first quarter, then stepped up the pace to lead EADF, 36-28 at halftime. Although EADF tried a comeback in the third quarter (47-43) they were never able to overtake COMM, largely due to the efforts of Scott and Stefancin, who scored 21 and 14 points respectively. EADF's attack which was always a pressing one, but never enough to take the lead, was paced by Hanley, 14 points, Richards 12; and Rizzo, who scored only nine points but was a giant under the backboards.

SPORT SPINS

As if Monday night's contest between 42nd COMM and EADF did not produce enough excitement; 42nd COMM and Prep School clashed Tuesday night and produced one of the most thrilling games of the season.

Prep School edged COMM 61-59, but it took a double overtime to do the trick. The score was tied 48-48 at the end of regulation play and 53-53 at the end of the first overtime. Day of the Prep School led his team with 19 points; while Stefancin of COMM was high man in the game with 27 points, followed by teammate Scott with 15.

306

'Allstars' Place 2d In 1.

Stewart Air Force Base "All-Stars" captured second place in the Northeast Area Air Force Basketball Tournament held at Loring AFB, Maine, last week.

After a two day weather delay at Stewart, the "All-Stars" left Stewart for Loring on Monday, 7 March.

The next day the "All-Stars" played their first game with Otis, rolling over them 80-64. Stewart, jumping off to a first quarter lead of 21-12, held that margin through the next three quarters for the win. The score at half-time was 48-30 and at the end of the third quarter 64-42. There were four men from Stewart in double figures with Pazera showing the way with 22

Steve Scott in for two points for Stewart in an 80-64 victory over Otis AFB, in the opening game of the North East Tourney at Loring AFB, Maine. Stefancin (17) of Stewart, in the foreground, is shown backing up the play.

THE NESTING INSTINCT

Two years earlier, on a Saturday afternoon in early spring, 1967, I was sitting in the sun room doing home work at our apartment on Fall Creek Parkway South Drive. The bright sun was lovely as it streamed through the windows on a struggling young family man. My lovely wife and her young son were busy doing what lovely wives and sons do on a Saturday morning . . . getting in each other's way.

I could see robins outside my sun room window gathering straw and wintered grass to build their nests. My wife must have been watching them as well because as she brought me a cup of hot tea, I noticed her eyes had a determined glow to them. It somewhat puzzled me, but I simply considered it part of her wifely charm. Terse and decisive as always, she said expressionlessly, "I want a home of our own. It's a pretty day, let's go house hunting." To steady myself, I took a long sip of tea, the cup and saucer rattling in my hands, the noise sounding like rattling skeleton bones. Another robin flew past my window with straw in its beak. She definitely saw it this time. This was not going to be a matter to take lightly, I thought to myself, and it wasn't. I was doomed. Over the next few months, I began to understand what I should have known all along about women. No matter how emancipated they are, no matter how intellectual and freedom-loving, nature has decreed that they must have a home of their own. Something drives them – no, COMPELS them, often without their knowing it, into thinking about a home. "Why not?" was all I could muster.

That afternoon we took a drive northeast of the city where many of the middle and upper-class sub divisions had been built. We were just searching for homes that were perceived to be in our price range. When we returned home later that day, I promised Marilyn we would have our own snug little nest in the near future, with a big yard, flower garden and all of the other amenities that constitute a "nest." This was not an idle promise by some insipid husband. Something was also gnawing at me to build my own home, but I couldn't remember why.

The year of this stirring for achieving the American dream was 1967. I had a good job and was earning a decent salary for the time period. In addition, I was receiving extra income from my fledgling broadcasting career. Marilyn was now a full-time teacher, so life was good. I no longer had feverish dreams of food and decent clothes. Over the following months, we looked at every quadrant of the city of Indianapolis. Marilyn was now in full passion for a home. On one particular day, after she and her friend, June Moss, returned from one of their house hunting forays, she dashed into our apartment in a rage and nearly in tears. The two ladies had made arrangements with a realtor to see an upscale house in an all white neighborhood. Her story unfolded something like this. The real estate agent, who arrived early for the appointment, was parked in front of the house. He saw the two black women approaching. He jumped in his car and sped away, blue smoke billowing from his rear exhaust. Now in full rage, my wife called the manager of the realty company and read him the riot act. She was not appeased by his weak apologies. Next, she hurled a call straight to the State of Indiana Civil Rights Commission. They in turn, and without delay, called the realty company to determine the issues involved. Now events moved into even higher gear as Marilyn received a call inviting her to come to a special showing of the home right away. She went, too, undaunted and unabashed.

We both knew, secretly, that building our home on our own lot would be the only answer. The search began anew for a lot on which to build our dream home. I knew that I didn't want to build on just any lot. A football field, if you like. It had to have enhancements, such as a location on a hill or near water. With these prerequisites, our best bet was to explore a new area, northwest of the city, which had thus far escaped the burgeoning home building market. We looked and looked, and looked some more, but nothing matched our desires or met even our minimum prerequisites. In the meantime, Marilyn had settled on house plans, having sent away to a developer in California who specialized in contemporary homes, our number one desire. She found the perfect design too, with vaulted cathedral ceilings, plenty of glass, picture windows in front and in the back as well. She found a first rate black architectural firm – Snyder, Blackburn and Associates, to build our home once we found the land.

In the meantime, I called a black realtor friend, Walt Howard, whom I knew to be an aggressive, talented and successful real estate agent. Having been given the parameters of the kind of land we were looking for, Walt went to work with hellish fervor. One day he called my office with a new spirit in his normally rich baritone voice. "Steve, I have great news for you! Your search is over! I have the absolute perfect lot for you. It even has a deep ravine in the rear with a small stream at the bottom. Can you get away around lunch time and I'll show it to you?" My soul did the eclipse that is prone to do under serendipitous circumstances. "Well, huh, sure Walt," I said, both my voice and hands trembling as if preparing for dental drilling.

Walt was talking a mile a minute as we drove to the site, just off Kessler Boulevard, 4900 block west, on a street named Seville Drive. It was March, almost a year after the house hunting process had begun. Since it was just prior to spring, with little greenery on the trees, it was too early to see robins building their nests. But I could see how the whole lot looked. It was nearly a one acre lot on a hill, and pie shaped. I was excited as we walked over the land that sat on a slight bluff surrounded by gorgeous homes. I never thought about it being in an all white addition because I never saw anyone coming or going. Walt said the plot of land was being held in reserve by the female owner of the development. She wanted the site for her own future home. So you know it was prime land. "Ok!

Ok! Walt, I love it and I have to have it. How much is it?" I held my breath, having first sucked in the cool March air in gulps. "She is asking fifty-five hundred dollars, and believe me it's a steal," Walt said with a grin too large for his face. "I'll call you this evening after I show it to my wife," I said with emotions running the gamut from exhilaration to exhaustion. I also felt dread because I recalled the great story credited to Tolstoy. It was a tale of greed and of knowing when to be satisfied with what is being offered.

The old King, in a faraway land, wanted to reward his four war commanders for being victorious in defeating his enemies in the northern reaches of his kingdom. One day, while strolling through his beautifully landscaped gardens and admiring the vastness of his territory, he came up with the ultimate solution. He smiled broadly at the beauty and simplicity of his solution. He would send each commander, on foot, to a quadrant of his kingdom – one to the north, one to the south, one to the east and one to the west. Each could have all the land he could traverse from sun up to sun down. But they had to return to the starting line in that elapsed time. Having called his commanders together early one morning, he gave them their instructions, including the final caveat that if they failed to cross the start/finish line by sundown, they would forfeit all the land they had covered and they would receive nothing.

Away they all ran toward the four corners of the kingdom. By noon each had traveled far. But the noon day sun began to parch their throats and they became tired and hungry. Still they trudged on, all save one, who had taken the northern route. He walked in measured steps, conserving his energy and strength. As a matter of fact, satisfied that he would have all the land he needed, he began his homeward trek. The others sped laughing with glee at the folly of the king who granted such a magnificent prize.

The northern commander arrived back at the starting line well before the sun set and the commander could see far away in the distance the other returning commanders. They were stumbling, falling and dragging themselves in agony toward the finish line. The sun went down. It passed out of sight first as the commanders, each in turn, collapsed and died within sight of victory.

What does that story have to do with anything, Steve? Well, the story means many things, but to me, only this: Either you know when you have enough and when to cease your quest and lay claim to your prize, or you may pay a supreme price.

When I showed Marilyn the land within our grasp, she must have heard the story because she triumphantly let out a scream of ecstasy, drowning out the croaking of a pair of blackbirds angry at our invasion of their territory. Over a year of searching and embarrassment was over. We would lay claim to that which we had found. But the story does not end there. The Goddess of Good Luck must have her own tribute from those to whom she chooses to pour out her favors. A series of events led to another of my spectacular blunders.

Having secured the land, my wife could now decide on the final plans for her nest – our dream home. After pouring over hundreds of books and magazines, she sent away for plans and renderings of a richly handsome design by Schultz in California. Enter my black architect friend David Snyder of Snyder and Blackburn. All of us spent the better part of three months pouring over the Shultz plans, adding here, cutting there, until we had the costs and the living space to manageable levels. We were seeking costs in the $50,000 range and living space of about 2,800 square feet which was a considerable price and space for a house in those days. We hit the targets. We were

312

congratulating ourselves with hearty handshakes all around. I took Marilyn to dinner that night for further celebration.

The next day, we received an urgent call from David Snyder. He had to see us right away. Upon arrival at his office, we could only say that he looked like a corpse that some apprentice embalmers had finally abandoned. He came directly to the point. "We've been looking at plans of the first floor only! This house is huge . . . it's a mansion!" he said, full of regret. Marilyn's heart turned to stone. Both of us were devastated. All that wasted effort. Sufficient blame lay everywhere. His office reeked with it. It was a shattering blow to all of us. We were back to square one.

On the way back to our apartment, I made my first real attempt to problem-solve. Was it possible, I wondered, that my residential home builder friend, Bill Myers, could save the moment for us? The next day I made the fateful call. "Sure, Steve," he said, "I'll be happy to work with you and Marilyn on this project." Project was not the right word. My life was at stake since I had steered Marilyn to David Snyder in the first place.

We showed Bill our list of prerequisites and our building site. "Matter of fact," he said with glee, "I have just completed a house in Greenwood, and its design is the perfect house for this lot. He drove us that same day to see it. It was perfect, exactly what we were looking for. Planning and financing began in earnest. Marilyn continued to read hundreds of books on interior decorating, lighting fixtures, appliances, carpeting and the like, all the while dragging me at least once a week to walk over the land. For some unknown reason, I had been feeling very apprehensive and self-conscious when we walked over the land. Suddenly it dawned on me. For the past few weeks, we were being watched, watched not only by the crows protecting their territory, but by unseen eyes from behind curtains and doors. I began to pay attention to the fluttering of curtains at windows, whenever we set foot on the land. I said nothing to my wife.

Construction began in March of 1969 with a completion date set for August. I quickly learned the phrase "a few dollars more," and it had nothing to do with a Clint Eastwood movie. I have a theory that would instantly save any failing marriage. Before the marriage starts to go sour . . . build a house. I guarantee it will be a catalyst for open and constructive dialogue with one's spouse. Every evening when you come home, the conversation begins like this: "We can have this kind of light fixture . . . but for a few dollars more we can have that one." "We can have this kind of carpet, but for a few hundred dollars more, we can have that kind." "We can have this kind of stove or oven, but a self-cleaning oven will cost only a few hundred dollars more." Trust me, this kind of talk gets your attention. Heaven forbid one is forced to talk with one's wife when building a home. In fact, one's tendency is to instantly say, "Okay, let's go for the convenience and luxury of the higher priced item." This dialogue continues through the entire building process. No more going home, grabbing the evening paper or watching television. I pray others do not fall into this trap. We ended up borrowing nearly $5,000 more to pay for the "few hundred dollars more" items.

The house was now complete. Because of the "few hundred dollars more," I ended up seeding and putting straw over the entire lawn to make up for the trade offs. I also had to hire a friend of mine from work, Bob Buck, to help me paint the interior of the whole house! Try painting the inside of 2,800 square feet of living space in July with no electricity for a fan, or an air conditioner. I was beginning to hate the house and I hadn't even moved into it yet. Moving day was no piece of cake either. The house was now demonic!

Moving day came on a Saturday. As was the habit in those days, one would solicit friends to help in this damnable exercise. Marilyn and I enlisted our friends and associates at work and several of my brothers and sisters, some fifteen people in all. Marilyn made a huge pot of

314

spaghetti and meatballs. I purchased three cases of ice cold beer for those tortured souls who had volunteered their services. In case those friends and family are reading this chapter, I had better mention a few of their names: Ted and Barbara Boyd, Ben and Alice Robinson, Florence and Allen Greene, and Hal Hyatt. With Ted Boyd at the helm of the rental truck and men hanging outside and inside, we made our way to Seville Drive. We must have looked a curious sight as we pulled into our driveway. One could again see blinds and curtains fluttering, ever so slightly, as incredulous, hidden eyes must have peered anxiously from behind them. I'm sure they hadn't seen this many black folk since watching Amos and Andy reruns. Even the crows who had been watching us for nearly three years now took up special perches on nearby branches to watch this spectacle, hoping, I'm sure, that something would prevent these invaders from taking permanent residence in their territory. They didn't have long to wait, and they were nearly vindicated.

After nearly killing ourselves moving the refrigerator and stove inside, the most damnable thing happened. The hydraulic lift to the truck bed broke. There it lay on the ground, spewing steam and oil like a ruptured water line. Luckily, no one was on the lift at the time, so there were no injuries. The driveway, made of white crushed stone, looked a mess. Even the crows, who by now had become my friends, choked at the sight, and flew directly to their nests. I made a desperate call to the rental truck service. They indicated they would dispatch another truck, and reimburse me for clean-up of the oil spill in my driveway. I groaned as I wiped sweat from my eyes. It was time to make an executive decision, and I did — a classic, tactical decision that was a blunder of the first magnitude. I opened a case of cold beer! The hot weather, parched throats and fatigue led to predictable results. Empty beer cans began to pile up in a heap. So did my helpers. One by one they began to offer up wonderful excuses for having to depart the disaster scene — things like, "I forgot, my mother-in-law is coming in from Jackass Flats, Utah, this evening." I didn't blame them. If I could have escaped, I would have. They were all saints for helping as much as they did. Nevertheless, a new truck arrived, along with several men to help unload the remainder of the heavy items from the stricken truck. We were able to quickly retrieve the other items from our apartment, which my wife had skillfully packed in boxes. We made sure we set up the beds first as young Steve, Marilyn and I now sought blissful sleep. It didn't come easy.

It began around midnight. Muffled, intermittent sounds, scraping and creaking noises. I chose to ignore them. My wife didn't. "What was that?" she would exclaim in a loud voice. "Nothing, dear," I grumbled. "It's just your nerves. It's been a long day." My wife wanted me to go downstairs to see what it was. I am told that men have heard that request since the caveman first crouched at night before the campfires. I stumbled downstairs, keeping the lights out, fearing all the while that a cross might be burning in our yard, set by some crazy race-hating night riders. I peered outside through a tiny crack in the curtains . . . nothing! It was now about 3 a.m. as I climbed back into bed, for the third time. After 30 minutes, I endured one more "What is that?" This time it was real. Steve was bounding down the hall from his bedroom. "What was that?" he cried, terror in his voice, eyes as big as saucers. Marilyn and I broke out in hysterical laughter. Tears filled our eyes and fell unwiped. "Come on, son, hop in bed, everything is okay," I said. As Morpheus, the Goddess of Sleep, finally intervened, I gave one last thought to decades ago when revelations of my young life to be were made manifest. "You will build your dream home before you reach your 38th birthday." My birthday, August 25, was just a few days away and I would be 38 years old. I was still on target with the revelations of the "shimmering bush."

CHAPTER 10

**Good friends around these hearthstones
speak no evil word of any creature.
Frank Lloyd Wright carved this
inscription over his mantel 100 years ago.**

EACH MAN'S LIFE TOUCHES ANOTHER

I have learned to accept the truism that most of mankind is permanently preoccupied with its own immediate concerns. These concerns may seem somewhat petty to the rest of us, mainly because we ourselves are probably occupied with some all-consuming interest of our own that may in turn appear trivial to others. In short, everybody in the world seems to be busy with his own business and only a scattering of saints seem to have any time left over for anybody else. I know that they exist though, these holy ones, because I have encountered a few of them in my lifetime.

Mom Mayes could not have had a better name. Her husband's name, logically enough, was Pop Mayes. I had heard of Mom and Pop Mayes as soon as I arrived on the campus of Indiana University. They lived in the city of Bloomington on the far west side, in a cluster of homes owned by blacks, none of which would be considered rundown or in a poor state of repair. Just plain, moderate housing would be an accurate description. The blacks in the city of Bloomington reminded me of those in my hometown, Lebanon: hard workers. But the city economy revolved around jobs at the university and small factories, service entry jobs which would not permit more than a low to moderate income lifestyle. Black people there made

317

their living in much the same fashion as most of the city's inhabitants.

Mom and Pop Mayes earned their living by opening their home to poor, black IU male students. When I say poor black IU male students, I mean poor, black male students, many of whom would have been unable to attend college at all, if not for the altruistic commitment of Mom and Pop Mayes.

The Mayes' house was a well-constructed bungalow. It had a long linear front porch where the guys could sit on warm summer days and get some relief from the confined quarters inside. What would normally be a living room was reconfigured into a dining area that would seat about twelve men. Down the hallway were three rooms that were made into sleeping quarters that contained three to four bunk beds, accommodating up to four men to a room for a total of some 12 to 14 students. The major advantage an individual student would have in these cramped conditions was that most students were out a great deal of the time, working at either odd jobs, studying, or involved in their own individual pursuits. Most studying was done on campus. Daily laundry was accomplished at a laudramat some three or four blocks away. It is my understanding that Mom and Pop Mayes had been offering students low-cost housing since the early 1940s. An impoverished male student, usually ended up at the Mayes' house for survival to finish school.

When I first entered IU in the fall of 1956, I stayed on campus in Cottage Grove, an army barracks housing unit. These all-male units housed Korean veterans like me and veterans of former wars, going to school on the GI Bill. GIs received $110 per month. Although tuition at that time was only $8 per credit hour, after three years of economic struggle, I abandoned the humble confines of Cottage Grove to find refuge at the even more humble sanctuary of Mayes' house. I was, and still am, grateful for these saints. I spent two years at Mayes' House along with my brother, Don. Pop Mayes would spend his afternoon and early evening hours sitting on his front porch watching television. He also watched me closely, I think because I spent a great deal of time chatting with Mom Mayes. I would walk up the steps after daily classes and immediately catch his wrath. "We don't need you here," he would say. "Go stay somewhere else, get out of here," Mom would hear his outburst and order him inside the house and down to the basement. That is where he lived, banished to the basement of his own home by Mom. Mainly, it kept him out of harm's way.

Pop, bless his heart, had a penchant for the grape and the barley and spent much of his time in another time and place, down in the basement, drunk. To me, his life seemed a simple routine: Chew Steve out, get chewed out himself by Mom and then get exiled to the basement. What a life for the poor fellow - a prisoner of his own circumstances. Pop was a small man, about five foot four and weighed about 130 pounds. He looked to be about 80 years old. The bottle had taken its toll on his spirit. In many ways he looked like an overdone baked apple that had been left on the window sill to cool.

Mom Mayes had not carried her later years well either. Mom was probably never a well-kempt woman. When I arrived on the scene, she too had become old. She was in her seventies. Mom had very light-colored skin, which was strangely unwrinkled. That could have been because she was a large woman, weighing nearly 200 pounds. Mom was about five foot nine inches tall, much taller than Pop. Her hair was always stringy and never seemed combed. She looked like an Americanized Indian squaw out of the old West. In her youth, Mom was probably a very attractive woman. Now she walked with a halting gait and stooped slightly; probably the burden of caring for "her boys" caused her poor health and disheveled look. She carried the burden and responsibilities of running the house on her own shoulders. Pop never helped. She never failed to cook two meals a day, six days a week. Her only break would come on Sunday when she prepared only one meal, dinner. That was an awesome responsibility. Just washing the dishes would be more than most would care to do at her age. The food – well, for the most part she served lots of casseroles, beans, franks, pork chops and plenty of potatoes. But it was filling, and what more could one really ask for under the circumstances?

In the conversation, as I sat on the front porch talking to Mom, one thing would always come through abundantly clear: she would rather do what she was doing than anything else on earth. Nevertheless, he would not accept the fact that over the years she was responsible for hundreds of black students' getting their degrees because of her benevolence. She would just say, "It's God's will." Some of the guys had no money to pay her at times, but she never kicked anyone out of the house during my stay. Occasionally, I would be one of them, but I always paid my rent on time except for one occasion, which I spoke about earlier. Why I found favor in her eyes, I don't know. She would even give me extra food from time to time. I think it was because I paid attention to her and often expressed my gratitude to her.

You would think that Mom Mayes would have taken summers off and not house "her boys" when regular classes were dismissed. No, not Mom Mayes. In fact, many blacks from Tennessee, Alabama, Mississippi, Louisiana and Arkansas would come to Indiana University during summer sessions to work on advanced degrees and would stay at Mayes' house. Many of these men were married, teaching school, sometimes principals working toward required Masters or Doctoral degrees. They were living on a shoestring, and Mom Mayes was saving them too. These black men could not go to the major universities in the South because of their race. It is hard to believe, as I write this in 1995, that only thirty years ago the almost impoverished Southern states would actually pay for black educators advanced degrees if, and only if, they went up North to school. The beautiful Southern woman that I married was one of them. Her advanced schooling was paid for by the State of Louisiana, Anyway, the result was that Mom Mayes' "sainthood" stretched beyond Indiana University and beyond the State of Indiana.

I would often promise Mom Mayes that I would come back to see her after my graduation, after I made something of myself. She would say forlornly, "Yes, yes, I know, but you'll forget me like everyone else." I promised faithfully that I would not be like all the rest. "I will come back," I said, and I did, one day nearly a decade later. My wife, Marilyn, and I drove down to Bloomington on a bright fall day, expressly to see her. I drove up to the house with a wide grin and a present for her hidden behind my back. I knocked on the door, and a young black lady answered my ring. I asked about Mom Mayes. "Why, she's been dead more than five years now. We're the new owners now," she said proudly. I went back to my car dazed, quickly wiping away tears so my wife could not see my despair. I was like everyone else after all. I returned as promised . . . but too late! What a sad, sad day in my life.

"HANG YOURSELF, BRAVE CRILLION"

King Henry said, after the battle of Argues to his comrade at arms, Crillion, who had failed to arrive in time to help him, "Hang yourself, brave Crillion, we fought at Argues, and you were not there." Unlike Henry IV, I hold no malice toward any man who didn't bother to give me a friendly hand when I was in desperate need.

Realizing there would be few Henrys out there but lots of Crillions, I had no misconceptions about what the odds would be for my entry into commercial broadcasting. There were no footprints for blacks to follow in those days. The success I had to this point was in non-commercial broadcasting, and for station owners to give me a break held great risk for them, even if they respected my talent. I held few illusions about a black person succeeding in broadcasting when I arrived at Indiana University. My experience with the American Forces Korean Network was a good beginning, but the realities of a black person making a breakthrough in commercial broadcasting would be a profound challenge. Nevertheless, I struggled on, sure that going to college at Indiana University would enhance my career potential. I could do no more to enhance my chances for success than be prepared. I paraphrase Abraham Lincoln's statement, made nearly a hundred years earlier, "I will study and be prepared, and then my fate will be in the hands of the gods." The next person in position to help the gods was Elmer Sultzer . . . and he failed miserably. I'll have more to say about him later.

When I arrived on the Indiana University campus and enrolled in their Radio Television Broadcast Journalism school, I would be the first black person to enter that department. I had worked at radio station WAIN in Lebanon doing news and sports. Having followed that background with one year as part of the American Forces

Korean Network, I quickly became a staff announcer with the IU station, WFIU radio. I was paid too! A dollar an hour. At that time only seniors were paid, and I was a freshman. I usually worked five days a week doing an afternoon disc jockey show, playing light popular music and several classical music shows and operas. I must say they were very popular shows and I would eventually receive several awards for outstanding achievement for announcing these programs. Several of my contemporaries went on to achieve national prominence. Dick Enberg, now one of the chief sportscasters for NBC sports, and I were considered top announcers at that time. Phil Jones went on to distinguish himself with NBC news. Several others went on to be outstanding local newsmen, including my friend Ken Beckley, who anchored local news in Indianapolis.

With this exposure, I quickly became known to the chairman of the Department of Broadcasting, Elmer Sultzer. When I arrived on campus, Elmer Sultzer was in his early sixties. Among his many idiosyncrasies (he liked for the female students to sit in the front row of his class so he could look at their long legs and arms). Elmer smoked constantly the world's most putrid cigars. I never saw him without one. I think he smoked them because he thought it gave him additional stature as a department head as well as masked the fact that he looked like something freshman embalmers had abandoned in disgust. He was about five foot three and had a face like a chipmunk. His jaws were distended as though he carried a walnut in each check. His eyes shone with the same sinister glow of a werewolf. I would remember that face anywhere, no matter how much time elapsed.

"Steve," he would say on numerous occasions, "I am going to personally see that you land a good position at one of the best stations in the country. I think you possess enough talent to even begin your career on the network level." He could have done it, too, because he had numerous connections with commercial broadcasters around the country by virtue of being a full professor and department chairman of a Big Ten University broadcasting school. He would invite me and Marilyn (my wife to be) to all his personal functions at his house and to several other academic occasions. I think he just wanted to show off Marilyn's beauty to his contemporaries. It was becoming fashionable at the time to show others you were not prejudiced, and of course we were black- the token blacks. Marilyn never trusted him, and to this day just mentioning his name in her presence can evoke her strong, negative reaction.

When it came time for me to graduate, he wrote a "To Whom It May Concern" letter of introduction. That was all. It was not much help. From that day forward, I knew that if I was going to be successful in broadcasting, I would have to do so on my own and it was going to be delayed. I never for a moment thought it wouldn't happen. Unknown to me, or to them, there was the "spirit guide" at the shimmering bush, and men in Indianapolis who would give me the nudge toward success.

> Orandum est ut set mens sana in
> corpore sano . . .
> We should pray for a sound
> Mind and a sound body . . .
> Anonymous
> Roman Poet

<u>2000 years ago</u>

There is a more modern saying by Dr. Benjamin Mays that is appropriate to cite here. "A young man may die . . . but an old man must!" As I drifted into my early sixties, reasonable men would not debate the fact that I still possessed a sound mind. However, I was beginning to receive garbled signals from my body that all was not well. Age was now nipping at my heels. And running faster didn't seem to keep it from catching up with me. Middle age is a time when a man is always thinking that in a week or two, he'll feel just as good as ever. Unfortunately, that is not true.

It was March, 1994. I was on a trip to New York City, attending the conference of the Association of Blacks in Energy. New York is still the "Big Apple" and I was looking forward to the trip, ignoring the fact that I had been experiencing occasional sharp pains in the lower quadrant of my right side. It would last for a little while and then disappear. "No matter," I thought, "The pains are too far from my heart to kill me." But, now that I was getting older, I no longer took comfort in this rationale.

My company physical examination was coming up in less than a month and I would be sure to advise my doctor of the pain. For those unfamiliar with company physical exams, let me say two things. First, they are extremely thorough. X-rays, EEG'S, EKG'S, and volumes of blood are taken for examination. Various probings and thrusts are done to every orifice one has. Second, the employee must sign a statement to release all of the results to the company's chief executive officer. If anything major is found, that person is automatically out of the race for serious vertical moves within the organization.

Over the course of 30 years in management I have had these yearly exams, and nothing unusual or scary had surfaced. I would get the usual advice like, "Stop smoking." "Stop drinking." "Get vigorous exercise for an hour, at least three times a week." "Watch your blood pressure and fat intake." The various doctors would always end their two-page narratives by saying something like, "It was a pleasure meeting with Mr. Scott. I have detected nothing in his overall physical condition that would give cause for alarm."

When I would receive my copy of the report, I would always go directly to the second page, last paragraph to see if these comforting words were there. After all, the annual report is akin to a new lease on life after a year of enduring life's struggles and indulging in a few of its excesses. This time in addition to other signs of foreboding that I had tried to minimize, I knew that I was in trouble for that final reassuring paragraph was not there. Instead the report ended with, "I suggest strongly that Steve undergo a colonoscopy to determine if there are any signs of blockage in the colon." He gave me the name of another doctor to see. I went.

After pulling and tugging, and terse verbal inquiry, the new doctor, an internist, agreed with the first doctor: " I suspect a problem in your lower colon. I want you to see a gastroenterologist right away." His voice had the sound of regret. I endured, nay, survived a colonoscopy; then this new doctor, after reviewing the x-ray results, called me the next day, indicating that he wanted to see me right away. I went to see him.

For the first time, I really noticed this doctor. He had cold-looking hands, but a soft voice, a gentle manner, and a wonderful attitude. He flashed a smile that could easily hide the real truth about what lay ahead for me. "You have a large polyp in your lower intestine. It will have to be excised," he said, avoiding any eye contact. He had the temerity to show me color photos he had taken of it. Yuck! But, the name "polyp" did have a certain crass elegance that suited what I was looking at. The picture reminded me of a "chuck hole" which Indiana highways are noted for following the spring thaws.

"I can give you the name of a fine surgeon, one of the best surgeons in the city. He wrote down the name of the surgeon: Dr. Frank Lloyd, Jr. What a coincidence, I knew him. In fact, his father, a prominent black pediatrician and entrepreneur, had delivered my son, Steve, Jr. Dr. Lloyd, Sr. was also my boss when I was the President and General Manager of his radio station, WTLC-FM Radio.

Over the next few days, I became reacquainted with young Dr. Frank Lloyd, Jr., who had been in undergraduate school when I first met him. I looked closely at this bright young doctor, the one who would undertake to make my "plumbing " operable again. Dr. Lloyd was in his early forties, with medium height and the athletic build of a tennis player. He was very handsome with bronze skin and strong facial features masked by large designer glasses. He moved quickly and assuredly, appearing and disappearing magically from the examining room. His cherubic smile and childlike laugh were perpetual and very reassuring. Dr. Lloyd's medical credentials were impeccable. He earned his undergraduate degree from DePauw University and his medical degree at Indiana University School of Medicine. He completed his general surgery residency at Howard University. He received a surgical oncology fellowship, which included research at Roswell Park Memorial Institute in Buffalo, New York. With a precise, staccato voice he outlined the procedure he would follow. "Steve, " he said, his tone inspiring extreme confidence, "We will excise the polyp area and rejoin the two sections" Somehow, I remembered what Chairman Mao said about Chinese dissidents. "If poisonous weeds are not removed, scented flowers cannot grow." Now why did I let such a distasteful thought like that creep into this serious consultation.

MY voice sounding like a dying quail, I asked, "How long will I be in the hospital and what is the expected recovery time?" I was hoping all the while for a one week's recuperating period. Dr. Lloyd continued, "You will be uncomfortable for a few days during your ten to twelve days at the hospital, but in three or four weeks you will be playing golf and back to work again." My soul did an eclipse. Having never been really sick, not even with headaches, I felt that this was now shaping up to be a real character builder. I was face to face with the undeniable truth that all men must face sooner of later. I was mortal!

Some thoughts added to my consternation. First, medicine has changed greatly since I was young. In the early days, one or two doctors treated the "whole" patient. A general practitioner knew anatomy! All of my brothers and sisters were delivered at home by our family physician, Doctor Kern. He even performed minor surgery. Each of his patients was ministered to in a "holistic" manner. As you may recall from reading back at the beginning of this chapter, I had already been seen by several doctors and had not ever been treated. Not even with a proverbial aspirin.

I guess I'm particularly prejudiced against "specialists." When you're sent to them, they don't know you and you don't know them. They glance with glazed eyes at a chart of the small territory of your afflicted carcass of which they have some knowledge and don't seem to know or care what has untangled somewhere else. This list of body parts and specialists to treat them is not meant to be all-inclusive, but it will give some idea of what a patient will encounter when something goes wrong.

The brain doctor knows the brain.

The optometrist doctor knows the eyes.

The ear, nose and throat doctor knows otolaryngology of those three orifices.

The orthopedic doctor knows the bones.

The allergist doctor knows what causes viscous material to come through the head and nose orifices.

The pulmonary doctor knows the lungs.

The internist doctor knows the ulcers and other viscera in the mid- section.

The gastroenterology doctor knows the food plumbing.

The urinary doctor knows his part of the plumbing apparatus.

The kidney doctor knows nothing north or south of anything but the kidneys.

Many doctors know nothing about the patient's psyche that holds everything together. That job is left up to the psychologist and psychiatrist.

The second point I want to make involves the risk of dealing with any of them. One should always discuss the risks involved with either ingesting anything, preparing for the surgeon's knife, or the eventual, welcoming kiss of anesthesia.

A group of psychologists who specialized in decision making ran a bunch of tests to see if doctors used their reference statistics correctly. Several groups of doctors were presented with the exact same statistics in totally opposite ways. One group was told that 10 of 100 patients would die of surgery. The other group was told that 90 of 100 would live. Now, that is saying exactly the same thing. Right? It is just said in a different fashion. It shouldn't have had much effect on their answers, Right? Wrong! Dead Wrong! Faced with the negative slant, they chose positively, opting for surgery. In fact, TWICE as many doctors in the second group chose surgery than those in the first.

Now, these doctors were experts in their respective fields. The test was run at Harvard Medical Center for Gods sake! That's really scary, isn't it? Harvard doctors, experts in their fields, manipulated not by statistics, but by perceptions. Think what psychologists or any medical practitioner could do to you and me under those circumstances. If you are presented with risk statistics, and you probably will be one day, stop. Analyze and see if you can spot the flaw, even if there isn't one. Fortunately, for me I had all of the confidence in the world in my surgeon and it was well entrusted.

I had a little chat with my son, advising him that it might be best if he would go to the hospital with his mother and me. I told him frankly that this was going to be a real bummer for me. For the first time, he would see his father down for the count. Not only would I not be a pretty sight following the operation, but they might find cancer in the colon, and I didn't know how his mother would react. I told him I wasn't afraid, and asked him to keep a stiff upper lip. He was a jewel and offered all of the correct sentiments one could expect from a son.

My son and daughter-in-law, Julie Perkins Scott, had given me a most wonderful Christmas present the Christmas past. A cap and sweater embroidered with the words "Lebanon Fighting Tigers," in black and gold no less, my old high school colors! They had never seen me wear them, probably because I had not worn them before. I was saving them for some inexplicable reason. I now had the perfect reason to wear them. Marilyn and I were sitting in the hospital waiting room, having just finished the mountain of paper work necessary for my star performance. As Steve, Jr. and my daughter, Wendy, sauntered into the huge waiting room packed with patients, they looked around nervously trying to spot their father. Eventually they spotted me in my "unrecognizable" garb. A muffled laugh of glee erupted from them as they hurled the biggest grins I had ever seen. My intentional act to break the solemn and turgid atmosphere of the moment had worked! I was now ready to meet my fate with a grin of my own.

I had nearly forgotten how cold it is in an operating room. I had been in one before for optional surgeries. That chill gets my attention, if nothing else does. I joked with the anesthesiologist as he placed a syringe in my arm. It would be the last joking I would do for weeks.

I heard a thin voice speaking from everywhere and nowhere. Where was it coming from? It sounded like a blur of mighty wings. One should pray he never hears sounds like that in his life. It stirred my very soul. I opened my eyes to shadows and shapes of things that seemed unreal. "Where am I?" The voice was the nurse speaking. She repeated again and again. "Steve, you're in the recovery room. It's all over! You did fine! Everything is going to be okay!" She seemed to be speaking through frozen lips. I fought back screams and sighs. I must be paralyzed, I thought. I knew that almost immediately. I opened and closed my eyes again, flicking them left and right, because my head wouldn't move. I licked my dry lips. The paralysis didn't bother me and it lasted less than a minute. I felt dreamy and removed from myself, content to just lie there in bed, or wherever I was, and let events take place around me. There was a distant humming sound. It was coming from an array of gadgetry over my head. Bags of clear and cloudy liquids streamed from them into my arms. I tried again to turn my head. This time I could move it. I was alive! Or, as Descartes put it, " I think therefore I am." This elated feeling would not last long, but I didn't know it then.

Young Dr. Lloyd came in for a little post-op chat. " You've been one of my best patients. Guess what?"I dared not ask. "No cancer!" he said. "By the way, while I was there, I removed your appendix too. Someday something else may go wrong in the area, but it won't be appendicitis. Get some rest. I'll see you later today. I'm going to talk to your wife and children now." He seemed to de-materialize through the door.

The next thing I knew I awakened in my room with those things hanging, and protruding, hooked up, somehow to me. I was sweating and I wanted to retch. I did, but nothing came of the effort. I retched again. Marilyn appeared at my side. She looked beautiful, but worried. I was worried too because nothing in my body worked. For three days I could do nothing. I woke up. I slept. Woke up. I slept some more. Each time I would awaken, there were Marilyn's smiling eyes locked on mine, as if she were trying to absorb some of the pain. I couldn't have been a pretty sight. This went on for three or four more days. Nurses came and went, pulling here, tugging there, all the while flashing smiles like shattered glass.

Finally, after a few more days, I decided I needed to walk. So, with the help of angelic nurses, I took my first tentative steps down a long hall, bent in an L-shape and carrying a small pillow clutched to my mid-section to ward off scrambling things within. I had not eaten anything for about seven days. The food that they would bring me a mountain goat wouldn't eat, and neither did I. Gradually though, I would down a little broth or Jell-O, then retch. The problem seemed to be the food. It couldn't make up its mind which way it wanted to go, north or south.

Somehow, after the first week, I started to feel a little better and the meager food I was able to eat decided it knew the proper way to exit. Then I made a terrible mistake. On one trip to the "throne" I decided to look at the mirror!

I sucked my lips and slowly stared into the mirror. I shouldn't have done it. I saw my shadowy reflection. A brown ghost stared back. I felt a deep chill when I saw the obvious major weight loss in my face. I looked like death eating a cracker, or a person stranded on a barren island in the Pacific for thirty days without a bite to eat. My soul's equilibrium shattered. I looked more closely at my image in the mirror, grimacing at the flaccid bones protruding through my face. I said something to whatever was staring back at me in the mirror, but it sounded like a reptilian hiss. YUCK!

I told the doctor I wanted to go home. And after two more days, he let me. But, devishly, I had one last trump card to play on fate and my family. I wanted to demonstrate to them I was still a heroic figure, an icon of courage and strength. I want to stop on the way home at Shapiro's delicatessen for a corned beef sandwich.

"You must be kidding, Pop," Steve Jr. said with a look of incredulity.

"I want a corned beef sandwich," I said, trying to summon forth my best commanding voice.

"Okay! Okay!" Steve, Jr. said. "A sandwich from Shapiro's it is. I'll just run in and get it for you and we'll be on our way home."

"No!" I said, ignoring his plea. "I'll go inside, sit at a table and eat it." I moaned beneath my breath.

I guess I was still in "La La" land by virtue of all the codeine and the other pain killers I had taken in the hospital. At any rate, I sat down at the table. The sandwich came and I began to warily crunch away. Suddenly, without warning, my protoplasm crashed! The knurled, bony hand of nausea was reaching out for me. I think it was the smell of all the different foods in the restaurant that did me in. But, I played it cool, simply saying. "Well, uh, guys, I think I will wrap the remainder of the sandwich and leave now. Very quickly if you will, please." Soon it was all over the office that I had gone immediately from a hospital bed to a restaurant for lunch. I smile deep down whenever the story is repeated to me.

I quickly mended at home under the watchful eye of my wife, the children and "Prissy" our coal black cocker spaniel. It was gratifying to know that my friends and associates at work cared enough to send plants, flowers and cards to wish me well and a speedy recovery. Fortune also smiled on me in that summer was coming on fast. It was now early May. I could spend many hours on the patio, reading and soaking up the sun's healing rays. But nothing simple and mundane happens to me. I had to endure one more indignity.

One bright sunny afternoon as I reclined on my chaise lounge on the patio, listening to the rustle of surrounding cotton wood trees, a very strange thing happened. I became aware that my little animal friends, the squirrels, rabbits and cardinals were not coming around as usual. I must have looked a sight. Even a huge black crow flew near, gave an ominous croak of regret and flew off in disdain. But no matter, life was starting to feel good again. Most important of all, I was getting comfortable with the fact my hegira would continue, even with the profound knowledge that I was no longer immortal. Wasn't it that sound philosopher Nietzsche who said, "One has to pay dearly for immortality; one has to die several times while one is still alive."

ME AND MY MENTORS

Dr. Carl Godeski was a tall, angular, brilliant scientist at Eli Lilly Company in Indianapolis. Marilyn said he looked like Robert Culp the actor in the old "I Spy" tv series. Carl and several of his associates started an FM radio station with the call letters WAIN. "The Lively Arts Station," it was called. Carl had convinced his associates that the City of Indianapolis needed a cultural arts' station to fill the vacuum of mediocre radio fare that currently existed. With a shoestring budget they obtained a Federal Communication Commission radio license, pledging to bring listeners classical music, jazz, opera and discussion programs.

For several years Carl, in his spare time, had been the disc jockey of a three-hour jazz program. The program was called "Jazz Flight-105." It was a very clever format. The opening and close of the program had the signature sound of a passenger jet taking off and landing with carefully scripted chatter of a pilot talking to the tower as the plane began its taxi and rolled down the runway. During this period I had been a regular listener to his show and to WAIN for some time, along with many other firm jazz devotees in Indianapolis.

At this juncture in my working career, I was working at the Marion County Welfare Department, as Director of the Food Stamp Program. Prior to that position I had been a caseworker and then casework supervisor. These were my first jobs right out of college. Since Elmer Sultzer was not able to use his prestige to assist me in finding a job, I took the first job available to me. The year was 1965. One day I wrote a letter to Carl and included an audition tape of a dis- jockey program I produced at Indiana University. Carl called me right away and asked that I meet with him while he was doing his broadcast.

That evening I drove to the old Dearborn Hotel, where the station was located, took a creaky old elevator to the third floor, and walked right into the station, since it occupied all the floor space. Carl was the only person there, and when he saw me, and realized that I was black, I noticed his eyes shrivel down to tiny Mongolian slits. I'm sure he thought to himself, "My God, this man is black." But his demeanor quickly changed. With his melodious voice, deep and resonant, suppressing his surprise, a light bouncy, "Hi, I'm Carl Godeski, come in." was the next thing I heard. He clucked several times to himself and continued to smile as he motioned for me to sit next to him while he gave a station break, read a commercial, and introduced the next two jazz records. All that done, he closed the microphone and with another wide grin of pride at what he had just done he said only, "It's a pleasure to meet you." We chatted. What happened next was truly amazing. "You're hired," he said. "I want you to do my show, and you start tonight." I could hardly believe that this was the man who owned the station. He showed me the record library, told me to pull twenty albums. He also showed me how to read the transmitter and sign the broadcast log, and how to turn out the lights. Then he left, telling me with another wide grin, "I'll call you when I get home." Can you believe that? That's all it took. Serendipity is wonderful. So are "shimmering bushes." Here were two people needing a break. Carl needed one and I really needed one. The "burning bush" was whispering again to me through my earphones. Carl later sold his radio station and moved to Florida in the 1980s. I would one day be its general manager, when the station became WTLC-FM in 1972 under the ownership of Frank Lloyd and Associates. Carl and his wife, Joyce [now deceased] would remain fast friends of Marilyn and me until his retirement.

Jerry Chapman, was station manager and Eldon Campbell, vice president and general manager of WFBM-TV AM & FM. Eldon Campbell had the appearance of a born leader, although he reminded me of a Ted Grant of

"The Mary Tyler Moore Show." Eldon had a little more hair, which was nearly silver. He talked in a staccato, Baritone voice. His eyes were a penetrating ice blue and he never spoke idly. When he did speak, his every utterance was one of brilliance. Everyone listened in reverence and awe. Time had left deep fissures on his brows. His cheeks were sunken, but his eyes, and the bound in his step, retained the full cunning of a youthful athlete. His left-hand man was Jerry Chapman.

Jerry was the antithesis of Eldon. He was extremely handsome and had the greatest baritone voice any broadcast announcer would love to emulate. As a matter of fact, Jerry had been my idol when I was in high school. Jerry, did a two-hour show at noon called "Lunch Time Melodies." The time period was 1951 and I had just won 3rd place in the State in broadcast announcing, and was working at the local radio station in Lebanon, WINL. I had asked my dad to take me to Indianapolis so I could meet with Jerry Chapman. You will recall that he was one of the judges of the contest. Dad was anxious to assist me in any way he could. I was very nervous that day; I had knots in my stomach all during the drive to Indianapolis. I never let it show, however, and found Jerry to be very cordial. He seemed genuinely interested in me and never appeared to be put off by the fact that I was a black kid from a little town. He even went out of his way to introduce me to Tom Carnegie, one of the elder statesmen in sports broadcasting in Indianapolis. Tom, of course, achieved acclaim for his announcing of the 500-Mile Race time trials. Everyone knew his name. I was shocked to see that Tom was physically handicapped in the lower extremities, but his strong over the air voice belied any such affliction. Little did any of us know that within a decade our lives would entwine again, professionally, mainly due to Eldon and Jerry.

During the 60's period life seemed especially good for Marilyn and me. My wife was a master teacher enjoying her position. God was good. Life was good, and I felt I was good at my job as Director of the Marion County Food Stamp Division. I was also having a great time doing the disc jockey program for WAIV-FM. One of my friends at WAIV, Dave Scott, had moved on to WFBM-FM radio. He was now Program Director for the station, reporting to Jerry Chapman. One day I received a call from Dave. He asked me if I would like to come over to WFBM-AM-FM and do the same kind of show I was doing for WAIV-FM. My heart did a total eclipse; I had a brief spell of shortness of breath and sweat began to rush from every pore. I was finally getting a big break! I am sure the "burning bush" of long ago began to shimmer. "YES!!!" I glowed. I was going to work for my dream station.

The Saturday night program for WFBM-FM was called the "Nite Hawk" show. I loved it. Listeners must have as well, because I received many calls and letters through the years. Listeners told me they enjoyed the jazz and vocal mixtures I served up every Saturday night. In 1967, I received another call at my office at the Food Stamp Division. This one was from Jerry Chapman offering me a full-time position with WFBM-TV and WFBM-AM & FM as Manager of Public Affairs and License Renewal. He asked me to think it over. I did. Marilyn and I discussed my current career and where it might lead. We explored the opportunities at WFBM-TV-AM/FM and the broadcasting career for which I had trained and aspired. In reality, there really wasn't much to be discussed, but I felt I had to play hard to get. Jerry was out of town in New York at <u>Time</u>, Inc. headquarters when I received another phone call from him. "How are you coming along with your decision, Steve?" he asked. "Are there any further questions I might be able to answer for you?"

"No," I said.

"Well, then, I'll talk to you about salary when I return to Indianapolis. Again, I hope you'll decide to join us." I did! My years at WFBM were extraordinarily happy ones for me. I was now in my chosen career.

Jerry Chapman and I became inseparable friends. A great deal of jealousy prevailed among fellow employees at the station, but everyone tried to hide these feelings, of course. Jerry was my mentor and I enjoyed or friendship (shame on me). I reported directly to him. Although it was never stated by Eldon Campbell, the Chief Executive Officer, Jerry Chapman was to be his hand picked successor. Chapman was the most laid back senior executive I ever met. He delegated nearly everything of consequence. Jerry loved life and was fun to be around. He and his wife, Susan, were made for each other. Sue liked me too, so that didn't hurt my favored personal status either. We had many delightful dinners at the Chapman home. Both Jerry and Susan liked everything to be perfect when they interacted with others. The delicious food, the muted lighting in the dining room, dinner setting at the table, all commonplace. Jerry's infinite jokes and hilarious stories all made for delightful evenings at their home.

He, especially enjoyed telling the "bonus buy" story when we both decided to buy our Thanksgiving turkeys at McFarland Farms Poultry Wholesale House. One chilly November day, Jerry stopped by my office with his usual, "Hey Steve, let's go to lunch. Then I want to do some shopping for my Thanksgiving turkey." He showed me an advertisement in the newspaper announcing tremendous holiday savings on turkeys that were slightly different. "Sure, that's fine," I said, thinking to myself that there was probably less to this than meets the eye. Away we went. When we arrived at McFarland Farms, we were both astonished to see what "extra pieces" meant. These were deformed, mutant turkeys! Some had extra long necks, I mean as much as six inches longer, some had three legs, four legs, five legs, it was incredible. Jerry bought a five legged turkey and urged me to do the same. "Hey Steve, just think of the extra drumsticks you will have, Marilyn will love it," he said.

"Not on your life Jerry," I said, "I can see it all now, I bring this damn turkey home. Marilyn opens the package and faints dead away – or she goes along with the charade, cooks the turkey, brings it to the table, unwraps the aluminum foil, places it on the serving platter in front of the dinner guests, and the women faint, the men grow weak in the knees, and my Thanksgiving dinner is ruined. No thanks, you buy the turkey and take it home to Susan." He did, and she nearly died laughing when she saw it, cooked it, and their guests got just the results I had predicted. What a guy, Jerry Chapman.

He eventually did succeed Eldon Campbell when Eldon retired to seek other business opportunities. Regrettably, Susan died unexpectedly in the prime of her life. Jerry died a few years later, also unexpectedly, I think from a broken heart at the loss of Susan. I will always be grateful to Jerry for easing my entry into broadcasting and teaching me a management style that was easygoing in nature. His style became pretty much my own through the later years. Believe in those around you. Believe that everyone can make a contribution to the team. No one comes to work to do a poor job, intentionally. These are great lessons just catching on in today's corporate world. But remember this period was decades earlier. Eldon and Jerry were men ahead of their time.

A VISIT FROM CASPER

. . . BUT, NOT THE GHOST

I was always very nervous prior to and during on-camera TV work; however, it never seemed to show in my voice or my physical appearance. It is incongruous that camera fright would be the case, particularly with all the experience I had gained over the years.

The year 1968 was a tumultuous year for the media. Most television stations were trying hard to change some of their old approaches programmatically to documentaries, news and talk shows. Most of these shows had been "talking head" programs of little substance. But slowly, things began to change. Many stations showed a strong commitment to aid the nation through its healing process by getting people to talk to one another and by raising important matters for debate, matters such as how to deal with the high unemployment rates for poor people and black people. There were some critical issues facing the nation. It did not go unnoticed by the proletariat or by the East coast powers that people became less militant if they were working and providing for their families. Surprise! Surprise!

In any event, in my position as Manager of Public Relations for WFBM-TV and radio, I became aware of a very successful innovative program called Job Fair aired by a major Chicago television station. I convinced Eldon Campbell, that our station could make a real contribution to the community and to those people struggling to find work if we aired a similar program. The basic format of the program called for a host to interview prospective job seekers, and determine their qualifications, ambitions and in some general information about them. The host usually also had guests from the Indiana Employment Security office who would describe jobs that employers had registered with their department. When job seekers were successful in finding a job, the host would prerecord interviews with them on the job site. Numbers were flashed on the screen during the half hour show, affording employers the opportunity to call in and ask for interviews with specific job seekers appearing on TV. I thought it was a great idea!

Eldon Campbell thought it was too and quickly endorsed the program, with one caveat. He insisted that I do it. This simple decision does not sound like much today, but it was precedent-setting then. There were no blacks on TV, except those that were heading for the lock-up. Not only would I host the show, but I was to have full control over its production and direction. In other words, I was to be the producer of the show. I called it "Job Line." Having worked most of my life, I had first-hand knowledge of what it meant to be working. Self-worth, ego enhancement and pride are just a few of the virtues that go hand-in-hand with a good work ethic. I also had a basic conviction that, given the opportunity, most men, black or white, would rather work. I saw an interesting documentary about the same time our show was being considered. It was a heart wrenching 30 - minute mini-documentary, which someone had sent to WFBM from one of our sister stations in California on what it was like for a black man to be going on a job search. It was called "The Sandclock Day." It had such an impact on me when I previewed it that I insisted that the program manager air it, which he did.

The story begins on a typically gorgeous day in Los Angeles, California. The camera captures a lower middle class black family as the family members begin their day. The home furnishings are spartan but neat. Eggs are sizzling in the frying pan, coffee brewing in a coffee pot. Viewers can almost smell the heavenly aroma of both. Then they see a stocky, overweight but handsome black man pulling on his tie as he bounds down the stairs. Smiling broadly, he kisses his wife and two children. Today he is seeking employment and has an interview at 8:00

a.m. in downtown Los Angeles. We see the clock – it is 6:30 a.m. He announces to the family that today is a very important day, his "Sandclock Day." He will know shortly whether or not he gets a job that will mean so much to his family. One gets a sense that he has a great deal of confidence and expects to get the position. His wife continues to look at him adoringly and with assurances that he will be successful. Something, however doesn't seem right. Tension seems to lie just below the light, homey atmosphere. Our hero is running late. He wolfs down several mouthfuls of the steaming hot breakfast and grabs for his coat. He gives a last minute stern lecture to one of his sons who is not eating his breakfast (more time is lost)! We watch him running to the bus stop–he has no car. The bus is late, fifteen minutes late! As the bus finally appears, approaching in the distance, the camera gives us a glimpse at what our hero cannot see: the bus is full! It passes our hero by. Now another fifteen minutes is lost before the next bus arrives. He is now in deep trouble and knows it. We know it too! He pulls a handkerchief from his pocket to wipe sweat that now is penetrating his eyes. He looks frantically at his watch – 7:40 a.m. Traffic is getting heavier and heavier and passenger pick-ups increase. Our hero is going to be late for his appointment.

The bus stops in front of a huge skyscraper that looks formidable and unfriendly. Our hero now races up to the entrance. One now worries about his health, as he is out of breath, panting furiously and perspiring profusely. There are several banks of elevators indicating different floors. Our hero is confused about which one to take, more out of anxiety than reasoning. He asks a white receptionist where the elevators are for Suite 907. The lady is casually adjusting her makeup and all but ignores him. Being black can make one invisible. He is beside himself as she now casually pours herself a cup of coffee and waves across the room at her associates as they begin their early morning rituals at work.

Our hero cannot believe his misfortune and neither can the viewer. "When is someone going to help this man?" we say to ourselves. Finally he has been given the directions to his destination. But first he must catch the elevator to the 9th floor. The elevator never seems to get there. We see the lights, indicating the floor numbers move like molasses as the elevator reaches the lobby floor. The time is now 8:30 a.m. The elevator is full and takes considerable time to empty. When it does, there are too many people, all white, waiting to get on. They muscle their way past him. The elevator door closes. He must wait for another one. Finally the elevator arrives. Our hero knows, and we know by the forlorn look on his face, that things have taken every possible turn for the worst for him. The swirl of circumstances and chain of events, all out of his control, is defeating him. The camera does a flashback and we see his lovely wife pacing back and forth over her kitchen floor with her fingers crossed and a look of prayerful hope etched on her face.

Our hero arrives at Suite 907 and approaches the receptionist at full gait, bumping into a white man who has a mysterious smile on his face. Our hero grumbles. He asks to see the employment director. She motions him to the door. He knocks and is told to enter. Our hero is now forty minutes late. The employment director looks quizzically at his watch and says to our hero that he is late. Our hero, totally exasperated at what has happened to him, tries to recount his problems to the director. It falls on deaf ears. "I'm terribly sorry," he tells him. The job was just given to another applicant, minutes ago. He just left, you must have run into him in the hall. Our hero is heartbroken and so are we as viewers. It was our hero's "Sandclock Day" and he was destroyed – destroyed primarily by events, the system, if you will, that was not sensitive to difficulties urban job seekers must face, just to get to a potential job. Sure, he could have gotten up earlier. Sure, he could have made a trial run prior to the day's appointment. There are plenty of what ifs.

Our hero was last seen trudging crestfallen down the street, void of hope, depressed and angry. The sand had gone out of his hour glass. Hundreds of viewers called the station to express the fact that they were very moved by the show. It opened many viewers' eyes to the difficulties many of the poor experience just getting to a job. Transportation is indeed a critical impediment for job seekers even today, some thirty years after the airing of the show, especially when so many good jobs are in the suburbs and one must either have a car or use public transportation.

One of my objectives for "Job Line" was to keep the show at a highly professional level, thus avoiding all appearances of a "slave auction." This, I believe, we were able to do. We were never at a loss for prospective job applicants to come on the show and discuss their talents. I made it a constant theme that prospective employers need to understand that many problems job seekers have are non-existent for those more fortunate. I was extremely pleased that through the efforts of "Job Line" hundreds of people, black and white, were able to find employment, and expressed their thanks to the station for being courageous enough to air the program and to use a black man as host.

My first show from a personal standpoint was a real adventure. I became painfully aware of just how hot it gets under the glare of the TV lights. The compounded anxiety of my first television appearance proved to be much more than I had bargained for. Many, many times I had done "off camera" announcing and narrative work, but being in front of the camera was another affair entirely. When the actual time arrived for the show to begin, I was a basket case. Inwardly my heart began to pound as the director pointed a bony finger toward me to begin. I had a hard time focusing on the hand signals being given to me and keeping a steady stream of conversation going with the guest. Sweat began to stream down from my forehead, into my eyes. The show was to be thirty minutes long, and there was no turning back. Everything went well, as I interviewed three guests. Somehow, I must have appeared calm to them because all three talked amiably with me and the time passed quickly. Suddenly, as the show wound down, the TV camera man began to give me closing signals. Most I didn't recognize, but there was one I did from my days in radio. The most dreaded signal of all – the S-T-R-E-T-C-H signal, a slow pulling apart of the hands. A minute and a half, he signaled when I thought I was through. What was I to do now? I had already thanked the guests for coming on the show and had completed most of the closing remarks. More stretch signals were given, including the ad-lib signal. I continued to talk about something or other and then arbitrarily just ended, thirty seconds short! So much for my introduction to television.

The show, nevertheless, was an instant success. During the course of the week all three guests had been granted job interviews. I felt really good and much of the dread had disappeared by the following week when the next show was to be aired.

There was plenty of curiosity in the TV viewing area about this young black man on TV. Since there had never been a black TV host on a local network station in the state of Indiana before. I was pleased at the white viewer reaction most of which was favorable. Was a star born? Not really – in my eyes, I knew that it was something I had trained for over the years. (Not on-air camera work though). Furthermore, I was really surprised by the warm wishes that blacks in the city accorded me when I went out in public. Many called my home to say how proud they were to see a talented black man on TV, instead of the usual visual images of blacks committing mayhem on the nightly news. I loved the accolades, but I knew that many people were responsible for my being there, particularly blacks in the South who had endured so many indignities and even death to make a better day and life for those who would come down the path at a later time and place.

In the second year of the program's existence, I was notified that the show, and I, as its host, had received the prestigious "Casper Award" for broadcast excellence. I was staggered! The award was to be presented at a gala community program and dinner. I was to receive $250.00 and a large, gorgeous plaque. The Casper Award has an interesting history.

The Community Service Council, a large human service organization, bewailed callous indifference from the community as well as negative attitudes regarding the problems of the people whom the human service agencies were attempting to help. It was felt that there needed to be a much better public interpretation and much more involvement by the community services in solving these problems.

One board member of the organization, Miss Mary Houk, then Director of Indiana University Division of Social Service, had a suggestion. Why not an awards program to recognize those outstanding efforts where news and communications media aggressively or forcefully tackled community problems? Such an awards program might first encourage community agencies to make a substantial effort to interpret services or problems on a year-round basis. The board appointed a committee representing the three local newspapers, other media, and community leaders to tailor this awards program. The program was restructured several times in the early years but it was not until 1961, when advertising executive George A. Saas was serving as chairman, that discussion moved to giving the program a better name and identity. Someone suggested it be along the lines of the Oscar-Tony-Emmy Awards . . . a "CASPER," spelling out Community Appreciation for Service in Public Enlightenment and Relations, plus a plaque created by noted sculptor Adolph Wolter, symbolizing the role of communications media in Indianapolis and surrounding communities. It was regarded as an award not to be "passed around" for the sake of touching every base just to make the media happy. It must be earned with quantifiable results required. CASPER is well known locally, but also it has been pictured and written up in many national publications, several times in full page color ads, giving credence to the esteem in which it is held by recipients. Donna Shea, consultant for years for the CASPER, has been an icon. She monitors strict adherence to policy detail. Her considerate attention to detail and her zealous production of the integrity of the award has kept it free from biased selection. Winning the "CASPER" was for me another morsel from life's bountiful table. I devoured it greedily and it tasted like a just-ripe melon!

IN THE LAND OF THE LOTUS EATERS

One spring day in 1968, an ordinary day which was a rare occurrence in broadcasting, Eldon Campbell suddenly appeared in my office. He had a dark, quizzical look on his face, a look that would indicate I had done something wrong and that ordinary day was about to become disagreeable. Then without warning, he broke out in a wide grin. "Steve, I want you to go to New York with me next week. I need to discuss some things with our owners. Then we will attend a three-day conference of the National Association of Broadcasters in Washington, D.C. We'll stay at the New York Hilton and then go to the Shoreham Hotel in Washington. Normally, about 1,500 broadcasters from across the United States attend the conference. On the final evening we will attend an elegant dinner and hear an address by President Nixon. By the way, we'll have dinner the first day in New York with Mr. Andrew Heiskell and Mr. Berry Zorthian." To say the least, my wonderment and perplexity grew to the point where my throat became as thick as cotton. I stared at him balefully, stalling for time to let the cotton balls in my throat clear.

Time Inc., with headquarters on the Avenue of the Americas in New York City, was the owner of WFBM-TV and WFBM AM and FM radio stations in Indianapolis. They also owned six other radio and TV stations across the country. But, WFBM-TV was considered the "Flagship" of all of the station properties. There was little doubt that this was due to the excellent leadership of Eldon. During this period, Time magazine was the most venerable of all the weekly magazines. Its chairman and chief executive officer was Andrew Heiskel. The broadcast properties were managed by Barry Zorthian. I was to be in their company. "Little ole me" from Pearl Street.

"Sure, Eldon," I said, trying not to appear nonplused about this wonderful invitation. This was not a powerful

349

answer from a communicator, but I was taken aback by it all. The following week we embarked on a marvelous flight to New York City. The skies were clear and I could see beautiful land forms of Ohio and Pennsylvania far below. My eyes stayed plastered to the plane window the entire trip. Suddenly the concrete buildings of New York stretched up to meet me. We landed at La Guardia Airport and headed to the New York Hilton. After more than a decade, I was back in New York, walking the broad expanse of the Avenue of the Americas.

The city had changed little during the intervening years. There was still the crush of people coming and going, seemingly without destination. It is like watching an ant colony at work. Beautiful young women fashionably dressed in dazzling colors of neon red and oranges, fuchsias, lime greens, golds and silvers. Was this penchant for loud colors an attempt to draw attention to lost egos? Perhaps an attempt to say, "Hey! Look at me! I am somebody among all of the teeming masses." The concrete wall of buildings leaning over and threatening any timid interloper. The city is so alive! Vendors hawked food from push carts. A thin white lady, in a hippy dress, strummed a guitar while her partner beat a drum. A large hat sat in front of them for collecting money from any grateful or benevolent passerby. I dutifully tossed three quarters into the hat. The drummer flashed a stained- tooth grin in my direction.

That night at the top of the Time building, I ate a wonderful filet mignon steak dinner with the giants Andrew, Berry and Eldon. Andrew Heiskel was a tall, immaculately dressed man with Eastern European features. As it turned out he was a very likeable person who spoke fluently of his vision of where he wanted Eldon to take the station over the next twelve months.

Barry Zorthian was a portly man with an olive complexion. I believe his heritage was Armenian. He discussed current and future revenue expectations. Eldon's favorable prognosis of these subjects brought

350

smiles of delight to their faces. Then the two moguls turned to me.

I shuddered quietly as they asked me about the progress I was making on getting the station's license renewed. I said something like, "The integrity and viewer loyalty to the station, under Eldon's leadership is exemplary. No serious challenge to the FCC renewal process is evident. Eldon recognizes that the station's highest priority, next to profitability, is its active role in insuring a favorable quality of life for the community. This means an active employee volunteer presence in the community. It should be noted that our news staff is motivated to maintain the highest standards of integrity and strict allegiance to the highest precepts of the journalistic fraternity." These comments appeared to impress them, as their heads bowed as one in general accord. As a matter of fact, I received the same smiles of satisfaction that Eldon did.

More drinks and cigars were passed around the table as my eyes fixed in wonderment on the gold leaf mahogany box in which the waiters presented cigars. They wore dapper tuxedos and spoke with a French accent. My mind drifted into solemn reverie, back to Ulen Country Club, where my dad had been a head waiter and my first attempt to be a waiter turned out to be such a disaster. Somehow I believe that the point Eldon wanted me to experience was to witness the opulence and splendid atmosphere of businessmen conducting their affairs in the "Land of the Giants."

I smiled with contentment as I leaned back in a heavily upholstered dinner chair, blowing blue cigar smoke in lazy circles in the air. "Well, kid," I said to myself. "You've finally made it. Mighty is the magic of the white man." I was wrong, of course. The following day we flew down to Washington, D.C. where we would interact with the giants of the fourth estate, the National Association of Broadcasters.

The Shoreham Hotel was like my hometown, with a roof over it: huge! Sitting on acres of land, with trees, shrubs, and flower beds, this mammoth greystone hotel attracted the greatest of conventions. I felt totally lost within its confines. Eldon and I attended several "breakout sessions" that, quite frankly, were boring. Broadcasting, at the time, had few real problems. They were "cash cow" machines, producing money beyond dreams.

The meeting boasted some fifteen hundred people from across the United States, who gathered together to congratulate each other on their unbridled success. I was merely a spectator to the pomp and pageantry.

Dumbfounded at the lavishness of the proceedings at the reception, I wondered "How long had people been living like this?" Food and drink were in abundance. It reminded me of a painting I had seen of a Roman bacchanal. There were ice sculptures of "flying" salmon and life-sized goats and steers made of brightly covered paper machè. And beneath each one were layers and layers of sliced meats. There were hors d'oeuvres of every description: tiny finger sandwiches, melons, stuffed olives, caviar. Waiters were everywhere serving chilled champagne and catering to the whimsical needs of the guests. The whole affair was obscene.

The men, whose soft, layered flesh hid their tough survival tactics, tried desperately to make themselves seen and heard. They didn't fool me. Some appeared programmed, trembling at the thought of doing or saying the wrong thing. Others, in small groups and out of earshot, held confidential and perhaps cynical conversations. They were the guardians of secrets passed along to them by the old ones of yesteryear. Most were drinking too much and belching like they had just finished eating walrus meat, although I saw none of that on the banquet table.

The women were really strange sights. Many were past their prime and had probably set their alarm clocks for 5am to brush and tease their overly coifed hair, to apply makeup, and to stuff themselves into dresses two sizes too small. They grinned at everyone through red lips that highlighted some impressive porcelain teeth. They would greet and hug old friends as they looked over their shoulders to see who else was there and was more important than the person they just greeted. I saw two elderly ladies do just that as they greeted each other like two ghosts past due for a haunting rendezvous.

I made my first contact of the evening with a middle-aged man who approached me with two glasses of champagne in his hands. His head was massive and pointed, forcing crinkled furrows in his brow. He slurred a "Hi! How are you?" Before I could answer, he followed with, "What do you do?" I have always hated that question, especially, if it is the first thing out of a person's mouth. It puts one on the defensive and permits the questioner to escape putting any energy into getting to know a person. Through the years I made a conscious effort never to do that. I would much rather probe to find out small details about a person. If I happened to enjoy their conversation, it would be too late to discover that their social standing was above, or below what I may have initially perceived. Nevertheless, I thought about his question for a second. Since I was the only black person there among the hundreds and hundreds of people, I answered, "Do you see that man over there?" I pointed to anyone in the vicinity. "I'm his driver, and he asked me to come in and enjoy myself." He gave the previously described "ghostly" rebuttal and went on his way. Perhaps, in search of someone more important to talk with than a chauffeur.

I continued to observe the masses, making a great discovery. Everyone in the room walked counter clockwise around the vast room. So, I figured that if I stayed in one place, everyone in the room would eventually come past my vantage point. Eventually, I engaged in brief conversations with a number of males and females. The more champagne I had, the more they seemed like decent human beings. By the time the President spoke, everyone was numb, so his speech was great!

So much for my first encounter with life among the "Lotus Eaters" I was invited back during the next several years and remained the only black person there.

SIPPING MINT JULEPS

A porcelain calm enveloped me as I crossed the Ohio River on the huge iron bridge leading into Louisville, Kentucky. It was early morning on a lovely, sun drenched day in October, 1969. Stressless breezes blew gently out of the South, of course. I sped along Highway I-64 East, my sights set for Lexington, home of the University of Kentucky.

I was slated to be one of the main speakers at the annual meeting of the Kentucky Broadcasters Association (KBA). Why me? Simply put, Eldon Campbell, my boss, could not attend, and he asked that I be his stand-in. I have good reason to consider this man a "Holy One." When I remember that the year was 1969, I know that few people could imagine a black broadcaster as a principal speaker before members of the "Fourth Estate," and below the Mason Dixon Line.

The country was in a sorry state at that time. Looking back from the vantage point of this writing, I find it rather easy to remember just how sorry. The 1960's produced the biggest civil, political, and military upheavals of my lifetime. There is more history to write about during this era than most people want or need to endure. Nevertheless, I am compelled to briefly summarize this period as a backdrop for my speaking engagement.

The decade of the 60's brought the assassinations of President Kennedy, Martin Luther King, Malcolm X, Bobby Kennedy, the student massacres at Kent, riots at the National Democratic Headquarters in Chicago, and the Vietnam War protests, cast the nation into severe torment. There were other subsequent race riots erupting throughout the land, with big and small cities alike incapable of escaping carnage. Despite these calamities, it was the role the broadcast media played in these dramatic events that concerned me the most.

355

For the first time we were able to watch, in living color, the four horsemen of the apocalypse. Television brought us the student riots at the Democratic National Convention in Chicago. We saw American white boys and girls being beaten and maimed by Chicago's finest. And if that wasn't enough, we were able to watch at the dinner table, nearly a dozen male and female student protesters being gunned down at Kent State by the National Guard. Equally pathetic were sights of America's finest and brightest young people strung out on drugs strumming guitars in trees and gazing all day at the sun over the skies of Height Ashbury, California. The "Chicago Seven" appeared on television giving Judge Abby Hoffman hell, and driving him nearly mad as they made him and his court a mockery that rocked the sensibilities of the American viewing public. But, for the moment, I was interested was more in the city of Lexington.

In preparation for my speaking engagement I speed read an entry in the <u>Encyclopedia Britannica</u> to learn a few things about Lexington. With a population of nearly a quarter of a million people, Lexington is located in central Kentucky. In an area known throughout the world as the "Blue Grass Region," it is a major center for horse breeding. Lexington is surrounded by rich farmlands. The city is an important market for beef cattle, sheep, spring lambs, bluegrass, and loose leaf tobacco. The grave site of the great race horse, Man-O-War is there, attracting thousands of horse lovers each year. Home of the University of Kentucky, founded in 1865, it is also famous for the U.S. Government Hospital for Narcotic Addicts and for Fort Knox, where the U.S.Treasury stores its gold supply.

Marveling at the rich beauty and bounty of the state, I passed what seemed to be miles upon miles of white fence rows [wondering who couldn't help but wonder] who in the world paints these. Palominos, dark grays, dark brown and ink-black horses cavorted among manicured pastures. My reverie was made easy. I had always admired the work

356

ethic of Kentuckians, as well as their old-fashioned virtues and values, as well as their seemingly constant search for any excuse to get together and have a good time.

I now reviewed in my mind what lay ahead. I was to talk on any subject of my choosing, as long as it involved broadcasting. I planned to speak for twenty minutes and then take questions from the audience. There were to be some two hundred KBA broadcasters there, mostly radio and television owners, their top executives and managers. So, the topic I would choose needed to have some relevance, some depth and significance to it.

One of the things I had deplored about many speakers on such occasions was the tendency to tell listeners what they wanted to hear, which, loosely translated, would be to tell them how wonderful broadcasters are. "Speaking to the converted," one might say. I tried never to do that when I spoke. The best speakers, the ones that I thought made a difference, were the ones who challenged their audience, or "shook-up," the system. I planned to do just that.

I had chosen to speak on the subject of the "Duality Principle of Television" - its propensity to elevate the consciousness of society toward a greater good, or dwell on the darker side of the nature of men through its programming. Powerful television visual images can compel individual viewers to respond in a manner known by psychologists as "emotional contagion." This response makes individuals feel as if they are a part of something much larger than themselves: it <u>connects</u> individuals from different parts of the country, making them of one mind.

For thousands of years mans choices and his freedom to act and think were made by someone else. What to do; how to do it; when to do it; what to think about; all handled, for the most part, by someone else. Wars have been fought, millions have died, legislation passed, men of persuasion continue their struggle to ensure man does have individual choices to control his own destiny. The cultural revolution of the 1960's cleared away a lot of social and psychological baggage our young people said they would no longer tolerate. The hypocrisies of past generations were swept away. Unfortunately it left a vacuum.

Now it seems as though we always have something to worry about. We then adopt the attitude that until there is nothing to worry about, there is nothing to be happy about, creating the opposite of happiness; anxiety and depression. Newspapers and newscasts give us news of what are mostly fresh disasters. It's not really what's new but what's bad that sells newspapers and gets TV ratings. All of this negativity is bound to affect us. It becomes easy to believe that the world is a much worse place than it actually is. Before we realize it, we are lost in our eternal dilemmas, our fears dominated by life's shadows. We complain of our circumstances even though our cups overflow with blessings. Nevertheless, we continue to drink in life as if it doesn't. In my view, that was the path television news was taking its viewers down, instead of how to make us better people, parents and community leaders. But the state of television news was worse than all of the above.

Television News was now taking a much stronger grip on America. The public couldn't seem to get enough of it, especially attack journalism during Presidential press conferences. I recall Sam Donaldson openly attacking President Nixon during a press conference, as if Sam was more important than the president. He was not reporting the news, he was making it!

The Vietnam War was raging during this time period and, for the first time in history, war came into our homes. The ugliness, the brutality, and the heart rendering images of women and children suffering the terrible effect of war as they became victims of the opposing combatants. We saw live pictures of close combat and air strikes of napalm bombs while our potatoes grew cold at the dinner table. These images were adding fuel to the growing dissidents revolting against the war. In my opinion, it prolonged the war causing many more Americans to die than necessary.

Most Americans had never witnessed death in combat situations. War is brutal and nasty as it has been for thousands of years, and yet, to see dead and dying men on the six o'clock news, was unsettling to say the least. We even witnessed American actress Jane Fonda, broadcasting live on Hanoi radio, imploring Americans to resist the War. It was unbelievable. While our Gi's were dying, she gave aid and comfort to the enemy. Such ruptures in our views of the role America played in the War have not healed to this day. Opponents of the Vietnam War still see America as abandoning the people of South Vietnam in their struggles to ward off a Communist threat. Certainly our abandonment left the Comer Rouge to commit genocide of more than a million Vietnamese and Cambodians.

Television, as you know, was in its infancy in the sixties, really less than two decades old. There were only three major networks: NBC, CBS, and ABC. They were giants and nothing less than money-making machines. That was fine with me- nothing wrong with making money. What troubled me was the creeping sense of arrogance developing among my colleagues, particularly those who ran the newsrooms. Unfettered, the newsroom was the perfect propaganda machine, often taking viewers into places and events far beyond their comprehension or control.

I did not like this vision for the future for television news. I had spoken out before that one of the dangers of the electronic media was that the images created were so fleeting. A word is spoken, and a scene is flashed upon the screen, lingers for a few seconds, then it is gone. But, it remains embedded in our memories, or taken out of context and often repeated as half truths by the viewer, such images are the truth. Years later, this point of view was to be substantiated, as these fleeting images were to be called "sound bites" that lasted but a few seconds, but their effect lingered. Politicians became masters of this tool. There was even talk at broadcast seminars that print media was dead-replaced by the electronic media. I was not one of them. I had spoken out before that one of the dangers of the electronic medias was that its transitory nature. Print media in my view has permanence

The flip side of the coin was the ability of television news broadcast to do good. For example there were the vivid images broadcast from Mississippi of Bull Connor and his deputies terrorizing and beating civil rights protestors; his attack dogs mauling little black children and other people as they marched-demonstrating for their human rights and dignities. These sights awakened liberal Americans and others of goodwill who never dreamed these things could happen in our country. The television footage of the above events, and Americas disdain for it, aided President Lyndon Johnson in his effort toward passing the Civil Rights Act of 1964 following the assassination of John Kennedy.

I told the KBA members that we should be aware of the future that we were helping to shape, that we should begin to discuss among ourselves with scholars what our role and proper conduct should be. Should it be proactive or passive? If we chose proactive, we needed to know and better understand that responsibility to a greater degree than we knew at this juncture of our burgeoning industry.

I also chided my associates about the need for them to act more responsibly and aggressively in hiring blacks. I would tell them that I had been to the last two National Association of Broadcaster's meetings and that of the more than two thousand participants, I was the only black person there. I would ask the KBA to survey their fellow broadcasters to determine how many blacks they had in their employment and to use the results as a benchmark for improvement. I submitted that they would find very few in their ranks beyond janitors. Finally, I spoke to the point that many black viewers were becoming frustrated at being unable to see an accurate reflection of themselves on television. All they saw on the six o'clock news was black men committing murder, rape, and mayhem or as buffoons, thus perpetuating the old stereotypical images of blacks being unfit to join the human race.

I knew this was very heady stuff for a young black man from Indiana to be telling powerful broadcasters in that day. I was attempting neither arrogance nor militancy. I was merely reminding them that they had an obligation to make a favorable contribution to society as a whole. In addition, I felt a strong obligation to use the opportunity to speak for all of the voiceless blacks who had marched and died in order for a person like me to achieve the modicum of success that had come my way. I spoke of these things, and to my total surprise received more than polite applause when I finished. I felt quite good. I wasn't too sure what word would get back to Eldon Campbell, but knowing him, I was sure he would have been proud of me. We both had talked about such things in the past.

I answered many questions posed to me during the question and answer period. Most were polite. For instance, "What do you see in the near future for listener interest in expanded news?" "If blacks were helped by the showing of the civil rights confrontations, why are you giving the industry such a bad reputation?" And finally this one, for which I will try to reconstruct my response. "With all of the destructiveness of the riots and civil unrest, what is it that you black people really want?" I replied straightforwardly, "We want what you want and already have. We want the opportunity to reach the fullness of our ability. We want to participate in the American dream of a decent job, a home, the potential to provide a decent life for our wives and families, decent schools. And the right to do what we want to do as long as we don't infringe on the rights of others." I nearly swooned when the questioner shot back, "You mean you want all of that? Your race isn't prepared yet for reaching those goals. Show me someone who is black and qualified like you and I will hire him in a minute. We've been looking for a black to hire in our production department but we can't find anyone that is qualified."

I said, "There is something called transferable skills. A manager is a manager, whether in a country store, managing a McDonald's restaurant, or supervising a production line at a factory. A person has only to be taught and given a chance, even to fail if necessary. Any black drama graduate can deliver the news."

Well, they may not have liked what I said, but they didn't lynch me or run me out of town on a rail. In fact, I've recounted this episode in such detail because what followed proved to be one of the great surprises of my life. When I finished and sat down, the chairman rose and asked me to come back to the podium to receive a gift of appreciation from the Association.

When I approached him, I noticed he was unwrapping a huge, flat object. He began to read:

"From the Commonwealth of Kentucky, Louie B. Nunn Governor

To all, to whom these presents shall come, Greetings:

Know ye, that Honorable Stephen Scott, Indianapolis, Indiana

Is commissioned a Kentucky Colonel"

My soul did another eclipse as it is prone to do under such circumstances. My mouth set itself in a generous and permanent smile. The Greeks worshiped the goat as a god. I would worship my elevation to the status of a black Kentucky Colonel. I floated back to my seat amid generous applause, thinking all the while, "What will my friends think about me now . . . Little ole me from Pearl Street . . . A Kentucky Colonel. Yes, I would insist they call me Colonel from this day forward. "Well kid," I thought to myself, "You've finally made it." I was wrong, of course, but it would have taken a lot of persuasion to convince me differently at that moment.

For Those who have tears
Prepare to shed them now...
William Shakesphere

THE RICHEST MAN IN ALL LEBANON

There is this little bit of queasiness in my innards as I prepare to relate this next anecdotal misadventure. As William Shakesphere said, "For those who have tears, prepare to shed them now." I repeat this quotation because, even today, it seems such an incredulous misfiring of my brain cells that I dread reliving the episode. My pen trembles.

A Friday night in the lounge of the Hilton Hotel in downtown Indianapolis that proved to be the setting for the worst mistake of my entire life. The year was 1971. Eldon Campbell, one of his entrepreneurial business associates, and I were meeting to discuss my potential involvement in a major business venture. The idea was to be the first group out of the blocks for obtaining the cable TV franchise for all of Marion County, Indianapolis. All franchises were granted by the Federal Communications Commission (FCC) in Washington, D.C. This would be a major initiative.

At this particular time in the country's history, a strong concerted effort was underway to involve minorities in the communication industry, particularly ownership of AM, FM, and television stations. Ownership, even partial ownership, by blacks was sweeping the country. Gratefully, many blacks were finally getting an opportunity to participate in these powerful, profitable communications industries. Even if a majority of ownership stock was held by whites, the FCC would still look favorably on awarding licenses to those proposals that involved blacks. I had a working knowledge of its potential, since at the time I was an executive with the local television station, WFBM TV, owned by TIME, Inc., in New York. TIME executives had made a commitment to enter this new technology. As a matter of fact, one of the business managers of WFBM TV, Bill Davidson, was their point man for developing cable TV in the markets where they owned broadcast properties. Despite the fact that this fledgling industry had mountains of problems to overcome, men of vision like Eldon had great faith in its potential. As a matter of fact, he had holdings in a cable operation somewhere in Illinois.

One of the great impediments to anyone is venturing into this new communication market was the heavy capital start-up cost. Land lines had to be laid. Many television sets already owned by TV viewers were not equipped to receive cable; therefore, Cable adapters were being hastily made for conversion of the sets. But the time line for any kind of home saturation was still years down the road. Finally, there remained the not so inconsequential fact that there was a limited product for viewers to watch. This was pretty much the state of affairs on this fateful night.

At the Friday night meeting, after making proper introductions, giving a brief personal background sketch of my career, and sipping a few drinks Eldon changed his ebullient mood to one of deadly seriousness. Ever-wise and full of care, he said, "Steve, I have come to know and respect you as a person and more importantly your professional capabilities. I want you to listen very carefully to what I am about to say." A dry heat enfolded me. I hoped it didn't show as I reached for my handkerchief and feigned wiping my fast-drying lips. He continued. "Steve, I have remained true to one abiding precept in my business career. Never, ever go to bed [enter a business relationship] with a man who has Vaseline on the nightstand." I furrowed my brow trying to see where this obscure metaphor was leading. Eldon continued. "What I'm saying to you is this, my partner and I have known each other for decades and have entered several business ventures together (come to think of it, they owned the very hotel we were sitting in) and we trust one another implicitly. We are now prepared to embark on another venture together: buying the cable TV franchise for this city. My partner trusted my judgement when I told him you would be the kind of person we need to complete our final licensing proposal. To be honest with you, we need a black person with some equity position in our corporation. We are prepared to offer you a 5% stock equity position. You will need to obtain $50,000 within ten days. I don't care how you get it, mortgage your house or find some rich uncles, but you have only ten days. We might be able to help you with some of the needed money, but not much. We have an NBA professional black basketball player who can raise the money in days, but we prefer to have you join us."

That was Eldon. He sized me up. He made up his mind and that was the end of that. He was terse and decisive. His mannerisms reminded me of Harry Truman's. A terrible tide of anxiety flooded my soul, my caution and my tact. I heard myself say, "I'll get back to you in a couple of days." I took a final look at the two shadowed faces, got up noiselessly and left, thinking all the while, "Scott, you need a plan, and in a hurry." Really, the first part of my plan was to try not to have a heart attack before the night was done.

Except for a few thousand savages scattered here and there over this planet, everyone else knows the second problem I faced. It is known by the time you're six years old. black, white, male, female, rich or poor. Christian, Jew, Russian, Tibetan, Korean, Chinese, Indian all have heard of my need. Money! And where to get it when I need it!

This part of my plan would not meekly submit to my bidding. Taking out an equity loan or a second mortgage on my home was out of the question. Marilyn and I had completed the building of our new house in 1969, so we had only a few thousand dollars in equity. Savings were meager as well and would yield only a few thousand dollars. Cash value in insurance policies would yield another few thousand. Probably a bank would lend me another $10,000 dollars. I would be woefully short of $50,000 dollars.

I next talked to several doctor friends and advised them of this once-in-a-lifetime business venture. I had to be frank and honest with them in advising that the potential was there for untold thousands, perhaps millions of dollars, but any investment would be long-term. They would not receive any residual return on their investment for many years. Most liked the idea and trusted me, but felt financially they could not wait that long for a return. I was through! There may have been other options, but I couldn't think of any at the time. And time was against me.

Reluctantly, as if surmounting some barrier and then free-falling at an accelerated rate, I called Eldon with the bad news. He was thunderstruck but understanding and demonstrated sincere regret. He now had no choice but to align himself with the famous black athlete. I should have been a professional basketball player.

Of course the cable TV industry grew to the prodigious heights envisioned by Eldon and is the tremendous communication force we all know it to be today. But why do most of us only dimly imagine what might happen in the future? I have no answer, only a piece from William Shakespeare: "Today's dream is tomorrow's reality." That's that's not quite the end of the story.

A little before sundown on a hot, steamy summer evening in New Orleans in 1980, I was relaxing on a chaise lounge on the patio of my mother-in-law's home reading the <u>Wall Street Journal</u>. I had taken the family down for a two-week vacation and was sitting on their patio surrounded by lovely rose bushes protected by large, overhanging magnolia and oak trees.

Suddenly, amid the semi-darkness, my eyes happened to settle on a short business article. As my eyes became accustomed to the sparse light, I read and reread the story. "Indianapolis Power & Light Company buys locally-owned cable TV franchise for $67 million." It was Eldon's cable company. Nay! My would-be company! An aura of blue funk came over me. I did a quick mental calculation. My 5

366

percent ownership that had slipped through my hands was now worth nearly $3.4 million.

I must have read the article a dozen times. For years I never told anyone outside the family this story. Such was the divine nature of the Goddess of Good Luck that too briefly alighted on my shoulders that day at the Hilton Hotel, and teasingly flew away to light on the broad shoulders of the already fortunate NBA basketball star. The would-be richest man in all of Lebanon was no more than that.

CHAPTER 11

THE COMING OF THE THIRD MILLENNIUM

It has always been compelling to think about the future. It is, after all, where we all hope to go. The future is the precursor of our hopes and dreams, but it is also the repository of our fears and insecurities as we contemplate what will become of us. What about our spouses and our families? Will we have successful lives? Will we succeed or fail at love? The third millennium is just over the horizon. January 1, 2000 will be the most unique day in the lifetime of readers alive at the time. Actually, February 29, 2000 will be a leap year day and only the fifth leap year day we could have had in our era, if we had always used a modern calendar, and at any rate the first millennial one we shall have ever had. Concern about the third millennium is growing, and it will soon join a long list of man's obsessions, beyond those listed above.

Intensifying and feeding our anxiety about the coming millennium will be words, words – like those of Herman Kahn, Alvin Toffer, and Nostradamus. Nostradamus knew how to play the word card very well. His prophesies are so obscure and wordy that his interpreters can make them fit many modern day calamities; World Wars I & II, AIDS, earthquakes, or the Nixon near impeachment are just a few. Toffer frightened us by telling us we couldn't cope with a fast changing world. Kahn held the nuclear cloud over our heads. More words will be issued by our modern day, self proclaimed prophets to be fatuously and carelessly repeated by opportunistic journalists, academicians, advertisers, theologians, and, of course, politicians. Prophecy is a powerful propaganda device because it is fun to read and, on the surface, harmless. But those who follow the prophets will come to believe that if we can predict what the new millennium will bring, we can control it. But contemplating the future can be fearful for many. The future seems ominous, not because it is rushing in on us and forcing us to fathom decisions about our unfathomable, but because we are paralyzed by the failures of the present and the immediate past. Although our failures haunt us, to avoid being terrorized by the past and traumatized by the future may not be as difficult as we think.

The paradox of prophecy is that is it almost always wrong, yet by playing on our anxieties, it has a powerful driving force on our daily conduct. What distinguishes the renown prognosticators like Nostradamus or the Oracle of Delphi from you and me is not that they are more knowing; it is because their pronouncements touch deep chords in the human psyche. In this sense prophecy is like music or poetry – teaching us about ourselves, provided, of course, that we abandon the notion that prophecy means anything. The well-kept secret is that no one possesses the secret to having a completely satisfying life; there is no magic formula. Life is still hellishly brutish, dangerous and imperfect. Woes, troubles, confusion and bad things will occur daily across the planet. But we all must still grope through life in our own clumsy way. We must still live alongside five billion other people. And to synthesize this pragmatic view, the millennium is coming, like it or not.

What does the millennium mean? The word millennium comes from the Latin word "mille," meaning 1,000; hence, a 1,000 year anniversary. The biblical millennium refers to the 1,000 year period after Christ's reappearance, after Armageddon, when the kingdom of God is established on earth. As many people see the new millennium, it is or will be the golden age in human history, a time to close the door on the past and embark upon a new era a "New Age."

There are many ways to contemplate the millennium and, as we get closer to that date, we will hear more than we want to about the promise of "The New Age." How many individuals and groups will set goals with reference to the third millennium? It will act as a deadline, encouraging us to confront and resolve our problems, so we can charter new lives. The fact is that humanity and the planet will not be saved at that time by a second coming or by friendly spaceships, or by a golden age. The answers to our woes will have to come from within those human beings who will people this planet. The young people will have to lead us into the third millennium, not the self-appointed prophets.

To listen to the prophets of doom, those wonderful self-anointed ones, one would never dream that despite all their alarms about fatal dangers to the planet, every food that we grow or develop or consume, the air we breathe, the water we drink, the earth we walk on, despite each new hot topic, the planet keeps revolving around the sun, with more and more people standing alive on it. Some people probably won't like my point of view on this, but I get a chuckle out of environmentalists waving placards saying "Save the Planet." The planet will save itself through renewal. For untold eras it has withstood mighty plagues: the biblical deluge, the Ice Age, the shifting of the continents, mighty volcanoes, and fallout from comets entering our atmosphere. What is most needed and what the signs should be saying is " Save Ourselves...From Ourselves."

So why are there so many prophets of doom? Because there are real profits in heralding doom. Prophesying penmen and penwomen have for generations sold their books to a credulous public as they predict that this or that calamity is imminent. The wonderful thing about it for them is that they don't have to refund the money when it turns out they are dead wrong. Prophets are never really held accountable when they are wrong! It is easy to predict that an earthquake will shake southern California within a year's time. There are many of them every year; sooner or later the prediction will be right. I remember the time when I was in the fourth grade and some prophet had predicted that at precisely 12:00 noon on Tuesday the world would come to an end. The disastrous, calamitous, and deadly end of all things would certainly happen at that time. Hey, that meant me! The newspapers and radio news hyped this miserable story for weeks, prior to the appointed doomsday. Some parents kept their kids out of school on that fateful day. The rest of us walked, zombie-like, through the morning. The teachers tried to teach (they were scared too) but no learning took place. We all were watching the big clock behind the teacher's desk. Some kids began to cry as ten o'clock came. But, by eleven o'clock, we were all basket cases. Whisperings could be heard all around the room. By eleven-thirty the room was totally, deadly quiet. The hands of the clock hit twelve noon. Again, muffled cries and the sucking in of breath could be heard. It was terrible. Then nothing, nothing at all happened. Cheers and laughter erupted. The world had been spared. The curious thing about this incident was the swiftness in which the adults and children alike said as one, "I knew it wouldn't happen." I asked myself . . . who saved us . . . and why? Whoever the prophet was, I hated him — hated him for controlling me and the rest of my classmates. Why did we believe it? Because it sounded reasonable to us, especially if we read about it in the paper and heard it on the news, it had to be credible, didn't it? All those words signified nothing in the end.

The most charitable thing I can say about this story is that it taught me, and I hope others as well, that prophets cannot predict the future anymore than you or I can, and to take actions as a result of their prophecy will result in pure folly at the least and may prove dangerous at the extreme. As Max Dublin says in his wonderful book, Future Hype, "Modern prophecy, with our consent, has developed in such a way that it has come to rob us of an essentially human right and responsibility: the right to dream our own dreams and set our own goals; the right to ultimately exercise freedom, individually and collectively, to make the decisions that will shape our own destiny."

There are many areas in which we relinquish responsibility for our own growth, development and regular responsibilities and pass it on to professionals, experts and prophets, thereby empowering them and, at the same time, rendering ourselves helpless and more irresponsible. An anecdote Bob Berger cites in his book, Beating the Odds, may help close our understanding of how the prophets can scare the daylights out of us by their pseudo knowledge. The story is about two men who attend a lecture in which a scientist predicts a time when the sun will burn to a crisp. The first man frantically asks his friend when the scientist had said the sun would burn out. "A billion years." "A billion? Oh." The first man quiets down. "Whew, that's better." "Better?" "Yes, I thought he said a million." Numbers carry no judgment, even the number 2000. They only describe the world as we know it, without condemnation or praise . . . that's left up to you and me.

A final example looks back on the events in history as the last millennium ended and this one began. One thousand years ago, before the last millennium, the Christians believed the millennium would rescue them from Roman persecution. Sounds pretty familiar in these contemporary times, doesn't it! Aren't we looking for something or someone to save us now from ourselves? During the Middle Ages, bands of peasants led by charismatic preachers expected the millennium at any moment. As Norman Whan, author of The Pursuit of the Millennium, argues, "The fourteenth century English peasants revolted, and the German peasant revolt of the fifteenth and sixteenth centuries fulfilled millennial expectations." It appears to be happening again. We see people believing the time is at hand for the "New Age." They cluster around colorful, eccentric leaders. Millions are attracted to unorthodox ends of the religious spectrum. New Age characters and TV preachers of all birth and kin are scaring us again. How many denizens of the l999's will they keep up at night staring at the ceiling. How many people realize that man who out thinks you rules you.

The young people will make it into the next millennium as we old ones did. Hopefully, as we look at the future, will remember the past and what those good people learned and can teach us about survival, because the same challenges of the past were there for them and for us. The old ones did not try to conquer life, they tried to accommodate it. I say to the young people that I, too, bounced on the knee of life, and it was like riding on a tiger's back from which one dared not dismount. I found out, as you will, that tigers get hungry.

There, I'm done with this passion I have with the coming millennium. When the slings and arrows fly and the winds of change tug at your collar, go to that quiet place that is your private sanctuary. It will show you the way. Then and only then will you be free to welcome the arrival of the third millennium.

WFBM – TV – AM – FM Executive Management Team annual Christmas part. Sitting in forefront – Casey Strange. That's me kneeling on the far left. Continuing left to right, seated, Bob Gamble, Ruth Hyatt, Dan Wieberg, Bev May. Standing, far left, Jerry Chapman, Bob Flanders, Eldon Campbell, Don Cripe and Bill Davidson

From the desk of **ELDON CAMPBELL**

4/30/71

Crispe
Chapman
Flanders
Davidson
Gamble
Strange
Scott
Hiatt

Confidential

This is it! You
will recall my last meeting
with you,

WTLC manager named to Ind. Broadcaster's board

Steve Scott, general manger of WTLC radio on Wednesday became the first black to be elected to the board of directors of Indiana Broadcasters Association, Inc.

Scott was elected to the IBA board by the general membership of the association at its annual fall meeting conducted at Evansville in October. Scott will also serve as a member of the board of directors of the IBA News Network, Inc., a 40-station radio network operated by the Indiana Broadcasters Association.

A native of Lebanon, Scott holds a bachelor's degree in radio and television from Indiana University. Prior to assuming the position as general manager of WTLC earlier this year, he seved as public af-

Steve – Thanks for the
report – and the fine
job you did for the City
Bill Hudnut

2/13/79

The Casper Award, received for hosting job line.

COMMONWEALTH OF KENTUCKY

LOUIE B. NUNN

GOVERNOR

To all to Whom These Presents Shall Come, Greeting:

Know Ye, That   HONORABLE STEPHEN SCOTT, INDIANAPOLIS, INDIANA

Is Commissioned A

KENTUCKY COLONEL

I hereby confer this honor with all the rights, privileges and responsibilities thereunto appertaining.

In testimony whereof, I have caused these letters to be made patent, and the seal of the Commonwealth to be hereunto affixed. Done at Frankfort, the 9TH day of OCTOBER in the year of our Lord one thousand nine hundred and 69 and in the one hundred and 78TH year of the Commonwealth.

By the Governor

Secretary of State

By

Assistant Secretary of State

Honorary Kentucky Colonel, (Black) that is.

379

COLLEGE OF ARTS AND SCIENCES
DEPARTMENT OF TELECOMMUNICATIONS

September 15, 1969

Mr. Steven Scott
WFBM
Indianapolis, Indiana

Dear Mr. Scott:

The Kentucky Broadcasters Association is pleased to have
you speaking to the fall meeting at Lexington, October 14.

So we may properly publicize and execute the various sessions,
we would appreciate having from you:

1. A short biographical sketch
2. A picture of you for publicity purposes
3. A list of any special audio-visual equipment
   necessary for your presentation.

We hope you will give this your immediate attention.

Hope to see you soon.

Sincerely,

Joseph H. Berman, Ph.D.
Assistant Professor

JHB:jd

ROBERT E. SLAUGHTER

December 10, 1971

Mr. Stephen L. Scott
Public Affairs Director
The WTDM Stations
1330 North Meridian
Indianapolis, Indiana 46202

Dear Steve:

Thank you very much for sending to me a copy of the October issue of the Black Communicator, which contains an article on McGraw-Hill. This had been brought to my attention by our Washington counsel. Nonetheless, I am deeply grateful for your thoughtful interest.

Thank you, also, for your Holiday good wishes. Gertrude and I want to extend to you and your family our best wishes for a merry Christmas and a very happy New Year. We remember with great pleasure being with you and your wife at the 1971 Indy 500. I hope we can do a repeat in 1972, but as associates in McGraw-Hill!

Very sincerely yours,

Bob Slaughter

RES:mkp
cc: Mr. Barry Zorthian
    Mr. Eldon Campbell

381

TIME-LIFE BROADCAST, INC.

A Subsidiary of Time Inc

TIME & LIFE BUILDING
ROCKEFELLER CENTER
NEW YORK, N.Y. 10020

(212) 556-1212
CABLES:
TIMEINC NEW YORK

January 22, 1970

Dear Steve:

It ever the domino theory needed proving, developments at WFBM the past couple of months should be sufficient. It seems to me I keep writing notes of congratulations to people out there. The nice part of it is that they are all very well deserved.

This is particularly true in your case. I am happy to see you moving up, both because of the job you have done to date and the contributions which you can make in the future. I look forward to working with you in the coming years.

My very best wishes to you and your family in the new assignment.

Sincerely,

Barry Zorthian
President

Mr. Stephen Scott
Public Affairs Director
The WFBM Stations
1330 North Meridian Street
Indianapolis, Indiana 46202

STATE of INDIANA

INDIANAPOLIS 46204

DEPARTMENT OF PUBLIC WELFARE
100 NORTH SENATE AVENUE — ROOM 701

February 23, 1968

Mr. Wayne A. Stanton, Director
Marion County Department of Public Welfare
1501 City-County Building
Indianapolis, Indiana 46204

Dear Mr. Stanton:

Food Stamp Federal Audit

I wish to take this opportunity to thank you and your entire staff for
the excellent cooperation and assistance you gave the federal auditors
while they were recently in your County performing their duties.

During the final discussion, the items mentioned were very small and
you are to certainly be congratulated for having an excellent admini-
stration and issuance procedure in your Food Stamp office.

I know that this should be a gratifying source to you to know that you
are helping so many in your County obtain better foods and a more nutri-
tious diet for their families.

If you should have any questions concerning the audit, please contact
this office.

Very truly yours,

Wm. H. Sterrett, Director
Division of Administrative Services

Perry H. Peck, Supervisor
Food Stamp Program

PHP:807

383

MARION COUNTY
DEPARTMENT OF PUBLIC WELFARE
1501 CITY-COUNTY BUILDING
INDIANAPOLIS, INDIANA 46204

Feb. 29-68

Dear Steve,

Attached will show that the extensive recent federal audit of our Food Stamp program came out beautiful. Out of about 100 cases they checked they could not find any error to report! None!

The only thing they mentioned is where the ~~State~~ Plan is out of conformity with our excellent practice — i.e. filing cabinet in different place, who (whatever) types I.D. cards, etc. State said they would change their plan. — about time.

Hope everything is going fine with you. Allen is doing nicely.

Best regards,
Wayne

384

R/TV's building, early 1950s

The Radio and Television Studios at Indiana University as they appeared in my student days in the late 1950's

Broadcasting from WFIU, Indiana University. The one dollar an hour I received was a great deal of money for a student during that period

385

It was a lovely day for a wedding, even by New Orleans standards. Marilyn looked even more lovely.

A Favorite picture of my family, Marilyn, Steve Jr. and Wendy, taken in 1979. I chose to be seated in the middle because Steve Jr. was in a growth spurt and was now several inches taller than me. Perceptions are real and a man must rule his manse anyway he can!

> God does not die on the day we cease
> To believe in a personal deity, but we die
> On the day when our lives cease to be
> Illuminated by the steady radiance, renewed
> daily, of a wonder, the source of which is
> beyond all seasons.
> Dag Hammarskjold, <u>Markings</u>

<u>FAITH FOR THE NEW AGE AQUIRIANS</u>

The tradition of the God of Christian Theologies was developed in large part by Saint Thomas Aquinas in the thirteenth century as a necessary, timeless, immutable, perfect, unchanging being on which the universe depends totally for its existence, but who, by contrast, is completely unaffected by the existence of the universe. The unique contribution of Christian thinking about the universe is that it was created ex-nihilo - out of nothing but God's love. It appears as if creation of the universe ex-nihilo, resolves the paradox of how a changing world can be explained by a timeless, unchanging being. When human beings choose freely, their choice is colored by their nature. So what can be said about God's nature?

To contend with the possibility that there could be many different types of gods is useless, for then we would have gained nothing by invoking a God in the first place. We would be left with the problem of explaining why that particular god existed rather than some other! The whole idea of invoking God as a necessary being is to ensure that he is united with us; nature could not have been otherwise. We should be content with God and leave the matter alone. Only faith is necessary then, or the certainty of faith. Faith in the laws of physics discovered in the laboratory apply equally well to the chair, a stone or a distant galaxy.

The early Greek philosophers recognized that the order and harmony of the cosmos demanded explanations, but they perceived these qualities as deriving from a creator working with a preconceived plan. My thinking is much simpler and outflanks the general question of religion. It is simply this – the fact is we are here, and by the grace of some pretty fancy arrangements that make us who we are in this vast universe. Our existence cannot in and of itself explain these arrangements. One could shrug the matter aside with the comment that we are certainly very lucky that the universe just happened to possess the conditions for life to flourish, but that is a meaningless quirk of fate. Again, is our place in the universe a question of personal judgment or fate? Until we have a proper understanding of the origin of life, or knowledge about alternative life forms elsewhere in the universe, the question must remain captive to what philosophers call "The Principle of Sufficient Reason." This principle states that everything in the world and in the universe is as it is for some reason. For example, why is the sky blue? Why do apples fall? Why are there nine planets (maybe more) in the solar system? We are not usually satisfied with the reply "because that's the way it is." Certainly it usually works all right – apples fall because of gravity, the sky is blue because of short wave lengths of light scattered by molecules of air in the atmosphere (but that does not guarantee it will always work out that way). The fullness of time changes all things.

So what are we to conclude? I am bewildered. Nevertheless, to my mind's rationale there is a rational, fundamental compatibility for a completely timeless, unchanging necessary God and a universe that can change and evolve and bring forth the new out of seeming chaos; a universe in which there is free will. If God fixes everything, including our own behavior then, free will is an illusion. The plan of predestination is certain, says Thomas Aquinas – or things happen over which God either has no control, or has voluntarily relinquished control. The arguments against predestination are far shakier than the arguments for a necessary being. Yet I also believe that there remain several difficulties relating this timeless, necessary being to the changing, uncertain world of experience. Nor is it obvious to me that this postulated being who underpins the rationality of the world bears much resemblance to the personal deity perceived by most of us today.

In fact, quite apart from the psychological need most of us have to embrace a higher power in our lives, we are going to find it exceedingly hard to find it in a single discipline. Neither pure science nor theology can satisfy the rational mind. Test tube babies, DNA unraveling, artificial intelligence and other exotic breakthroughs in astronomy and space exploration will all have profound theological, cultural and social consequences as we enter the next century. Helping the religious community to understand the scientific issues and to find ways to talk about them in a theological context is a must.

Is this, then, where scientific explanation breaks down and God takes over? Astrophysicist Robert Jastrow described such a prospect as the scientist's nightmare: He [the scientist] has scaled the mountains of ignorance; he is about to conquer the highest peak; and as he pulls himself over the final rock, he is greeted by a band of theologians who have been sitting there for centuries."

I hope that each of us, but especially the young people, can find, after your spiritual journeys, a mind set that will comfort us as the millennium begins. For as T.S. Elliott so succinctly stated, "The end of all our exploring will be to arrive where we started and know the place for the first time."

> The end of all our exploring will be
> to arrive where we started and know
> The place for the first time...
> T.S. Elliott

THE END OF ALL OUR EXPLORING

It's time to end this book and for the both of us to get back to the rest of our lives. I admit you will be missed as my companion on these late night writing sessions, looking over my shoulder as I sat writing in my comfortable, easy chair by the fireplace. You have been in many libraries, hotel rooms and on my patio on warm summer days. It has been nice having you along on airplanes, by quiet streams and heaven knows how many other places. I ask that you permit me just a few more closing thoughts before we part.

It is amazing how much a book has a trajectory of its own. It takes both the writer and the reader to places neither originally intended to go. It simply beckons with thoughts and ideas different from those one had when he began. I started this work as an exercise in recall, practicing flights of illusions and escape from reality. Now, as I end my Walk Through Time, the exercise has proven to be one of exciting self- rediscovery. After all, how many of us can say we lived our lives twice without, at some point, contemplating jumping off a cliff in disgust, despair, or just plain disbelief at having survived this valley of tears for any length of time at all.

In my journey through the world of men I have witnessed nobility, power, obscenity, intelligence and folly. There are a couple of other observations as well. One is characterized by humility, or the notion that all humankind and all its institutions matter very little to the continued evolution of the human species, or to softly, very softly, say that it has been nice to feel wanted and needed on most occasions.

Through the writings of these pages there also trembled in my heart a sort of submerged hope that the story of my life would finally come to form a meaningful pattern, a signpost, if not exactly a guide, for some of my alert progeny. As author Robert Bloch said in article in the October 1994 issue of OMNI MAGAZINE, "One would think after a long lifetime, I'd at least have learned a little something to pass on to future generations; a little counsel, advice, or just plain common sense."

Alas! I have no control over the direction their life will take. The great joys and ecstasies in my life came from surprises and achievements which were the result of certain risks that I was willing to take. There are no guarantees for the reader that life will be as merciful or kind. However, there is no reason to believe, with any kind of certainty, that it won't be either.

It's a funny thing, but maybe all I can offer by way of philosophy is that human beings are wonderful on an individual basis. It's when as a group the mob becomes the monster. There is no absolute truth here, as truth does not lend itself to absolutes. The world itself has had enough dogmatism. This book is about spirit and is written for those of spirit. The known and the unknown concerning the spirit of awe and wonder of life is addressed by the famous Zen parable. "Before I studied Zen, mountains were just mountains and rivers just rivers. When I first studied Zen, mountains were no longer mountains and rivers were no longer rivers. But now that I've really some understanding of Zen, mountains are once again mountains and rivers are once again rivers." Even if one wrestles with the many interpretations which this parable presents, one cannot exhaust them all. Perhaps that is all we really need to know about life — keep it simple. Go through life like a tourist. Live it, grab it by the tail and hold on. And there is nothing wrong with being a maverick for good measure, as typified in one of my favorite poems. Farewell, and God Speed!

I'm tired of sailing my little boat far inside the harbor bar
I want to go out where the big ships float out on the deep
Where the great ones are, and
Should my frail craft prove too
Slight for waves that sweep those billows over
I'd rather go down in the
Stirring fight than to be bored to death by the sheltered
shore.

Anonymous

ABOUT THE AUTHOR

Steve Scott, a native of Lebanon, Indiana, is the fifth of twelve children born to Lawrence D. and Violet E. Scott. He is a graduate of Lebanon High School and Indiana University, obtaining a bachelor's degree in radio and television. He was the first Black to graduate from that department and garnered three awards of merit for radio and television announcing.

After gradation from Lebanon High School in 1952, Scott served as a communications specialist with the Air Force and was the first black accepted by the American Forces Korean Network during the war.

He began his business career in Indianapolis as a supervisor for the Marion County Welfare Department and then became the first Black executive with a major television station in the state of Indiana, the NBC affiliate, the former WFBM radio-television station as director of station license renewal and public affairs. He retained that position when the stations were sold by <u>Time-Life Inc.</u> to <u>McGraw Publishing Company</u>. He was the first Black in broadcasting to receive a "Casper" award for his work in hosting the tv program "Job Line." He also received the honor of being named a Kentucky Colonel by the honorable Louie B. Nunn, governor of the state of Kentucky. Scott held the position of vice president and general manager of radio station WTLC-FM. While with WTLC, Scott was the first Black elected to the board of director of the Indian Broadcasters Association. He later became the first Black executive appointed to a position with a major utility in the state of Indiana, Director of Public Affairs at Citizens Gas & Coke Utility.

Scott has served on numerous boards in the Indianapolis community, including Boys' Clubs of America, Welfare Service League, Children's Bureau, the United Way. He also has been active in the Urban League, NAACP, Black Expo, and headed the Mayors Task Force to review the performance of the Federal CETA program.

He currently serves on the Methodist Hospital Medical Group, Board of Directors.

Married to the former Marilyn Gayle, Scott is the father of a son, Steve Scott, Jr., and a daughter, Wendy. He is a member of the Witherspoon Presbyterian Church.